TONETTA LAKE

A Memoir *of* My Life *in* Brewster, New York

AND
HISTORY OF THE
YOUNG SETTLEMENT
THROUGH WORLD WAR II

Dolores Beal Stephens

HERITAGE BOOKS
2009

HERITAGE BOOKS
AN IMPRINT OF HERITAGE BOOKS, INC.

Books, CDs, and more—Worldwide

For our listing of thousands of titles see our website
at
www.HeritageBooks.com

Published 2009 by
HERITAGE BOOKS, INC.
Publishing Division
100 Railroad Ave. #104
Westminster, Maryland 21157

Copyright © 2009 Dolores Beal Stephens

Other Heritage Books by the author:
Those Who Served, Those Who Waited: WWII Experiences as Told by the Veterans and Civilians of Brewster/Southeast, New York

All rights reserved. No part of this book may be reproduced or transmitted in any form or by any means, electronic or mechanical, including photocopying, recording or by any information storage and retrieval system without written permission from the author, except for the inclusion of brief quotations in a review.

International Standard Book Numbers
Paperbound: 978-0-7884-4372-5
Clothbound: 978-0-7884-8068-3

Dedication

To my husband, Mallory, and to our two children, Mal and Diana. They have always made my life full with their love.

And remembering with love my parents,
Florence Letitia Simms Beal and William Ross Beal Sr.

Also my siblings, who made life interesting!

Contents

List of Illustrations vii
Acknowledgments ix
Introduction xi
Early History 1
P. F. Beal and Family 21
Late 1920s and Early 1930s 49
The Great Depression 91
1939 159
1940 169
1941 178
1942 209
1943 216
1944 248
1945 259
Post-War Days 266
Epilogue 276

List of Illustrations

Walter Brewster House	3
St. Andrew's Church	3
Town Hall, "Laugh Night," ca. 1915	4
Howes Castle, "Morningthorpe"	4
Postcard, ca. 1950, of Main Street, Brewster, New York	5
Grandmother Nellie Beal, ca. 1939	23
Grandfather Philip F. Beal Sr., ca. 1941	23
Home of Nellie and P. F. Beal Sr., Brewster, New York	25
Cousin Malcolm T. Beal, World War II, 1944-1945	30
Philip F. Beal III, World War II	30
William Ross Beal, Nellie Wilcox Beal, Moses Clay Beal, during World War I	30
Philip F. Beal Jr., Philip F. Beal Sr., William Ross Beal in their office at P. F. Beal and Sons	31
Charcoal Sketch of Florence Letitia Simms	38
"Story Picture" for *Colliers* magazine. Ethel Lovey, Florence Letitia Simms	38
Florence, age twenty	41
Baby Dolores	54
Oil portrait of Dolores by her mother	55
Dolores (Dodie)	55
Dolores (Dodie), age four	61
Dodie and Jane in the latest fashions	61
Beal Cousins	67
Ross, Florence and the three girls	67
William Ross Beal, my father	67
Mother with Joan Ross and Norma Jane	68
Mother with baby Dolores	68
House at 12 Putnam Avenue as purchased	78
12 Putnam Avenue after renovations, 1939	78

Dodie, unhappy about vaccination and no swimming 134
Norma Jane Beal, Knox School Graduation, 1940 140
Joan Ross Beal, Knox School Graduation, 1940 140
Dodie 143
Cousin Malcolm 143
Dodie in her Brewster High School Band Uniform 149
Dodie holding her baby brother, Ross Jr. 153
Louise Vanderburgh 168
Muriel Pinckney 183
Charlotte (Cha) Tuttle 183
Dodie with brother Ross Jr. at 12 Putnam Avenue 208
Mom, war years 210
Dad, war years 210
The three sisters send a picture to Dad overseas, 1943 218
Dodie, High School Senior (two photos) 220
Captain William Ross Beal and drilling crew
 on site in North Africa ca. 1942 221
Louise Vanderburgh, Muriel Pinckney and Dodie Beal 226
My father recuperating, Atlantic City Army Hospital, 1944 247
My sister Joan in her WAVE uniform, 1944-1945 261
Dodie at Blackstone College, 1946 267
Dodie's Blackstone Graduation, 1947 267
Young Married Couple, Mallory and Dodie Stephens 275

Acknowledgments

My husband's family in this country and before goes back much further than mine. It was therefore convenient that I could ask him questions or double-check my knowledge with him. His sister Alice also answered some questions relating to the early period of Brewster, especially the Howes family. My husband encouraged me in my efforts with his patience.

My thanks go to my editor, Roxanne Carlson, for all the work she did in preparing my manuscript for the publisher. Her help and patience are most appreciated.

My thanks also go to Robert Pare for his computer expertise and for his work on my old photographs.

Thank you to the friends who went through school with me and remained my friends.

Introduction

Brewster, New York, during the 1930s and 1940s was a good place in which to grow up. A good family with aunts, uncles and cousins made life full and comfortable. Its history includes mining, the coming of the railroad and the namesake of the village, Walter Brewster, whose beautiful house has been restored.

It was the era of radio, as there was no television. We listened to "The Bob Hope Comedy Hour" with Frances Langford, serials with Orson Wells as Lamont Cranston in "The Shadow" (1935), "The Lone Ranger," and daily soap operas. Movies and newsreels in the theatres were shown in black and white. We paid fifteen cents at the movie theatre, and my mother told me she paid five cents when she was a child.

The Great Depression affected thousands of United States citizens, yet my life was barely touched by it. Whatever I did not have, I did not miss. What I had was a good mother who did not over discipline but made sure we learned civil behavior and compassion, and a father who showed his love to his daughters with his warm smile, making picking up hickory nuts for his penuche fun, taking us ice skating and passing on his love of flowers, plants and trees. Occasionally my mother referred to her three daughters as "daddy's girls."

My friends and acquaintances became a part of me – even those with whom I did not stay in touch.

World War I had its affect through the Decoration Day parades, as I walked holding my mother's hand and listening to the marching bands.

World War II slid into my life as it did others', as we learned what was happening in the world – and then, literal bolts from the blue as Pearl Harbor was attacked. The citizens went into action either in the defense industries, Civil Defense or on the battlefields. I believe that much of the bad news and my personal feelings at the time were suppressed, as it was too much for this sensitive teenager to embrace. After all, our local newspapers printed notices of the deaths of a classmate, the brother of a friend, my sister's young love; and boys came home without our knowing what they had been through.

I write these reflections trying to be true to the life around me, trying to honor those family members and friends with whom I shared sadness and not forgetting that we all had a good life and much fun during those years.

If one wonders why I chose the title, *Tonetta Lake*, it is because I spent so many hours, days, years at this small lake fishing, swimming, sun burning, dancing, ice skating and growing up.

EARLY HISTORY

Some History of Brewster in the Town of Southeast, New York

As a small child, I knew about the Hudson River, the Great Lakes, the Atlantic Ocean and the Pacific Ocean. It was when I was in school, specifically taking geography, that I studied New York State with its Finger Lakes, the Erie Barge Canal and the location of the cities of my state. I learned all the products made in the cities of New York, like gloves made in Gloversville, shoes made in Johnstown and shirts made in Troy. New York State during my youth was very busy commercially and very prosperous from one end of the state to the other. Geography fascinated me.

Having crossed the Hudson River at New York City but not having seen it upstate nearer its source gave my imagination something to work on. Then in my studies I learned about Henry Hudson, who had come upon the mouth of the river where New York City is now, and then explored in his small ship this river I would cross possibly hundreds of times.

Before the English drove the Dutch out and renamed the city New York, the Dutch had named it New Amsterdam after their city in the Netherlands.

Although I would often hear about the Phillipse Manor on the Hudson River, it would be later that I learned of the Town of Southeast, north of Westchester County and West of Connecticut, having been included in the Adolph Phillipse Land Grant of 1697. It was not until 1812 that the final act was passed by the New York State government making Putnam County (named after Revolutionary War General Israel Putnam) its own entity. The new county of Duchess (later to be spelled Dutchess) included the area that would become Putnam County.

In learning about the early settlers who came to America on the *Mayflower* in 1620, I found that one of the leaders was Elder Brewster. His son Nathaniel Brewster graduated from Harvard College. A house on Oak Street that I passed frequently walking or in an automobile was built by Walter Brewster, a descendant of this brave settler in Massachusetts. Being a skilled and enterprising citizen, he not only constructed this columned building that faces the schoolhouse and overlooks Main Street, but built at least fifty buildings along Main Street. The unusually wide Main Street was laid out by Walter Brewster in 1849. The Walter Brewster House, renovated by dedicated town citizens, is now listed in the National Register of Historic Places. Up to this time, the settlement had no name. It became Brewster after many shipments of needed materials were sent to Walter Brewster, addressed to "Brewster's Station." Earlier settlers made their homes northeast of Brewster, known as Sodom, on Turk Hill Road, as well as in the village. The village was incorporated in 1894.

Walter Brewster House, courtesy Denis Castelli.

St. Andrew's Church, courtesy Denis Castelli.

Town Hall, "Laugh Night," ca. 1915, courtesy Denis Castelli.

Howes Castle, "Morningthrope," courtesy Denis Castelli.

Postcard ca. 1950 of Main Street, Brewster, New York, courtesy Denis Castelli.

The Howes Family, the Circus, and Their Contributions to Brewster and the Country

As I was growing up, I often heard the words, "the Howes Castle on Turk Hill." I thought, "Do we really have a castle in Brewster?" In my early teens, I would see two elderly gentlemen and their mother amongst the congregation of St. Andrew's Church sitting in a pew on the right side. The two men were Reuben Howes and Townsend Howes. What a history these people had.

Descended from Thomas Howes, who sailed from Yarmouth, England in 1635, this family lived a true emigrant's dream. Hard-working people as the early settlers were, one of the family members, Thomas Moody Howes came to Southeast (Brewster) in southern New York State in 1748. He was a descendant of Jeremiah who had been born on board the ship that took these emigrants to the new world at Yarmouth, Cape Cod, in 1638.

The seventh son of Thomas Moody Howes was Daniel who married Ruhamah Reed. Their sons Nathan and Seth, nineteen years his junior were the names known to the people of Brewster as "circus people." At the age of fifteen Nathan learned the art of rope walking done without the use of a balancing bar. In 1815, he married Clarissa Crosby of Southeast, whose mother was a direct descendant of Elder William Brewster. She was, therefore, a descendant of the Brewsters who emigrated to Southeast.

Because of family relationships, it is interesting to local people that there is a connection politically between Nathan Howes and more recently D. Mallory Stephens, his son, Willis H. Stephens and his grandson, Willis H. Stephens Jr., all of whom served in the New York State Assembly for many years. Nathan, who built his home, "Stonehenge," in Sodom, east of Brewster, served as supervisor of the Town of Southeast (1840–1841 and 1849–1850) and later became a New York State assemblyman. Nathan's son, Elbert Howes, served as supervisor of the Town of Southeast from 1881–1888. The connection was my mother-in-law, Grace Hine Stephens, who was descended from the Howes.

During the late 1700s and early 1800s, menageries and traveling equestrian shows sprang up in many places. From these grew the circus, and the area around Brewster was struck by an entertainment mania with people investing in or joining the touring company as employees. Daniel Drew from Carmel, New York, was an early participant. He became a Wall Street financier, endowing what became the Drew Seminary for Ladies in Carmel, four miles west of Brewster.

I remember hearing about the elephant, "Old Bet," purchased by Hackaliah Bailey of Somers, New York, and I passed the statue that stands atop a tall column of stone in Somers as have thousands who travel on Route 22. Old Bet was killed by an angry farmer in Alfred, Maine, on July 26, 1816, unaccustomed as he was to seeing such a large "exotic" animal. A second elephant, "Little Bet," was also shot ten years later.

As a young person, when I attended the Barnum and Bailey Circus, I did not know the connection of P. T. Barnum and Seth Howes of Brewster. They became partners in 1853 in what was called the American Museum and Menagerie.

While in England with his circus, Seth appeared before Queen Victoria, a circus enthusiast, and was presented with a bloodstone ring by Prince Albert. This ring is now in the Stephens family.

For seven years the brothers communicated by letter, and these letters are in the possession of descendants living in Missouri; in fact, the family of my deceased cousin, James White. His mother, my Aunt Norma, read many of these letters to me in her later years. On returning home, Seth Howes with his English bride toured the United States, hauling beautifully colored wagons for the next show of the Great London Circus, also called Seth B. Howes' Great European Circus. It was an elaborate spectacle, a theatrical extravaganza being turned loose when these wagons rolled into town. In time the circus was moved by rail, but the people saw the wagons—if not in their town then in pictures, in movies and now in museums. They were true showmanship, designed by the Howes.

Tom Thumb, brought from England, was an outstanding attraction of this early circus. I saw one of Tom Thumb's chairs as it was in the possession of a Howes descendant, Elbert White, who married my Aunt Norma. Since Tom Thumb, sometimes called General Tom Thumb, was a midget, this chair was the size of a child's chair, and was folding with canvas for the seat and back, very like the folding lawn chairs adults used in the summertime when I was a child.

Seth no longer partnered with other circus entrepreneurs in the area. Nathan's twin sons, Egbert and Elbert, did continue the tradition after he died in 1901.

Lilly Deacon, half-sister of Mrs. Egbert Howes, married Adam Forepaugh, whose father owned the Forepaugh Circus based in Philadelphia. She was known for her training of horses and dressage. I remember seeing this renowned lady as she sat on her front porch on Peaceable Hill Road in the 1930s. I also saw her after she moved to the home of Mrs. Fred Ives, Egbert's daughter. She resided at the home of Mr. and Mrs. Willliam Ives on Railroad Avenue (North Main Street), always seen on the porch dressed entirely in black from head to toes.

The offspring of the Howes brothers were mostly girls, and after a few generations the name of Howes in the area disappeared. Nevertheless, numerous Brewster families are descended from the Howes family. (Today, with the advancement and current use of DNA testing it would be possible to discover what Brewster people are descendants of the early Howes brothers.)

Seth B. Howes left his home, a copy of an English castle named Morningthorpe, and it is still in existence on Turk Hill Road, well cared for by the residents of the rehabilitation center that purchased the property in the 1980s from the Howes family who did not reside in Brewster. On that property hidden under the weeds, there are three circus rings that were used for training in those early years. The other Howes residence, Stonehenge, is privately owned. In the 1940s, the property was used for a boys' camp where my brother Ross was a camper.

In the late 1870s, Episcopal services were held in the Town Hall. The beautiful stone St. Andrew's Church was not dedicated until 1901. It was Seth Howes whose generous gift made possible the completion of this church that stands at 6 Prospect Street with beautiful stained glass windows and fine wood beams and pews. The building went through a devastating fire that year but was quickly rebuilt and dedicated in 1903. I often studied the very colorful stained glass windows in St. Andrew's.

While the Howes Family of Cape Cod held reunions every so often and had collected much history of that part of the family, it was not until 1993 that they learned about their circus cousins in Brewster, New York. The reunions are held every three years either in Massachusetts or New York.

Dolores Beal married Mallory Stephens, a descendant of Nathan and Egbert Howes, while Norma MacLean, the author's aunt, married Elbert White, the descendant of Nathan and Elbert Howes, Egbert's twin. There are no descendants of the White family in Brewster, but there are many children and grandchildren of the Stephens family, thus the Howes family line continues. There are also descendants of Elbert Howes living in Missouri.

The name "Howes" can now be seen inscribed along with other early circuses on the outside of the new museum on the grounds of the John Ringling north complex in Sarasota, Florida. Seth Howes and his circus had many associations with other men and their circuses, the names changing as Howes became partners with other circus men.

Gail Borden, the Creator of Condensed Milk, and His Contribution to Southeast and the Country

Having a large house and three girls who wore dresses to school, my mother was able to hire Emma Birdsall to help out with ironing. Miss Birdsall, as we called her, lived on Route 22 between the Borden factory and Turk Hill Road.

There were only one or two occasions when I was to stay overnight with Miss Birdsall in her house that was so different than our house. It was very old and she had a privy in the back and a chamber pot under the bed.

I was glad that I did not have to be her guest more than I was. As I sat at the linoleum covered kitchen table, I was given a piece of bread and was told that I could spread the bread with the condensed milk from her jar. It was thick, syrupy and very sweet. This was Borden's Eagle Brand Condensed Milk made in Brewster.

Gail Borden was a direct descendant of Roger Williams who established Rhode Island. Although we learned in school that Roger Williams settled Rhode Island, he was not connected to Brewster's Gail Borden in our lessons.

Gail Borden, knowing that non-sterile milk caused illness and death to babies, decided to build a factory that would condense and preserve milk.

When he moved to Brewster, a land of dairy farms, he partnered with wealthy Jeremiah Milbank, and he began to prosper in the mid 1860s. The dairy farmers of the area also prospered. Mr. Borden resided with his family living on Main Street in the house built by Walter Brewster that was known as the Brewster House.

In 1870 Mr. Borden built his condensed milk factory using the waterpower of the East Branch of the Croton River, as factories in the Northeast used streams and rivers to run factories of all sizes. They gave employment to millions of Americans.

Many Brewster people were employed at the Borden plant both in production and management. The farmers in the surrounding area transported their containers of milk in horsedrawn wagons to the factory where the milk was turned into condensed milk. Willis Hine, my husband's grandfather, was one of the farmers who sold milk to the Borden factory.

During the Depression years of the 1930s, condensed milk was often a substitute for butter and was a favorite sweet for children. It is now mainly used as an ingredient in desserts.

The factory closed its doors when the number of farms in the area decreased, as their land was condemned for the New York City reservoir system that encircles the village of Brewster. Our next door neighbors were ones who had a home that had to be abandoned for that reason. Yet there were farms that survived into the 1940s and 1950s. During periods of drought or when water has been drawn down, the old stonewalls of these long-gone residences become visible. The reservoir close to Brewster on the east side is the East Branch Reservoir. The Bog Brook Reservoir is immediately north of the East Branch. The Middle Branch Reservoir is between Brewster and Carmel, west of Brewster. The Croton Falls Reservoir is to the south and west of Brewster.

During the early 1930s farmers also delivered milk to the cheese factory at the intersection of Route 124 and Allview Avenue just south of Brewster. The cheese maker was James Tavino who lived on Route 124 and was the father of my classmate Peter Tavino who was a well respected general contractor.

Mining in and around Brewster

During the 1930s and 1940s, people who lived in Brewster could still relate stories of the mines and their importance to the area. As a child when I heard that there was a mine under Main Street, it registered, but I did not know the significance of it or the extent of the mining. I knew Marvin's Mountain was the hill behind the railroad station and somewhere on the hillside there was an opening to the mine.

The opening to the mine under Main Street was in the center of the village behind some stores, but it was hidden. The names of the mines were: Brewster Mine, Tilly Foster open pit mine and the Theall and McCollum mines on their farms two miles southwest of Brewster on the west bank of the Croton River.

The only road going up Marvin's Mountain, Hillside Avenue was not far from my home. Part way up this steep road was a dead-end crossroad, and this area was residential. The rest of the mountain was forested except at the very top was the home of Aaron B. Marvin. This area intrigued children, and we used to venture into the woods at the end of the crossroad to see what we could find. What we discovered may have been a brook that did not seem to run anywhere. In the water was a wood raft made by previous explorers. Perhaps at that time there had been more water than what I was seeing. We did not come upon the mine entrance. Boys found more than one entrance to the old mine and did some dangerous exploring.

One of the young explorers was my husband, Mallory, who with his friend went down into the mine opening located in the area of the spillway not far from Croton Falls. They found an old, rusting metal pot used during the mining process. Ten years later another boy who explored the mine opening was my brother Ross, who today says that he and his friend went several hundred feet into the mine, and if there had been a collapse, no one would have known where they had gone and they would never have been found.

One day I with friends hiked to the top of that mountain past the home of my friend Gabriel Blockley. Like her father, a World War I veteran, she was an excellent snare drummer. We cautiously followed the road to the top and found we were in the driveway of the Aaron B. Marvin home. It did not seem to be occupied. Somehow, it seemed mysterious to us, and I was a little frightened by being up there in the woods at the top of the mountain by ourselves. We decided we should not approach any closer and retraced our steps toward home.

The Importance of the Railroad to Brewster

Twelve years before the Civil War, two railroad lines came to Brewster. The New Haven & Hartford ran east to west along the shore of Lake Tonetta and within view of the Brewster school, and the Harlem Railroad whose name was later changed to New York Central Railroad ran north and south. By 1849, the Harlem had extended to Pawling. It ran from Grand Central Station in New York City north, stopping at Chappaqua, Mount Kisco, Katonah, Goldens Bridge, Purdys, Croton Falls, Brewster, Pawling and north to Chatham. In time there was an express train from Grand Central to 125th Street then to White Plains continuing non-stop to Brewster—and the reverse. The express train was welcomed by commuters and others using the Brewster station. I can remember riding the local train, and it seemed to take forever.

The importance of the coming of the railroad cannot be overstated in the development of Brewster and the commerce of the area. It carried commuters from Brewster and surrounding communities to their places of business. It also brought vacationers from New York City to the lakes in the area. People vacationed at Peach Lake, Putnam Lake, Lake Carmel, Lake Mahopac, Peach Lake where Doctor Vanderburgh and his family had a cottage and Tonetta Lake where my family had cottages.

In the bloodiest war our country has ever experienced, the one in which countrymen fought against countrymen, Putnam County gave its share of men to fight and die. Tens of thousand of volunteers from New York state left their homes to fight. The New Haven & Hartford became crucial in transporting newly manufactured wartime equipment to military destinations, and the New York Central carried thousands of recruits from their home towns to their first assignments for training in the Army, Army Air Force, Marine Corps, Navy and Merchant Marines during both World War I and World War II. During World War II the railroads played an especially vital role as our war plants, gearing up to an unbelievable capacity, turned out the needed vehicles, tires, guns, ammunition, airplanes and parts and moved them on the freight lines. I saw hundreds of trains with hundreds of cars carrying war supplies during World War II when I was on the shore of Tonetta Lake.

Brewster is fifty-two miles north of New York City with the commuter line running through and dividing the village, the village proper being located on the east side of the tracks and Marvin's Mountain rising just west of the New York Central tracks. Half a mile north of the station and west of the tracks was always residential as was the area east of the village except for Main Street. As the tracks run north from the station (the street that ran parallel to the track was of course called Railroad Avenue), the land rises, and there was an iron bridge for access between the two parts of the village. The old firehouse was a short distance south of the bridge. In 1936 the cornerstone of a new concrete bridge was laid, this one being about a quarter mile north of the old bridge and could accommodate automobiles and trucks more safely. Route 6 is the main road from Danbury, Connecticut, through the village of Brewster and across this bridge to Carmel, the county seat and to Mahopac and beyond.

Train travelers went to the Tudor-style brick building at the foot of Marvin's Mountain and there was a concrete platform connecting to a longer wood platform that ran the length of the train. One could step out the station door and take only a few paces to the steps of the railroad car. There was always a conductor standing to take our hands and greet the many Brewster citizens with whom he was acquainted. And often the engineer leaning out his cab was a familiar face. Since one could board a northbound or southbound train, it was sometimes necessary to cross one set of tracks to reach the second set, but that would change.

My friends were children of trainmen employed by the New York Central Railroad as engineers, firemen, ticket masters, conductors as well as those who worked at the roundhouse a mile north of Brewster. There repairs were made, cars cleaned and trains turned around to be headed back to New York City.

During the 1970s and 1980s one could see changes being made all along the New York Central, when it became Metro-North, emanating from Grand Central Station to Brewster. Passengers could no longer walk across the tracks to take a train, but for safety reasons had to climb stairs, cross over the tracks below and descend to the new platform. Brewster Station has been refurbished and a lovely village clock is now there for all to see, thanks to the insight, interest in history, motivation and love of Brewster by many citizens and this trend is continuing.

Aqueducts and Reservoir System

It is undoubtedly true that we all take water for granted for drinking, laundering, cooking, bathing and so forth. Besides having village water in our home, we also had a hand pump near our back door. It was an F. E. Myers pump, and my father used to have fun with us about their logo, "Take off your hat to the Myers" with its picture of a little girl having her hat taken off by a spray of water. My father, being in the well drilling and pump business enjoyed the water from this well and often asked one of us girls (I took my turn when my sisters were away at school) to fill our pitcher at the pump. It never felt like a chore to do this.

I was also used to seeing the lakes and many reservoirs that enhanced the beauty of my surroundings.

One can only imagine what it was like for the early Dutch and then the early English settlers with no running water. They were fortunate that streams, rivers and lakes dotted the area. Later water was obtained from wells. But in those early days, with a growing population, problems arose as to health and safety. The need for ample, clean water became an economic and social issue for the counties north of New York City including Putnam County, as the population continued to grow.

In 1837 almost four thousand immigrants began work on the aqueduct system and reservoirs called the Croton System for New York City. This was to impact almost everyone in the town of Southeast in one way or another. There was not only a need for laborers but also for housing. The town of Southeast was affected not only geographically but also socially as the East Branch Reservoir, the Middle Branch Reservoir, the Bog Brook

Reservoir and the Diverting Reservoir were built within its boundaries. Yet this system was only a small part of the extensive aqueduct system for New York City.

Irish and Italian laborers and artisans, recent immigrants, were used on this vast project, many of whom were experienced masons. Many of these families came to Brewster, and their children attended and graduated from Brewster High School. They served honorably in the military of World War I and World War II as well as attending and graduating from college, conducting businesses and serving in government on all levels. Many of their children were classmates and friends of mine, and really wonderful people.

The Village

For me and for many people a mental picture of Brewster village is to see the single brick building "in the middle of Main Street." Being a small island on which the American flag prominently flies, for many years it served as a traffic circle around which automobiles drove in a counterclockwise direction. This is no longer the case, as traffic has been redirected. As a child, I often accompanied my mother, as we crossed the street to the First National Bank, where my mother greeted the tellers and other people going in and out of the building. This building became offices of the Town of Southeast.

Another historic building on Main Street is the Town Hall, a large two story building erected in 1896. The first floor below street level, during the 1940s housed the Brewster Police. The Chief and only policeman in those days was Charles Schaefer, uncle to my friend, Ruth Orton. James Durkin was a policeman for a time. After World War II, Gene Blaney was a policeman at the time my father was appointed Police Commissioner, an unpaid position, as I remember.

Once the place where the local people cast their votes in elections, it is now the home of the Southeast Museum. The main floor that housed the auditorium is approached by climbing a wide stone stairway and passing through columns and a wide doorway. As a child I saw my first show, the operetta "H.M.S. *Pinafore*" and also a minstrel show performed by local thespians. Some of the actors/singers were in blackface with lips painted white, as was the case with the comedian, Eddie Cantor, in his vaudeville acts. That was before the population understood how demeaning this was to our black citizens. Traveling shows, movies and local performances were attended there for many years. It is a building worthy of preservation.

Walking through the village in the 1930s and 1940s I passed Millar's candy store, where for a few pennies I would buy my favorite candies. There was Duffy's Hardware Store, Hope's Drug Store, Anderson's Drug Store, both with soda fountains. Diehl's Bakery turned out the best cinnamon muffins, but I never saw anyone using the soda fountain. It had been a very popular place in the 1930s, however. Mr. Leo Susnitzky ran the New York Store, a dry goods store where one could buy fabrics, work shoes, denim overalls and shirts. It was stacked to the ceiling with clothing. There was Durkin's Feed store next to the station, Goossen's Furniture Store, a shoemaker who did a good job of replacing soles and heels, Blanco's Taxi Service, Prisco's Taxi Service and bus company, Scolpino's Liquor Store, Benny Rosenberg's Stationery, Oxman's Stationery, the Brewster Diner, still in operation, Genovese's Bowling Alley, a shoe store, Feinson's for ladies, the post office next door to the Ritz movie house, later renamed the Cameo, Putnam County Savings Bank,

The First National Bank, and other small stores, dental and doctors' offices and law offices. Morehouse's Wood Mill was on the north edge of Brewster on Railroad Avenue. I often passed Mr. Morehouse as he walked into the village, a very pleasant man. P. F. Beal and Sons, my family's water supply business, was the only business on Carmel Avenue. Brewster Lumber Company was on Route 6 on the left between the old Borden's factory and the New Haven trestle bridge on the eastern edge of town, while the Hollywood Café was just after the trestle. It became Love's and later was purchased and is run as Sciortino's Restaurant. As these pages are written, it is a fine restaurant with facilities for banquets and weddings.

There was no seafood store in town, but there were plenty of fish in the brooks and lakes. Salted mackerel and cod could be purchased in a small wooden bucket and by soaking could be turned into a good meal. My father prepared mackerel this way, and I learned to like it with fried potatoes for breakfast, but I never learned to like cod.

There were several grocery stores including an A & P and First National Stores, all run by local men. I recall going to the grocery store across from the station run by Mr. Foster whose daughters were schoolmates of mine. Mr. Foster would put the brown paper bag flat on the counter to write in pencil the cost of each item, as he put it on the counter. The written numbers were large, and he would quickly add up the long list using his pencil and write down the total. He would then place the pencil behind his ear. With the total figured, the bag was filled with the purchased items. Mergardt's Market was also popular with food and meat shoppers.

The cookies were loose in bins and were picked out and put in brown paper bags. There were also some packaged cookies.

Calculators, credit cards and computers were still glints in the scientists' eyes, and plastics had not been developed for these and other purposes. These storekeepers took telephone orders and made home deliveries in their trucks without extra charge. Sometimes my mother would make use of this service. Many people did not drive, or had only one car used by the husband in his business. Therefore, this was not only a convenience, but in many cases a necessity. It would not be accurate to say that women did not work outside their home, since there were those who were teachers, bookkeepers, secretaries, dental assistants, nurses and shop owners. But on the whole most married women were in the home taking care of children, keeping the house and laundry clean and doing the shopping for clothing and food. There were also many who, being skilled at the sewing machine, made clothes for themselves and the children.

This is some of the history that is the background of my growing up in Brewster and had some considerable effect on my life.

P. F. Beal and Family

Nellie and Philip Franklin Beal, My Grandparents

Philip Beal settled in Elyria, Ohio, after arriving in the United States from Germany in the early 1800s. At nineteen years of age on December l, 1862, Moses Beal, son of Philip, volunteered and was "mustered in" the 15th Independent Battery, Ohio Light Artillery to fight in the Civil War. The records show that he was 5 feet 9 inches tall, had brown hair and grey eyes. His advanced one-month salary was four dollars. In 1891, Moses invented and procured a patent on the first Rotary Core Hydraulic Drilling Machine used for obtaining ground water, but after the seventeen-year period he let the patent lapse. This machine drilled with a circular motion extracting in smooth cores the stone through which it drilled, thus its name. Philip, the son of Moses and the namesake of his grandfather, decided to go east in 1893 and first settled in South Dover Plains, New York, now Wingdale where he made test holes for the South Dover Marble Company. In fact, he went further, making test holes, as there was interest in finding marble as far north as Vermont. After a few years he moved to Brewster, New York, with his bride, Nellie Wilcox, who came from Ohio. The first water well drilled by this method was on Prospect Street in Brewster about 1894.

Philip started in the business of drilling for water, a necessary and welcomed commodity at that time in American communities that were at the beginning of their growth. They resided in a rental house on Prospect Street, which like all the streets was unpaved and dusty. While living there, their first son Moses Clay was born in 1895 followed by William Ross in 1897. In time three other children came into the family: Philip F. Jr. in 1901, Aileen in 1905 and Helen (known as Babe) in 1908.

P. F. Beal had a brother, Moses, and a half-sister, Louise. Moses and son had a well drilling business in Harriman, New York. When I was a young girl, I met them when they came to visit my grandfather. Other family visitors were my father's cousin William Beal and family who came to visit from Elyria, Ohio.

Nellie Wilcox was the descendant of Daniel Wilcox, born in England about 1565, and Elizabeth Cook, who arrived in Massachusetts in the 1600s. Her male ancestors as well as her children and grandchildren served in the wars in which America was involved, including the Revolutionary War, the War of 1812 and the Civil War.

Nellie and Phil, my grandmother and grandfather, had a Dutch colonial style house built in the village at the base of Putnam Avenue with brown stained shingles, white trim, a wide porch and porte-cochere. There were times when visiting at Christmas time, and it was wet and snowy, my father stopped the car under the roof of the porte-cochere to let us run up the stairs and across the front porch to the front door. Otherwise, we would all use the back door of the house. It was behind this house that Philip Franklin Beal carried on the well drilling business that in my lifetime grew, became P. F. Beal & Sons, Inc. and was passed down to the fifth generation.

Grandmother Nellie Beal, ca. 1939, left, and
Grandfather Philip F. Beal Sr., ca. 1941, right.

On the first floor of the house was a living room that had a small built-in overhead library with glass-windowed doors. Under that was a built-in velvet-cushioned bench, a place where one could curl up in comfort to read. By the time I was aware of this corner, it had seen use in the family of children who were now grown and gone, the old books still located behind the windowed doors. There was also a fireplace with a mirror over the mantle; the woodwork around it was painted white as was much of the woodwork in the house. In time that room became the office of Philip and Ross Beal where desks replaced the Victorian furniture.

The front door led to an amply sized foyer with a fireplace and overhead mirror. Two steps led to a circular landing with windows and the curving stairway to the second floor. In the late 1940s that room became the reception room where the receptionist used a PBX telephone switchboard that connected the business telephones from in-office to the service department in the back yard.

A wide opening led to the dining room that had a fireplace, a side door to the front porch and large windows looking out to the back yard. The view encompassed a green island with a sour cherry tree, the garage and business building. On one side of the yard was a stone wall where Nellie had her fragrant, pink climbing roses. On the other side of the driveway were the apple and sour cherry trees. What was the dining room became the office of the bookkeepers with files.

There was a small breakfast room with table and shelves and the electric refrigerator that replaced the wooden icebox. This was a labor saving appliance as the icebox necessitated a block of ice to be replaced on a regular basis as well as having the water pan with the melted ice water removed and emptied daily. In the kitchen stood the cast-iron stove that had to be constantly fed with wood. When the electric stove was purchased, the large cast-iron stove was not removed. There was a small, glassed-in porch leading to the back yard. Today it would be called a mudroom. Between the kitchen and the dining room was the pantry that housed all the chinaware, glassware and silverware used for family holidays and for company. The woodwork in this room was stained dark brown and varnished. There was also a sink and at the end of that narrow room was the door leading to the back stairway.

On the second floor were three modest size bedrooms and a large master bedroom with tiled bathroom. One room that was connected to the master bedroom was used as an office and had an oak, rolled-top desk. There was a second, green tiled bathroom off the hallway. It is believed that medium green or black and white were the popular bathroom colors of that time.

The tiling was done by a master tiler, Frank Thorpe from Brewster, whose work has stood the test of time, as work done around 1910 was still beautiful sixty years later. From the top of the stairway to the end of the hall lay an oriental runner.

Home of Nellie and P. F. Beal Sr., Brewster, New York.

The third floor could be reached from the back stairway. There were three rooms: one a spare bedroom, one housing a billiard table and one small room used for a live-in maid. A story told when I was young was of Nellie finding that the perfume on her dresser was emptying faster than it would have simply from her infrequent use. She found that the maid had been taking sips to get a buzz. Another time, her delicate underwear would disappear and then reappear, as her maid used it, washed it and then returned it to the drawer. This story was told as a matter of fact and with humor, but of necessity this person was replaced. As a child, I was not aware of a maid. I believe my grandmother needed the help when the five children were young.

As a boy, Ross watched horse or horse and wagon races on the dirt road that was Railroad Avenue. When, as a child I heard him tell of this, it was hard to imagine, as we had an automobile, and the roads were paved. Before he was old enough to join the Boy Scouts, he used to envy those boys who were. One summer day the scouts walked to Peach Lake, about five miles to the southeast of Brewster, and there made camp. Knowing about this trip, Ross tagged along. When he was discovered at Peach Lake, he was told he could not stay and that he must walk back home. Eventually he became a Boy Scout and received a copy of the book, *Black Beauty*, as a reward for collecting and naming the most wildflowers. This love of nature, trees and flowers became life-long.

When Ross was a young boy, his father purchased a second-hand violin so that his son might take lessons. Fairly accomplished, Ross would be asked by his mother who was then president of the local Women's Christian Temperance Union to play a solo at a monthly meeting in their home, and he did as he was asked. He took his violin with him when he entered the Pawling Preparatory School. One day when some boys were tussling in Ross's room a boy picked up the violin and hit something or someone with it cracking the wood. Ross had to report this to his father. The violin was repaired, and he continued to play it, at least through his high school years.

Each evening parents and five children sat around the large dining room table eating the dinner their mother had made. Food was plentiful for this growing family. There were vegetables from the large family garden as well as sweet and sour cherries, a variety of apples, peaches, pears and grapes. Vegetables and fruits were canned in the summer and fall for winter's consumption. Grapes were made into grape juice and grape jelly. In the summertime, there were fresh cherry and apple pies as well as pears and apples to eat out of hand.

Consumption of alcoholic beverages and Sunday card playing were taboo in my grandmother's household. Nevertheless, she was a tolerant woman. My grandfather had ordered a cider press from Sears and Roebuck and had assembled it in their basement. Of course, he had plenty of apples and grapes for making juice, and a press was exactly what was called for. Unknown to Nellie, however, he was trying his hand at making wine, bottling it and putting the bottles on the shelves.

There was never a reason for her to go down the dimly lit stairs to the concrete and stone basement. One day as Nellie sat rocking in the dining room, she started hearing popping sounds coming from the basement. Phil's wine was fermenting and the bottles were blowing their corks, red juice splattering all over the room. Nellie sat rocking and rubbing her thumbnails along part of the arms, knowing what was going on below. Despite her strict adherence to prohibition doctrine, she gave Phil his leeway letting him have his fun. Nellie could be found daily sitting in her favorite rocker lightly letting her thumbnail slide back and forth until many years later she had created a noticeable two-inch lengthwise groove on both rocker arms. This rocker remains in the family, lovingly preserved.

The two younger boys were energetic and fun loving to the point of playing jokes on one another and their siblings. Sometimes the joking got out of hand, and it was often at the dinner table. On a hot summer evening while enjoying their dinners, there was a dish of melting butter on the table, undoubtedly for the fresh garden corn and homemade bread. When one sister across the table requested that her brother pass the butter, he picked it up and handed it to her. Just as she went to grasp it, the butter dish was tilted and with a little help the soft butter slid into his sister's lap. One can only imagine the reaction it caused.

All the Beal children attended Brewster High School, Ross graduating from the Pawling Preparatory School, and Aileen going on to graduate from Syracuse University. Babe also attended Syracuse University. It was their mother who knew the importance of education, and I suspect that she had dreams of becoming a music teacher or continuing in music in some way.

The eldest son, Moses Clay, served in the Army in World War I, and his brother William Ross served in the Navy. Ross also served in the Army in WWII, as did his daughter Joan Ross Beal who served in the Navy (WAVES) as a corpsman.

During WWI while serving on the USS *Amphitrite* and being denied enough liberty time to get home while in the Navy, Ross, age eighteen or nineteen, wrote his parents, "I figured on coming home tonight, and I washed my blues up and got all ready and then they spring it on us. We probably won't be gone over a month or two anyway. I don't suppose I want to come home any more than you want me to…Don't worry about me mother. I'll be all right and come back to you all safe and sound if it pleases God. Don't forget that I love you and Dad and that the things that you have told me all along thru life help me more than you would think."

When Mose and Ross came home after the war, Mose went to the University of Pennsylvania Dental School and upon graduation set up his dental practice in Poughkeepsie, New York. He married Edna Vreeland, who lived on Prospect Street. Their son, Donald Ross, started pumping gas for Mobil Oil Company and ended up an executive in the company. Their daughter, Barbara, went to Mount Holyoke College. The other Vreeland family, (Edna's uncle) had a home on Turk Hill near Morningthorpe, the Howes Castle. Ross joined his father in the well drilling business as did his brother Phil, both learning the ropes from their father.

Philip F. Beal Jr.'s two sons served their country in the military during WWII. Philip F. Beal III with a major in chemistry was in the accelerated program at Williams College, class of 1943, graduating mid-December 1942. In *Those Who Served/Those Who Waited,* he said, "Amongst my interviews, one was at the Winthrop Chemical Company in Rensselaer, New York, and one was at Columbia University. The job at Columbia was so secretive I couldn't tell much about it. It later turned out to be The Manhattan Project (the development of the A Bomb). The one in Rensselaer sounded much more interesting to me," as they were producing penicillin.[1] After a year and seeing that other chemists were being drafted, Phil joined the Navy. After officers' training, he "was ordered to join the USS *LST 40* as the Gunnery Officer." The ship went to the Pacific, taking part in the invasion of Okinawa. During his post-war career at Upjohn Pharmaceuticals, he was the first to synthesize hydrocortisone, which benefits the world community. He subsequently was nominated for the Nobel Prize.

Malcolm T. Beal, Philip's brother, after training at Fort Belvoir, Virginia, served in the Army Engineer Corps stationed in the Aleutian Islands during WWII.

---

[1] Dolores Beal Stephens, *Those Who Served/Those Who Waited* (Bowie: Heritage Books, Inc., 2003), 171.

Philip F. Beal III, World War II.   Malcolm T. Beal, World War II.

William Ross Beal (left), Nellie Wilcox Beal, Moses Clay Beal during World War I.

Philip F. Beal Jr. (left), Philip F. Beal Sr., William Ross Beal in their office at P. F. Beal and Sons.

Although not during wartime, two grandsons of Florence and Ross Beal served in the military. The son of Joan and Paul E. Peckham Sr., Paul E. Peckham Jr. served in the Army Air Corps. Mallory Stephens Jr., son of Mallory and Dolores Beal Stephens, wanted to join the Army. Having graduated from Hamilton College, he took the Westchester County, New York, examination hoping to win the one spot offered to attend Army Officers' Candidate School. The highest grade would receive this commission. Mallory received the highest grade given in the previous four years but did not receive the commission. Unfairly it was given to a female who placed second on the examination. Determined, he went into the Army as a buck private and applied for Officers' Candidate School. After graduating as second lieutenant, he went through Airborne School and then completed Ranger School. He was assigned to Korea for one year and returned to the states just as the invasion of Panama was taking place. At the time, the Army was reducing its size, and after serving three and a half years, Mallory chose to return to civilian life. He and his wife Claudia live in Wells, Maine. After teaching many years, she is now Dean of Faculty, and Mallory and a colleague hold classes at their Maine Primitive Skill School for teaching survival and primitive skills, a fascinating field. Those attending these gatherings range in age from school children to older adults.

A grandson of P. F. Beal Sr., William Ross Beal Jr., after going through the military program at Norwich University, served in Korea, and during the Vietnam War served in Laos and Vietnam as a member of the Army Special Forces. He retired a lieutenant colonel. Having served in Europe and within the United States, he and his wife Elaine eventually retired in Waterbury Center, Vermont. They have two children, Catherine Sheryl and William Ross III.

Florence Letitia Becomes Fatherless

Florence Letitia Simms was born on August 1, 1900, in Newark, New Jersey, to Florence Cox Simms and William Bross Simms. Her grandfather, Guy Simms, served in the Civil War and was marooned, having no food, on a small island in the Caribbean watching his ship, *Planter*, and others being ripped apart by pounding surf. With no navigational systems, they did not know of the coral reefs below. In his diary he talked about carpenters and a few sailors from the ship; I assume that he was a carpenter. When Florence was five years old, her father, a veteran of the Spanish American War, having served as a nurse/army medic and in civilian life a railroad motorman, was killed while boarding his train. After his death, Florence and her mother lived with Grandmother Susan C. Cort Cox, a widow who had nine children. She had been born in Manchester, England, in

March of 1858 and immigrated to the United States in the late 1800s with her husband, Joseph Cox. Susan's father was a physician. Three of her brothers arrived in this country, one of them going west to California. The other two settled in New Jersey where they carried on the successful Cort Shoes business. These were the handmade high-top shoes popular at that period. Of Susan's nine children, George died at the age of six and Edward, with no protective gear, died of a rugby accident on his nineteenth birthday. The siblings' names were Joseph, Florence, George, Anne, Edward, Susan, Edna, Charles and Edith. Not all the brothers lived at home.

To support her large family, Susan, now widowed, ran a boarding house in Newark, New Jersey, having to provide meals not only for her family, some of whom worked, but also for the boarders. Grandmother Cox's youngest daughter, Edith, was born the same year that her daughter, Florence, gave birth to a baby girl she named Florence Letitia Simms. The older children with whom Florence lived were her Uncle Charlie, Uncle Joe, Aunt Sue, Aunt Anne and Aunt Helen. One of the chores given to Florence (called Flossie or Wassie) and her aunt, Edith (called Dee Dee), as young girls was to heat the water in large pots to be used for bathing. Often one child would have to use the bath water of another. With Edith and her uncle Charlie, six years older than the girls and the ringleader, they were known as the terrible trio. One of the pranks was to rig up a slide using the dirty coal chute for sliding into the dark cellar where coal was dumped. For this Charlie charged one penny, the two girls, "Dee Dee" and "Wassie," being his best customers. Daily life was one lacking in conveniences as we know them, so life was difficult. Yet life was happy in this love-filled and fun-filled home.

Every other week Flossie looked forward to a special treat. Her Grandmother Simms would come by in a black horsedrawn carriage and take her for a ride and to spend the day. Her circumstances were considerably better and her manner more formal than those of her other grandmother. Flossie told of going to the dressmaker with this grandmother where she chose fabric for the season's new dresses. Nothing is known beyond this. Her real family was the Cox family who nurtured her with love.

Florence's mother met Tom MacLean after completing nursing school at the Essex County Hospital. He was a nurse, and they both worked at Overbrook Hospital in Newark, New Jersey. They married, leaving "Flossie" with her grandmother and moving to Westport, Connecticut, where he was offered a job with the trolley company. Infrequent trips were taken from Newark to Westport, Connecticut, where young Florence was able to visit her mother. When the family acquired a new Overland Touring Car with snap-on side curtains for rainy days, it wasn't long before there was a yearly vacation trip from Westport to New Jersey. On February 3, 1912, Norma Helen MacLean was born. The family moved to Norwalk, Connecticut, after her father received a promotion to superintendent. The two half-sisters, though twelve years difference in age, developed a life-long mutual affection.

It was in her twelfth year that one day her stepfather and mother arrived at the house in Newark to take Florence away from her Grandmother Cox's care. There had been no prior communication regarding this, and it struck Florence with gut-wrenching sadness at leaving the loving home environment of her grandmother. Of course, the compensating factor was being with her mother and half-sister who was only an infant.

Florence had a somewhat rebellious personality as a schoolgirl. In the eighth grade one of her classes was cooking. One day the students were being taught to make oatmeal. (There was no instant oatmeal at that time). They were sitting and while the teacher stood with her back to the students, Florence took a spoon, filled it with oatmeal and flipped it onto the column that was out of sight of the teacher. The classroom erupted in muffled giggles. It seems that the oatmeal running down the column was not discovered for some time. In telling of this childhood prank in adulthood, one could see the devilish glint in her eyes. At the time, I knew I would never do something like that, but it was enlightening to hear my mother revisit her youthful escapade.

Although a good student, at the end of the eighth grade, it was necessary to contribute to the family's financial needs. At this early age, Flossie (Florence) started working in the office of the trolley company where her stepfather was superintendent. She then found a job as a telephone switchboard operator, where she would answer the call, then push and pull plugs on the board in order to connect one party to another. The telephone system at that time made it necessary to ring the operator who would then make the connection to the number given her. She would say, "Number please, just a moment, here is your party," and so on. It was entirely possible for the operator to listen in on the conversation with this early system, and in small towns gossip was easily spread in this manner. Did my mother listen in on any conversations? I am sure she could have; however, working in a city there may not have been the breaks between calls as there would have been in a small town with one operator.

Being a pretty teenager and having an occasional date, she would invite the boy into their living room on her return home. From the time they entered the house her stepfather would drop shoes on the floor above or otherwise make it unpleasant for the young people below. It was his way of saying he was upstairs and did not want his stepdaughter to have a boyfriend. It was not a pleasant household. Still, she wouldn't leave her sister and mother, as the three of them were always happy together.

At eighteen years old, Florence met a young man who was attending a preparatory school and headed for college. They fell in love and were seeing each other frequently until their romance was severed. Florence always felt that the parents had the final words in this relationship. The boy was from a very wealthy family who owned a flourishing glass works business in upstate New York. The parents undoubtedly felt that their boy was too young and should not become serious with a girl not on their social level. Florence thought this was the real thing, and she was heartbroken. He was her first love.

Her stepfather barely provided for her mother and half-sister, Norma. Because of this situation, Florence gave her mother money from her earnings. Her mother also worked at home using her skill as a dressmaker. When Norma's school needed a new auditorium curtain, her mother was engaged to create one using material of heavy velveteen and sewing it on her treadle machine. Although Norma was a joy for her mother and half-sister, Norma's mother and father were not happy together and were destined in time to divorce, a rather rare occurrence in those days.

A favorite pastime for young people was to take a bus to the beaches on Long Island Sound in Connecticut. As a child, going to the beach with her mother was greatly anticipated. One day

Flossie came out of the dressing room to report that there was a "bad lady" in there. When asked about it, she reported smoke coming from the bathhouse. Someone had been secretly smoking a cigarette. Women did not smoke in public, as it was considered "unladylike." It was at one of the Connecticut beaches that Ross became acquainted with Florence Letitia Simms, who was by then eighteen years old. She was swimming with girlfriends, wearing the bathing fashions of the day: silk bathing suit and hat, stockings and bathing shoes.

The Young Model

One day the artist, Henry Raleigh, came into the telephone company office and saw Florence while she was working. He asked her if she would like to pose part-time for him in his studio in Westport, and she accepted. Mr. Raleigh and other artists earned their living as illustrators while their true interest was oil painting. He would draw Florence in a pose and the clothes that depicted the essence of the story, called the "story picture," and it would appear above the title of the story in such magazines as *Collier's* or *Saturday Evening Post*. One of the stories was about a young woman who was preparing to leave home and was saying goodbye at the doorway to her home. It was my mother at the age of eighteen, standing at the open door with coat and hat on and carrying a small traveling case. Another picture shows a young girl sitting in an attic reading a letter that had been stored or perhaps hidden away. The preliminary sketches were in charcoal, and Mr. Raleigh gave four of these sketches to my mother. In later years, each of us children was given one of the oak-framed sketches.

Charcoal sketch of Florence Letitia Simms.

"Story picture" for *Collier's* Magazine.
Ethel Lovey (left), Florence Letitia Simms (right).

Besides Mr. Raleigh, whom she greatly respected, there were other struggling artists who would drop by Mr. Raleigh's studio to visit. She was sometimes "borrowed" to pose for another artist. Growing up, I often heard her tell about the various artists with whom she became acquainted; one whose last name was Lietchtenauer. Another was Arthur Dove, who eventually became known for his work. It was a thrill for me to find his paintings being exhibited at the Phillips Academy in Andover, Massachusetts, and a few years later at the Currier Art Museum in Manchester, New Hampshire. It is said that he was one of our country's first abstract expressionists. My mother would have been very happy to have been with my husband, our daughter, an artist, her husband and me during these visits.

Florence's modeling was part-time work, and she enjoyed it. She was learning from these talented artists. There was a time however when she was put in an awkward situation. One of the artists came a little too close and made a proposition to her that embarrassed and shocked her. She was still a teenager and still had much to learn about life and adults, but she handled that situation well.

While in her late teens, Florence decided to leave her work and modeling. There was a traveling theatre group that she decided to join and try her hand on the stage. (In 1985–1986 her granddaughter, Diana Stephens, was in her high school theatre company, singing and acting but not getting a leading part until her schoolmate Vanessa Williams had graduated. She decided against theatre life and pursued writing and painting.) Florence went to Boston with the troupe, and it is believed that her career on the stage was not a long one. When she returned home, she received a letter from one of the artists who wrote, "I heard today that you had quit trouping and were back in Norwalk and going to take a job. Now we need figure drawing badly and wondered if you would care to give us a half-day or Sundays. Or any other time convenient. I didn't write you before as I heard you were an actress and wouldn't need artists' names in New York. Please let us hear from you, and if you can possibly see your way clear to pose, you'll not only be earning some money but helping two struggling geniuses to learn to draw. Sincerely, Lee Townsend."

In 1918 Flossie was still posing for the artists when her other job permitted, and Ross was courting her with plans to marry. Being from a small town and knowing its ways, he asked Florence to stop posing for fear of "raising eyebrows" in Brewster.

Florence Letitia Simms Becomes Mrs. William Ross Beal

Ross and Florence were married on April 17, 1919 when she was nineteen years old and he twenty-two years old. He never liked the name "Flossie," so loved by her family, but preferred to call her Florence and did so his entire life. Ross was learning the business and had charge of his own drilling machine that went from one job to another being pulled behind a truck. A job might take two to six weeks to complete. At the time of their marriage, the machine was at a farm in Peekskill, New York. Going on a trip was not an option, both because he had a job to finish, and because Ross had no money saved. Besides, spending money for a honeymoon would have been frivolous. Ross and Florence spent their honeymoon boarding at the home of the people who were having the well drilled. They were young and happy.

Soon after their marriage, P. F. Beal Sr. started to plan the house to be built for the young couple on Putnam Terrace. While they were waiting for its completion, they lived in an apartment on the corner of Oak Street and what was known as Progress Street or Post Office Hill. (The U.S. Post Office at that time was located half way down that hill. One entered it by going down a flight of stairs on the outside of the building below street level.) Florence was young and very sensitive and wanted to be accepted by the community. One day two older ladies of the community called on her, and she prepared to serve them tea and biscuits. While the hostess was preparing the tea tray, she overheard one of the women remark to the other, "I see she has a mirror on the wall!" Florence found she had moved into a community where the Victorian ethic was alive and well.

Florence, age twenty.

Florence found her mother-in-law to be welcoming, kind and helpful. Although her mother, Florence Simms MacLean, kept a neat and clean home, there was little money for extras for decorating or entertaining. So Florence, though courteous and having been taught table manners, at nineteen years old knew nothing about the finer household objects such as quality bed linens, china dinnerware, silver place settings, crystal serving pieces or how they were to be used. Nor had she been amongst a large family after leaving her Grandmother Cox and her many uncles and aunts.

Nellie, Florence's mother-in-law who was a refined lady, helped her to learn many things about housekeeping. Nellie had her own little stash of cash that she kept tucked into the top of her silk stocking. Sometimes she would reach up and under her dress and extract a roll of bills and hand forty or fifty dollars to Florence. Then she would tell her to go to John McLean's Department Store in Danbury, Connecticut, ten miles away and buy herself "some nice lingerie." I am certain that she did the same for her other daughters-in-law and her own daughters.

Although Nellie had a lovely home, her entertainment was confined to the Women's Christian Temperance Union, church affairs, her growing family and later on the ladies' bridge club. She played the piano for her own enjoyment and perhaps for the meetings. Her beliefs in the tenets of the WCTU must have been keenly felt. It was a movement led primarily by the women of the United States, many of whom saw the men in the family throwing good money after bad—and usually money they could ill afford to waste.

The windows of their dining room looked out the rear of the house where the business was located. Nellie sat each afternoon in her rocking chair and could see what was going on in the business yard. In the early days, the accounting books for their well drilling business were kept on the dining room table by Nellie. After finishing for the day, the books were stored in the desk that had its place against the wall nearby. Later, when her sons Ross and Phil worked in the business, the office was moved to the large garage building, and it occupied only two small rooms. The rest of the building was used for the shop where repairs were made on the equipment.

Philip F. Beal Sr. was fortunate to have his sons working with him until his retirement. In the 1940s, he was a member of the Brewster Board of Education. His friends were some of the "village fathers," and in his later years four of them would get together to play cards. He spent hours working in his large vegetable garden and tending his fruit trees. After time spent in the garden, he would sit down on a nearby log and look over the large array of vegetables: carrots, beans, tomatoes, corn, beets and other plants that would in time bear fruit. Sometimes I would look for my grandfather and be told that he was down in the garden. He would walk over to the row of carrots, pull one out, wipe it on his trousers to take off the dirt and hand it to me. I would eat the carrot, even though it had not been washed, because my grandfather had given it to me, and I knew he would eat one that way himself.

My grandfather stored his beautiful Buick sedan in the garage area next to the office. The car was nicely upholstered, and a plush, gray car blanket hung from the strap behind the front seats. My grandmother dressed in her summer Sunday best would sit on the rear seat, and my grandfather in his Panama hat, white trousers and dark jacket would sit behind the wheel and drive to the Methodist Church. I am certain that Phil only did this for Nellie, although his religious beliefs were never made known to me. And these clothes had the mark of Nellie, as Phil was most comfortable in the clothes he wore working in the business or in his garden.

In 1921 Philip Jr., who was working for his father, married Helen Tuthill, the only child of James Foster and Anne Lape Tuthill of Brewster. As a young couple Helen and Phil lived on Putnam Avenue about a block away from Ross and Florence. One of the boys would scout out a fine place for a picnic on a warm Sunday in summer, and they would head out in Ross's black LaSalle. The two girls would have prepared fried chicken, biscuits, fruit and homemade cakes and the four would find the field out of town, where they could spread their blankets for their feast and fun.

The Young Mother and The Cow that Came to the Door

While living in their new home on Putnam Terrace, Florence gave birth to her first child, Norma Jane, in 1921. While Jane was a baby, her great-grandmother Susan C. Cox visited them and was probably in her mid-seventies. It was the first and last time she was to make a trip to Brewster. Florence was especially fond of her very kind and loving grandmother, the person who had been so good to her when her father had been killed. On May 30, 1923, a second girl baby was born and was named Joan Ross Beal.

While in her early twenties, Florence decided to have her brunette hair cut and styled in a "bob." This style was appearing in cities, whereas in Brewster the style appeared more gradually. Older women still wore their hair long, twisted into a bun or rolled off the neck, but hair was never left hanging straight and long to the shoulders or below. But Florence was adventurous and liked the new style even if it raised eyebrows. Short cuts became popular, but it was a long time before long flowing hair was accepted. From all reports, however, she was considered to be "a beautiful girl" with blue eyes and a pretty smile. I do not believe that her carefree daring lasted, as she was integrated into the small town environment.

When the permanent wave came into vogue, I believe it was worth one's life to be subjected to having hot clamps attached to the rolled hair, each roller having an electric wire from the head to the electrical source. It was also quite a sight, judging from pictures. In case of flood or fire, this mass of electrical wires would not be easily removed. Nevertheless, curled heads started to appear, and eventually a safer permanent waving process was developed. For home use, curling irons were used, but they were not electric, and had to be placed on a hot stove, sometimes becoming too hot and singeing the hair.

In 1919, Brewster was a small village that was surrounded by dairy farms, and a few people kept one or two cows for their own use. Florence used to enjoy the visits of two young boys, the sons of Doctor and Mrs. E. R. Richie, who lived in a large house close to the village. The property lay between Main Street and Oak Street. His young sons Don and Bert took their cow from house to house selling milk directly from the animal. My mother bought milk from them when they came, wanting to be good to the boys. Consuming raw milk is not considered healthy, as it can contain disease-producing bacteria, usually from unclean cows. My mother probably used it in cooking, rendering it safe for consumption. When pasteurization became the law declaring that all milk must be pasteurized, it meant heating for a prescribed period of time and temperature. I remember young friends mentioning that they drank raw milk.

These two likeable boys became well educated and well liked, Donald becoming a physician who practiced in Croton Falls, New York, and Bert a professional photographer. They had three younger siblings, Jane, Beth and Doug. My parents were fond of Don and Bert, and when Dr. Don came to our house, my dad enjoyed visiting with him. On one visit my father had to give him some fatherly advice about the danger of driving in a convertible car because of the hazard of rolling over in an accident. He had just purchased a very handsome convertible that he drove with the top down in nice weather. I do not think he was convinced.

P. F. Beal & Sons

By the fourth generation, the owners of P. F. Beal and Sons, Inc. were college educated in accounting and engineering. (Nellie Wilcox Beal, being the exception, studied music at Oberlin College.) After World War I, my father was working with his brother Phil in their father's business. They both had a sense of humor, were fun loving and were known to play the occasional practical joke on their siblings. Ross knew how to relax when the workday ended, although I can remember times when he appeared concerned. He often talked about his work with my mother. I learned that it was not simply a matter of taking a drilling machine to a site, drilling a hole and producing water.

Experience had taught them about the topography, where there was rock likely to produce veins of water and whether the requirement could be satisfied. He knew the areas of Putnam, Dutchess and Westchester counties so well, that by walking around a prospective site, he could decide exactly where to locate the drilling machine. This knowledge was true for Philip and later his son, Malcolm, and then passed down. In one case that I recall, a large amount of gallons per minute was required for a manufacturer in Yonkers, New York—that is, several hundred gallons—and Ross worked out the process for this to happen. The answer was to drill five wells in a large circle, each one producing enough water to bring the total to the required amount.

He and his brother were conscientious about doing good work for their customers. The drilling machines had to be kept in good running order and be towed by truck to each job. It took between two and six weeks to complete a well. Sometimes a good flow of water was obtained at sixty or seventy feet. For other wells, a depth three hundred feet or more might have to be drilled. Following the completion of the well, pumping equipment and a water storage tank were installed in an underground concrete pump house. The experience of both these men weighed heavily in estimating what depth might be necessary and therefore how to write the contract. In time Phil's son Malcolm came into the business with Ross, as did Phil's widow in 1946. Philip Sr. was greatly saddened by his son's early death, and he died in 1948.

The business grew under these three men until they employed twenty-eight men as drillers, pump installers servicemen and in the office a secretary, bookkeeper and receptionist. It was after the death of P. F. Beal Sr., that the entire office was moved into his vacant house, utilizing the three main rooms on the first floor. Ross learned about the development of the new high-speed drilling machines and presented the idea of purchasing one to Malcolm and Helen. That first machine cost in the neighborhood of sixty thousand dollars. It was a lot of money, but it could drill most wells in one day rather than four weeks. So they did invest in that fast drilling machine, which in time negated the need for so many of the older models. Another innovation that came along was the submersible pump that was installed within the casing of the well, making the concrete pump house an unnecessary expense for the owner.

Both men were heavy smokers, which led eventually to Phil's death at age forty-six and in time to Ross's as well. The business continued under the same standards with Malcolm, his sons and their families. William Ross Jr. chose not to go into the business although he worked as an assistant serviceman during his high school years. He chose the Army as his career. Malcolm never smoked, but my sister, Joan, started as a teenager, and in her seventies she succumbed to the same fate as her father and uncle from cancer.

LATE 1920s AND EARLY 1930s

The Third Child Enters

We lived at 12 Putnam Avenue in a mid-Victorian style house that my parents had bought from Marjorie and Herbert E. Hazzard, who were building another house on Garden Street. These kind people moved out of their home into my parents' house on Putnam Terrace before their house was completed, so that this eager couple could start the renovation in their newly acquired house. At the time there was one baby daughter, Norma Jane, in the family, followed by the birth of my sister, Joan in 1923.

In 1927, I was born at the Danbury Hospital, ten miles away in Connecticut. I was given the name Dolores, because my mother thought the actress, Dolores Del Rio, was very beautiful. It rather embarrassed me, when she later told me. By that time my father wanted a boy baby, and having spoken of his wish before my birth, he arrived at the hospital with a gift of a beautiful platinum bar pin set with diamonds. He had let his preference be known but was sensitive to my mother's feelings. When going out for the evening, she dressed tastefully, wearing this pin on her plain black or navy blue dresses. Except for her engagement ring, it was her only valuable piece of jewelry.

Florence Reacts to Humiliation

Throughout the years, I have learned of people changing their religious denominations, and the reasons vary, ranging from religion, the liturgy, the formality or plainness of the service. When my mother married, although she had been raised in the Dutch Reformed Church, she became a member of her husband's church. There she met some of the local and old Brewster families.

There are occasionally dark times in peoples' lives, and for Florence as a young married woman, she was faced with a humiliating experience in church, of all places. Having three little girls to bathe and dress and one of them in a baby carriage, it took a good deal of effort to have her children and herself dressed in time for the service. Saturday evening was bath night for the children, and the next morning they were dressed in their Sunday dresses, coats, white socks and patent leather shoes. That is the way it was; nothing casual or sloppy. Cleanliness is next to Godliness.

One Sunday she walked with her family into the village to attend church. She sat with her children while the service was being conducted, and at one point, an elder of the church was speaking to the congregation when Joan, age four rose from the seat and ran down the aisle to the front of the church. The elder, known to all, stopped his comments and spoke these words: "Would the mothers of children please keep them in their seats." I can see my mother's face flush in anger, as she retold this story. She had to retrieve her daughter without help from anyone.

At the end of the service, she walked home to Putnam Avenue. As she passed the house before ours, she turned into the driveway where her older friend, and an Episcopalian, Mariah Birch lived with her widowed sister, Esther White, and her brother, Fred Birch, whom I only saw wearing his golfing outfit: knickers, stockings and brown and white saddle shoes. As soon as they greeted one another, my mother, undoubtedly still fuming from the humiliation, asked Miss Birch, "Do you want another member in your church?" Of course she was welcomed, and from that week on she and her family were Episcopalians. My father soon joined her, and they both became active members of St. Andrew's Church, my dad later becoming a vestryman. This was not the usual reason for changing denominations.

One of the first things Ross and Florence did in the house was to sand, stain and wax the oak parquet floors. They worked hard to put the house in an immaculate condition. Without funds for new furniture and rugs, they visited antique shops and purchased second-hand Persian rugs that were to have further wear as the family grew. It was about this time that my mother fell from the ladder while house cleaning. The treatment for a fractured spine at that time was to lie flat, and spend many hours, even weeks lying on an ironing board.

The exterior of the house, which was painted in two tones upon their moving in, was in time painted entirely white. The driveway was gravel as was the walk to the front door on Putnam Avenue. The porch was wide and wrapped around from the living room to the dining room with granite steps at each end. There was a back porch to the kitchen. The freestanding green kitchen cabinet was an important feature, as it held the flour bin in the upper part, a bread drawer below and storage as well. The enameled pull-out counter or the large kitchen table was used for rolling pie dough and kneading bread dough.

Next to the kitchen was a pantry where dishes and glassware were stored, with a swinging door between the pantry and the dining room. The living room looked out across the porch to Putnam Avenue. These rooms seemed so large to me as a child. A stairway with a landing led to the second floor, where there were four bedrooms. One bathroom was off the hallway and one off my parents' room.

The third floor fascinated me. After reaching the top of the stairs, there was a Dutch tip-top table against the wall. It was one my mother had found in an antique shop and was probably used as their dining room table in their first house. My father eventually put a pool table in the main room and had friends come to play with him. As a small child, I liked to climb the stairs and sit in one of the high, wire chairs to watch my dad play until my mother called me for bedtime. There were two other rooms, one having a curved wall as the rooms on the second and first floor had. In time a kitchen was installed as well as a bathroom, and when my grandmother lived with us she had her own apartment there.

Tonetta Lake

My grandfather and Nellie built a summer cottage on the western shore of Tonetta Lake. My husband's great-grandfather, George Hine, owned and farmed the entire area surrounding the lake plus the area south of it for many years. My husband's grandfather, Willis Hine, and his uncle, George Hine, cut ice from Tonetta Lake, stored it in a large building on the south side of the lake and delivered it to the residents of Brewster. He later sold the business to the Palmer family of Peaceable Hill who also ran a dairy farm.

They cut the winter ice, stacked and stored it in the large barn nearby. The brothers Ed and Henry Palmer continued the business of delivering ice to homes in and around Brewster.

They were generous to the many children who ran up to the truck on a hot summer day asking for a piece of ice to suck on. From frequent deliveries Mr. Palmer knew what size block of ice would fit. He chipped the piece at the end of the truck until it was suitable. The large ice tongs would be hooked onto the block of ice, and be carried with one hand to the ice compartment. Ice was delivered until the 1940s when electric refrigerators were being introduced to replace iceboxes.

Many of Brewster's citizens enjoyed swimming and picnicking at Tonetta Lake in the summer and ice-skating in the winter. It was surrounded by trees and farmland with marshland and inlet located at the north end. The New Haven railroad tracks ran along the northwest side of the lake, the rest being wooded, where there are now hundreds of houses surrounding the lake.

Tonetta Lake Park, barely two miles long, was the first and oldest development of homes in the Brewster area built as summer cottages by people from the boroughs of New York City, Long Island and Yonkers. Most of these homes are still in use, and although they were built on small lots, many have been upgraded and additions constructed becoming year-round homes.

Once called Tone's Pond, Tonetta Lake was named after freed black slaves, Tony, who lived with his freed wife, Etta, on the shore of this lake. Tonetta Lake was to become my summer home, my father's respite from his business two miles away and more work for my mother.

When I was about ten months old, judging from an old photograph, I was an obese baby. There I was, a little round blob sitting in an oval, porcelain bathtub that was on a table in the screened-in porch of a rented cottage at Tonetta Lake. In another photo several months later, I was sitting, dressed in a pretty, feminine pink dress with puffed sleeves, my face with puffed cheeks and puffy, fat little legs. If someone had given me a gentle push, I would certainly have rolled.

Apparently my mother was concerned and consulted the doctor who proceeded to ask what she had been feeding me, and if she was preparing me for a career as a sumo wrestler. My mother was young, without the information available that would have made her understand about calories and fat. She had been giving me a prepared formula, probably the only brand available in 1927, without diluting it. Fortunately, our small town doctor helped her to see that what she had been feeding her baby was an unhealthy amount of nutrition, and the slimming process began.

Baby Dolores.

My grandfather built a second cottage on the west side of the lake next door to his first, and it was this bungalow on the water where I remember spending time with my Grandmother and Grandfather Beal. Before I was born, my father had a cottage built next door to my grandfather's with only a few feet between the two. Large panes of glass for "picture windows" were not in use, and the small windows usually were screened. As they were built for summer use, they were small and functional. There was no air conditioning for hot days, so a screened-in porch was useful in catching any breeze.

When I was a child, my mother decided to arrange for painting lessons with an artist in Danbury, Connecticut, where she drove the ten miles once a week. Her only oil painting from this period is a portrait of her youngest blonde child. At that time portraits were done with a background of landscape, and this portrait was done in this manner.

Oil portrait of Dolores by her mother.

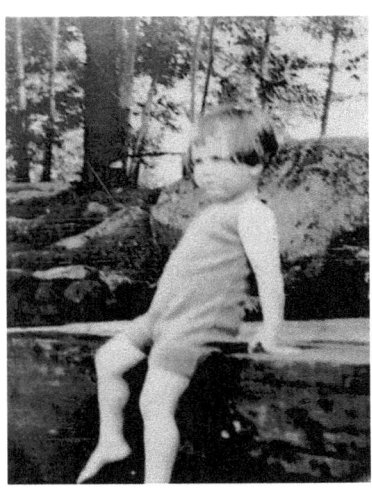

Dolores (Dodie).

At a later period, she enrolled in an art correspondence course, sending in weekly assignments. However, because of her growing family and involvement in the community and church affairs, her painting ended until in her later years, when she studied in Jensen Beach, Florida, with Emil Gruppe, a prolific painter who also worked in Rockport, Massachusetts. (His paintings were collected by Frances Langford Evinrude, the actress/singer who toured with Bob Hope during World War II. We saw them both in movies.)

At that time my father was making very beautiful hatbands using pheasant feathers, each one applied individually. Mr Gruppe admired my father's hatband and wanted one. My father wanted one of Mr. Gruppe's paintings. They negotiated, exchanging a hatband for a painting that from then on hung over the fireplace at their Tonetta Lake home.

Pulling Worms

At a very young age, I became interested in learning to fish. This pleased my grandfather who always had a couple of long bamboo poles under his porch. They each had a line with a red and white bobber and hook, and there was always a small wooden bucket of night crawlers in damp soil with grass on top. Whenever I wanted to fish, I went to my grandfather who would direct me to the poles and bait. I learned to row the boat and to drop the anchor overboard without burning my hands on the rope so that I could still fish. When I brought my first sunny or perch to shore, my grandfather taught me how to clean it by removing the scales, the head and the innards. One day I caught my first bullhead. That fish had to be skinned, and my father did it with alacrity as I looked on. Trolling at the north end of the lake, with my father rowing the boat, I caught a pickerel. and I had never caught such a long fish. I didn't particularly like to eat the fish that I had caught, but I received encouragement.

Seeing my grandfather walking around the lawn at night after it had rained, leaning down pulling worms from the ground, I decided I wanted to do the same. It was especially fun when there was rain falling, and I was covered with a rain coat and hat. Leaning over with my flashlight directed on the wet grass, I would spot a night crawler slowly exiting its hole. As taught, I quickly put my hand on the worm with enough pressure that the worm would not retreat into its hole. Then slowly I would pull it until it was well out of the hole and in my hand. Into my soil and grass-filled soup can it went. There were times when the worm was only partially above ground and, though I knew it could break, I tried to capture it by pulling on it, and sure enough it broke apart. Another lesson learned! It was bedtime when I had enough worms to fill the can. I also learned that worms did not stay alive for very long in the can. If they were too wet for too long, they died, and if they dried out, they died. They had to be replenished periodically.

While living at the Tonetta Lake cottage, my mother went weekly to our house in town and laundered our soiled clothes and bedding in her 1930s electric washing machine with the rollers through which she had to feed each individual piece in order to squeeze out the water. The socks were scrubbed by hand on the corrugated, glass wash board. I remember the use of yellow soap for very dirty clothes and shaved soap or a product called Oxidol for the washing machine. Detergents were not on the market, nor were electric dryers. Then the heavy basket of wet laundry was taken up the stairs to the outdoor clothes lines. When the clothes on the line had dried in the summer breeze, they were folded and put in the car, ready for ironing. They had an outdoor fresh fragrance. It was an all day production. (There were many times when I was older that I removed clothes that had frozen on the clothes lines and were like boards when being removed.)

Poor "Wow"

I was told that before I was old enough to remember, my sister Jane had a pet German Shepherd. She spoke fondly of the dog she had trained to do a few tricks. Frenchy was taught to carry a lunch bag from our house to my grandfather's house at the bottom of the hill. If there was food inside the bag, he would not stop or try to tear it apart, but would deliver it. It is not difficult to imagine my sister teaching him, as she was very patient in such endeavors. Her method of training would have been to send Frenchy with the bag in his mouth while she took a different route and then calling him from two houses away.

When the time came that Frenchy was no longer alive, and I was about four years old, not yet in school, I was given a black and white Cocker Spaniel puppy with an affectionate personality. The name I had given him was Wow, undoubtedly from the expression that came from my mouth upon receiving my puppy. He was definitely my dog, and he followed me in my travels. Wow would sit outside the door of wherever I was visiting, and my mother by looking out our door could tell where I was in the neighborhood. I would sometimes play with my friends, the Bruen brothers, when they were with their grandmother. David was older than Donald. One day when it was very cold, and there was snow on the ground, I trudged up to Putnam Terrace to visit my friends. I knocked on the door, and it was answered by their grandmother. She told me I could not come in, because my galoshes were too wet. So I trudged back home. David has lived in Brewster his entire life, becoming the first Putnam County Executive and serving for many years; and so I have known him for a long time.

Wow did not grow to be very old, as one day he was in the road and was struck by a car. He came back to our back porch critically injured. My mother did not want me to see him as he was, and she knew that he would not survive his injuries. After making a telephone call, she told me to walk down to my grandmother's house only two houses away. It wasn't much later that Wow died, and my father buried him. I didn't have a chance to say good-bye. My parents thought they did the right thing sparing me his suffering.

Aunt Norma

In 1929 my mother's half-sister, Norma MacLean, began studying music at Marshall College in West Virginia. One summer she donned her new orange bathing suit made of rubber. This curiosity wasn't seen past the one summer, as it undoubtedly succumbed to the summer sun. She was probably eighteen years old, and I adored her.

When I was about five years old I understood from conversations that something was going on in my Grandmother MacLean's home—that she was very unhappy with her husband. I heard the name Tom frequently. My Aunt Norma was in school in Norwalk, Connecticut, where they lived. My grandmother had to do alterations and make clothing in order to have enough money for herself and her daughters. When Norma became accomplished, she became the accompanist for the dancing classes, earning money for her piano lessons. My grandmother told of the heavy velvet curtain she was commissioned to make for the high school auditorium. Later, when I was familiar with that sort of stage curtain, I was greatly impressed with her accomplishment. She was my dressmaking teacher.

She and my Grandmother MacLean were by then living with us. I loved sitting on the piano bench, when she played

Chopin and Schumann. Her Steinway piano was being purchased by time-payments with her mother's hard-earned money, but the time came when my father decided to pay the balance due. A teenage girl with her talent and interest had to be encouraged with a fine instrument. Norma's mother was also paying the thirty dollars per semester for college tuition plus another thirty dollars per month for room and board. Ross and Florence gave Norma money for the many extras needed beyond the tuition. Norma was always grateful for the help and love of her sister and Ross. She said she felt she was treated like one of their daughters.

There was a rocker in the foyer just below the stairway, one that my Grandmother MacLean would go to when she deemed it time to rock me. Rocking would make me sleepy and ready for a nap. I am sure she did that when I was a baby, but I recall many times being held by her as well as my mother, even after I could walk. As she rocked, the rocking chair would "walk" across the floor, and often she would rise from the chair and slide the chair back from where she started. When my grandmother stood up to carry me up the stairs, my mother would call to her and say, "Mother, she is getting too big for you to carry." I believe that she did not want to give up this loving gesture.

Pussy Willows Where They Do Not Belong, and Family Activities

With two sisters in the elementary grades, I was alone in the house with my mother, when my father was at work. It was a big house for a little girl. Just inside the front door, my mother had placed a large urn with pussy willows my father had brought home. They intrigued me. I felt them, and they were soft yet fuzzy. I picked one from the stem. It fit nicely in my nostril, and

I pushed it. Then I picked another and pushed that one into my nostril. This was fun. So I did that several more times, until I tired of it.

Dolores (Dodie), age four.

Dodie and Jane in the latest fashions.

The next day my mother noticed I was not acting normally. Perhaps it was a stuffy nose or a fever. She called Dr. Alexander Vanderburgh, and he came to the house to see me. During the examination he looked up my nose, and saw something that did not belong there. He took tweezers and extracted a pussy willow. He looked again and saw another and pulled that one out. In all he removed about five pussy willows. My mother told me that as he was going out the door, she told him she thought there might be another one. He came back and looked again way up, and sure enough he found the last pussy willow.

I do not remember when I first noticed that we had a grandfather's clock in our house at the bottom of the front stairs. It seems as though it had always been there. When I was old enough and tall enough, my father taught me how to wind the clock, slowly and steadily so that the three weights of different sizes lined up at the correct place.

To keep it running it was necessary to remove any dust that found its way inside the case. In order to do this, he stood on a ladder or chair, removed the top square board, and carefully dusted everything within reach with the end of a feather. It was always referred to as "Dad's clock." My mother told me that a large, long box had arrived one day looking much like a casket. This was to be their anniversary present. On opening the box and finding it was a new Herschedy grandfather's clock, she knew it was for my dad. Of course they both enjoyed it throughout the many years they were married. She probably would have preferred perfume or a bouquet of flowers. My brother has that clock today. (My parents gave a more recent version as a wedding gift to my husband and me many years later). I am always reminded of my father when winding our clock.

We three young girls were always outgrowing our clothes and shoes. My mother liked to make the trip fifty-two miles south to New York City on the New York Central Railroad and outfit us for Easter clothes. This meant a new dress and coat for each. Hand-me-downs worked for school and play, but in one year we had all outgrown our spring coats. My mother liked to dress my two older sisters alike even though they were two years apart in age. One Easter they both had new navy blue coats with double capes that came to their elbows. Until recently my memory was of the most stylish, beautiful coats I had ever seen. They were about twelve and fourteen years old at the time, but they weren't exactly the model types, and the old picture changed my mind.

Each one of us anticipated the Saturday that we would be riding the train from the Brewster to New York City for our shopping trip except perhaps Joan. We climbed aboard the train with the help of the conductor, whom I am sure we knew, and found our seats. The seats of the trains could be moved so that one double seat faced another double seat. Thus, my mother and I could be seated next to each other facing my two sisters sitting together.

Taking the train from Brewster took an hour using the express train and about an hour and a half using the local train that made stops at all the small towns to White Plains and several stops after White Plains, all the way to Grand Central Station. It was exciting riding the train, but that was a long time to expect three girls to sit quietly. Inevitably, my two sisters would start swinging their legs, bickering, poking one another, standing up and fidgeting, especially Joan. When my mother felt things were getting out of hand, she would give my sisters "the look" that we all remembered. Her mouth would purse slightly, as she stared at each daughter. This meant, "You do as I say, or else." But the "or else" never came to pass. We knew what that look meant, and it kept us in line. At other times, when one daughter became obstreperous or would start to argue with her, she would say with a meaningful look, "DO as I say," or, "Don't talk to ME that way." We understood.

When I was about five years old, the shopping trip resulted in a new lavender spring coat and hat for me. Most of my clothes are lost in memory, but that coat and hat set is a colored picture in my mind. We called these new clothes our Easter outfits, as after the cold months had passed, many people were anxious to buy something new for spring and to wear on Easter Sunday. It was a national custom for those who could afford the expense. In the newsreels we saw the Easter Parade on Park Avenue where ladies and gentlemen strolled on the avenue in their latest colorful garb, pretty shoes, suit or dress and spring coat and always a special hat and gloves.

After my lavender coat and hat were no longer new, I wore them to school on chilly days. One drizzly day I was coming home and had crossed over the railroad tracks on the old iron bridge from North Main Street to Carmel Avenue along with children who lived on Carmel Avenue. Just as I was about to cross the road to reach the sidewalk on Putnam Avenue, Joey Mitchel, walking ahead of me turned, grabbed my hat and threw it into the running water in the gutter. I quickly retrieved it and crossed the road. For several years subsequent to that event, I would think of what he had done, because it upset me at the time, and I really could not understand it. I avoided him. As I became older, I could see that boys sometimes behaved that way. I did not hold it against Joe, as I could see he was a good person.

Before I could read I had stories read to me from my favorite large book of children's stories. Some of my favorites were: "Rumplestiltskin," "The Three Bears" and "The Teeny Tiny Woman in the Teeny Tiny House."

Summer at Tonetta Lake

During the summer we were at our cottage at Lake Tonetta, rarely referred to as Tonyetta. It was a typical cottage with three small bedrooms. In the bathroom there was a hand made tub lined in metal. I do not know the story behind that unusual tub, but I suspect that the plans did not allow for the usual long tub, and so my father had a square one made locally. The entire interior of our cottage was not bright, because the walls were paneled in bead board with a medium brown stain. We preferred to be out of doors, but on rainy days we had to occupy ourselves indoors with puzzles and playing cards. We always ate dinner indoors at the table in the kitchen next to the window.

It was about the year 1931 that my father had a motorboat on Tonetta Lake. I never saw my mother in it, although she may have taken a ride when it was first acquired. I was very small, when I learned that the motor was too powerful for the boat, especially on this small lake. One day he was driving around the lake, going very fast, and as he made a quick turn, the boat overturned, throwing him into the water. The motor went down to the bottom of the lake, and he could be seen waving that he was all right. (As a boy he was taught to swim by being pushed out of a rowboat.) I remember seeing an old life preserver hanging in the garage, but my dad was not wearing one that day. Everything that floated could be seen coming to the water's surface. There was no motor boating after that.

My father was good at capturing "the moment" on his 16-millimeter camera or box camera. He took many pictures of his family, as they grew. One was taken of my mother, and it could very well have been on or just after the occasion of my father capsizing his motor boat, nearly costing his life. In the picture my mother was sitting in a chair on the lawn facing the water. The expression on her face was one of anger, and my dad could not resist it. He had to snap that picture. If the occasion was after the boat event, it would be understandable.

It was always fun when my cousins, Malcolm and Philip, called Phip or Phippy, would come for the day. We swam and played on our yard swing, slide and teeter-totter. Sometimes other cousins would come with our aunts and uncles. My father's brother Dr. Moses Clay Beal (a dentist) and his wife Edna

Vreeland who had been raised previously in Brewster, occasionally drove from Poughkeepsie with my cousins Barbara and Donald. My father's sister, Helen (Aunt Babe) and Uncle Don Outhouse (later changed to Oothouse which was Dutch) from Croton Falls and their girls Jacquie, born in 1932, and Donna, born in 1938, as well as my father's other sister, Aileen and her husband Edmond Hawley and their son Buddy from Danbury, Connecticut, would all visit my grandparents at the lake.

We were especially close to the Beal family in Brewster. Phip was close to my older sisters in ages, and Malc and I were close in age. When we were in school Malcolm was one year ahead of me. I always felt a great fondness for him, as he was a kind and gentle person with a good sense of humor. We got along well, and he was always good to me.

One day at about four years old and apparently tired from all the play and swimming, I sat on the sloping back yard at the rear of our cottage. Soon I fell sound asleep on the grass in my woolen suit that had a tear in the lower back side. Having a tear in my suit did not concern me.

Woolen bathing suits did not have the life span of the nylon and latex fabrics which would come along years later. With use the woolen fabric tightened and shrank. Whether silk or woolen, the bathing suits worn by adults were shapeless and without much color. They tended to make even an attractive body look formless, leaving much to the imagination of the observer.

Each summer my two older sisters, Joan Ross, Norma Jane and I spent most of each day in our woolen bathing suits. At the front of the cottage there were wooden plank steps, where often my mother would on warm, sunny days place our lunches of sandwiches and milk. We faced the cottage with the lake behind us and our legs hanging through the steps. How happy we were.

Cousins (top to bottom):

Barbara Beal
Norma Jane Beal
Donald Ross Beal
Philip F. Beal III
Joan Ross Beal
Malcolm Tuthill Beal
Dolores Beal
Edmund (Buddy) Hawley

Ross, Florence and the three girls.

William Ross Beal, my father.

We were told we must wait one hour before going swimming, as a stomach cramp might occur causing us to drown. This was a hard and fast rule for many years. Later it was found to be an over-zealous concern. At the end of the day it wasn't unusual to see bathing suits spread on the back lawn drying in the sun.

There was no lifeguard but a family member who kept a watchful eye on us children, and until the age of four I swam with a rubber tube around my waist. A family movie captured the day I decided to swim without the tube. I was taking a big step, but was determined, because I loved the water and wanted to swim, as my sisters did. As I doggie paddled to shore, took off my tube, tossed it away and headed back to deeper water, the film in the camera ran out.

Mother with Joan Ross and Norma Jane.

Mother with baby Dolores.

As a small child, I wore white shoes that came to just above the ankles. I can remember seeing my mother applying a white liquid on them, especially on Saturday evening, so that they would be ready to wear on Sunday.

One summer day we children were playing and sitting on the back lawn of our cottage. I always insist that I must have been about four years old but my cousin Phil tells me I was older. Let's say five for my sake. For some reason there was a hammer nearby, and I picked it up and struck Phip on the head with it. Certainly he never forgot it, as he was about four years older, and I have a fairly clear recollection of the incident. It seems that I must have been quite young, otherwise I would have known the consequences of using such a lethal weapon.

Kindergarten: It Will Be Fun

In 1923, fire swept through Brewster's wooden school building while school was in session. In my book, *Those Who Served/Those Who Waited*, Joan Larkin tells about the day the school was burning. She said, "Harry Wells was in my class. The kindergarten and first grades were held in the basement, and when the schoolhouse was burning, Harry ran back into the building. He had forgotten to bring out his coat. Mary Connors, who was half-sister to Frank and Dick O'Brien was in the high school. She must have seen Harry run back into the school, because she ran in after him and brought him out, saving his life."[2] Classes were then spread throughout the village buildings.

The year of my birth in 1927, the new school at the end of Garden Street was completed. It housed all grades from kindergarten through the twelfth grade. My fourth birthday was March 5, 1931, and that fall I started kindergarten. My father had told me that my teacher, Miss Anna Crane had been his teacher as well as his sisters' teacher, and she was well liked—in fact he was fond her. My mother drove me to school and walked with me to my classroom that was in the basement of the school at the bottom of the stairway. My mother explained that she would be shopping and would be back at half past eleven to pick me up. I watched the clock. I had never been away from my mother.

---

[2] Stephens, *Those Who Served*, 250.

There had been no nursery school or preschool, and I am not sure whether I had been given any verbal preparation except perhaps that "it's going to be fun."

My friend, Charlotte Tuttle started kindergarten the same day. Charlotte's home was on Carmel Avenue and her Aunt Sara Hopkins lived on Putnam Terrace, only a few steps from our house. We must have become acquainted when Charlotte's mother visited her sister. At any rate, it was comforting for both of us to start our first day at school having a friend.

Mothers had left, and we were now a group of about fifteen boys and girls who did not know one another, a new experience for me. I started to cry, and Miss Crane tried to quiet me. As I was crying, my four-year-old friend Charlotte started to cry as well. We were alone with little strangers and an old lady in a figured dress. To distract us we were given pencils and paper to pass out, but we were not to be pacified. When one started to cry the other faithfullly followed. Apparently feeling desperate, Miss Crane told me to go into the boys' bathroom, and she directed Charlotte into the girls' bathroom. They were merely closets with a toilet, each at opposite ends of the "cloak room." (For those not familiar with the term cloak room, it was on the back side of the wall of the kindergarten room, about two yards wide with pegs on the wall for coats and hats. In years past, cloaks were worn.) It was totally dark without any light that I knew of.

I remember the teacher telling us we were to stay in there until we stopped crying. Eventually, the realization came that if I stopped crying, I might be allowed to leave my dark confinement space, or was it that I had spent all my emotions? Eventually we were allowed to join the class. It was an extreme measure, and one that produced a child who kept her distance from teachers, even to her own disadvantage.

We drew pictures and whatever else kindergarten children did, and all the time I watched the clock, waiting for half past eleven to arrive. As it neared the time, I was feeling relief that my mommy would soon appear. But half past the hour came, and she didn't come. The children were leaving, and I kept watching the glass in the door. At around twenty minutes before twelve she arrived, much to my great sense of relief. She explained that she had been delayed shopping. My tears had stopped, and I am not sure that my mother ever knew the extent to which I had been punished. My mother drove me home, and I was to face another day in school.

When I was an adult and my father a member of the Lions Club, I recall that he was instrumental in having benches placed in the village. He especially wanted one or two on the old post office hill, where he would see the aging Miss Crane and I believe her sister walking to or from their home. He was compassionate, and I appreciated what he was doing. The name of Miss Crane however always gave me a flashback.

Another situation occurred in my early school years, and that was in the first or second grade. I still believed in Santa Claus or at least liked the idea. One day our teacher who was motherly and likeable, with forthrightness told the children in my class that there was no Santa Claus. I don't remember my immediate reaction or whether I told my parents. There were things that as a child one had to accept, not being equipped to do otherwise. As an adult I have strong feelings that a teacher would be so insensitive, lacking in feeling and compassion in this matter. I believe she felt it was her duty and her mission to start her charges off on a path of honesty, without illusion.

There was one Christmas when my father had arranged to have Santa Claus visit us. I do not remember his entering our house, only seeing Santa in his red suit and white beard pass the window of our porch while we were in the living room. What a brief, exciting moment!

Young Beggars

Charlotte and I knew several of our neighbors and routinely we made calls on these ladies. We would knock on their doors hoping we would receive a freshly baked cookie. Charlotte's Aunt Sara Hopkins lived on Putnam Terrace, and we were quite sure we would find her at home. Sometimes she would invite us in, but usually she went straight to her cookie jar that she kept on a shelf at the top of the stairway to the basement. We would watch her as she opened the jar and held it while we reached in and took a cookie. We thanked her and said good-bye.

Next door was the home of Mr. and Mrs. Benson. (Both Fred Benson and Ernest Hopkins worked for the New York Central Railroad.) We knocked on Mrs. Benson's back door knowing better than to use the front door—besides that was near the cookie jar. Mrs. Benson knew why we had come. We thought she was a nice lady, and I guess she thought we were nice little girls. We took our cookies, thanked her and said good-bye.

Sometimes we would go to two houses in a day. Usually we would save a house for another day. One day we were near my grandparents' house at the foot of Putnam Avenue and decided we would try knocking on the door of Mrs. Ralph Diehl next door. We went to her back door. We did not know Mrs. Diehl very well and were being brave in going to her house. One time we were told that she did not have any cookies in the house, and we were not invited into her kitchen. We didn't go back to her house.

There were days when Charlotte and I would push our "baby carriages" on the sidewalk, playing "Mother," talking to our babies, holding, dressing and redressing them. We both had special baby patchwork quilts made by Mrs. Emma Birdsall who sometimes helped my mother. I still have mine and treasure it. On rainy days we would carry on this activity in the basement of the Tuttles' house on Carmel Avenue. There was a double door that opened to their lower yard, and it would be opened for light and air. We were hardly aware that we were in an unfinished basement. We were together and carrying on our important business. It amazes me how serious we were at this play of being a grown-up.

One of my favorite activities as a three- and four-year-old was "playing house" with my playmate, Charlotte Tuttle. We would have my child-size table and chairs set up in our dining room and "serve tea," re-enacting all the things we had seen our mothers do or imagined they did. My child's electric stove was given me by my mother's friend, Mrs. Frank Pinto, as her daughter, Evelyn, had grown beyond using it. Sometimes I would make oatmeal (there were no instant cereals), and at other times I would pick my grandfather's ripe plums from the ground and stew them in my little pot. Once I had done that, I had learned everything there was to learn about cooking. So, that ritual ended.

Another Friend for Life

Another life-long friend was Louise Vanderburgh, who was close to my age, and our mothers were fond of one another. Her mother, however, died when Louise was quite small. Louise was born in China on the island of Hinan, while her father was a medical missionary. I would have liked knowing her mother, as I was very fond of Doctor Vanderburgh, the kindest of men.

The Vanderburgh home and office were on the opposite side of the village on Main Street. There were several times when Louise played with me in my sandbox making mud pies. My mother said that she would look out the back window and see two little rear ends, as we bent over to play in the sand, and she could not tell one child from the other. Not seeing her for a long time was undoubtedly due to the fact that her mother had died, and my mother found it difficult for us to get together. After that we didn't become good friends until seventh or eighth grade. Louise had two brothers, Alexander and Ned. In time her father, Dr. Alexander Vanderburgh, married Gladys Meldrum, and Louise acquired a stepmother and stepsister, Shirley. When a baby came into the family, Louise then had a half-sister, Faith. Louise's step-grandfather, Rev. Meldrum, was an Episcopalian minister who sometimes substituted at St. Andrew's Church. I thought he was a very kind and gentle person. Louise and I remained life-long good friends.

Damn, a Bad Word, or, the Floating Soap, Please

One thing that was not permitted in our house was the use of swear words. But it was impossible not to hear these words outside our home. I was at home playing on the second floor, and for some reason, with an increasing vocabulary, I used the word "damn." My mother heard me and didn't waste a moment coming to me. She said, "Now Dodie, that was not a nice word you used, was it? We are going to get rid of that word so that you never say it again." And taking my arm, she marched me to our bathroom. She probably said, "We are going to march into the bathroom" for extra emphasis. She took my toothbrush, rubbed it on the Ivory soap and brushed my mouth with soap and water. I was crushed and crying. I had no idea that I had done something terrible. Nice little girls didn't say words like that. In later years I learned that this punishment was a general punishment used on children. I wonder if the Ivory people knew of the other use for their soap.

So, a threat to have one's mouth washed out with soap was a real one. My sister Jane had witnessed this ordeal and felt very sorry for me. When my mother left the bathroom, she told me she would help me get rid of the soap and started using the brush with water. That made it worse, as my mouth filled with more suds. Eventually my mouth was rinsed clear of soap suds, and the experience kept "damn" out of my mouth for a long time. Not forever, but for a long time.

Throughout my pre-high school and high school years, it was inevitable that walking along a sidewalk one would come upon a coarse four-letter word written in chalk across the concrete, so that it would not be missed. It might be a short sentence including a word "gentlemen" and "ladies" did not use. Some of the time I did not know its meaning, but knew that seeing it on the sidewalk meant that I should not use the word. And I accepted it with the attitude that some "kid" was "being smart."

Cherry Trees, Flower Gardens and a Backhouse

On the side of our house there was the sloping door to the basement. The lawn was flat with a peach tree that we children were warned not to climb. When I became bigger I climbed my grandfather's cherry trees and ate the cherries. The Oxharts were sweet, but I would eat the sour cherries as well. My grandfather did not mind that his cherries were eaten by his grandchildren. My father, however, did not want to have his fruit trees climbed, mostly because his children were small and could get hurt, and also, because climbing would break off small branches. There weren't many trees: one peach and one apricot behind the garage, one winter pear in the strip of garden between the driveway and the property next door and that one by the cellar door.

There was quite a hullabaloo one day, when I learned that my sister Joan had taken a saw to the peach tree near the cellar door. She must have done considerable damage, as my father was disappointed and perhaps a little angry at the desecrations that he witnessed. I think a scolding took place—in today's language she was "read the riot act." Somehow I equate this incident with the tale that George Washington had cut down his father's cherry tree, and perhaps this is what she had in mind.

Many incidents that occurred were retold, when I was very young—too young for me to have witnessed them. They were told and retold enough times that they were as real for me, as when they first occurred. That was likely the case with the peach tree as well as another day in the life of my sister Joan. Our neighbor Miss Mariah Birch and her widowed sister Mrs. Esther White and their brother Fred, until he died, lived in a large brown shingled house with a wide porch, where they often sat on summer afternoons. Their original house had to be abandoned when New York City took the property for a reservoir east of Brewster. This village house was located between my grandfather's house and ours. Their driveway came up from Putnam Avenue and made a circle at the back of the house. Further back from the driveway were Miss Birch's flower gardens. (My mother called her Aunt Ry, although she was no relation.) Miss Birch had many separate gardens, a formal garden area and cutting gardens with grassy walkways throughout. There was a great variety of flowers, and she tended them with loving care.

My mother used to admire Miss Birch's flowers and complimented her many times. We could look down at her gardens from our pear tree and view almost the entire garden area. One day as a small child my sister Joan brought my mother a present of lovely flowers. She thought it would make my mother happy, as she knew my mother liked having flowers in the house. Upon questioning and finding out that Joan had picked the flowers from Miss Birch's garden, my mother apparently was on the verge of being apoplectic. The only punishment I ever knew about was my mother telling Joan that she should not have picked Miss Birch's flowers, and that she must take the flowers to Miss Birch and tell her what she had done, also saying she was sorry. I hope that she received a big hug for her effort to please our mother.

Near the wall that separated our property from the Birch/White property was their garage that Fred used for his car. (After Fred died I do not remember a car coming into their driveway until Mrs. White's son, Elbert, had a car.) Next to that was a privy no longer used, now that there was indoor plumbing. I peeked in there one time just to make sure that, yes, that's what it is. In the same area as part of the garden was a small pool in which there were gold fish. I do not know how old Miss Birch was, but she looked old to me. She tended her garden, and it was as beautiful as a garden could be, spread out around that circular driveway.

House at 12 Putnam Avenue as purchased.

12 Putnam Avenue after renovations, 1939.

My mother conveyed the message that we were not to cross this property to reach our grandparents' yard, and so we always, almost always, walked using the sidewalk on Putnam Avenue.

There were a few times when Joan was tempted to climb one of their cherry trees that were located close to my grandfather's yard below. I remember being concerned that we would be caught and scolded. This did not worry my sister.

As little children while playing in my own yard, we found it great fun to jump from our wall across a small divide to the roof of the outhouse. To miss meant a hard fall between that building and the wall. I was bigger before I successfully made the jump. There were a couple of times, when Miss Birch saw what we were doing and called out to us not to jump onto her backhouse (outhouse), although she did not call it her backhouse. She liked my mother, but not having children herself, she most certainly thought we were misbehaved girls at times.

When my sister Joan was playing on Putnam Terrace, I always wanted to join whatever it was she was doing. Jane and Joan had matching wicker doll carriages, and since they had outgrown them, there was always one available for me; they were stored in our cold storage room next to the pantry and back porch. I could always go in there and help myself. I walked on the sidewalk pushing "my" carriage with my doll inside, occasionally stopping to adjust the doll's blanket.

Joan was closer to my age than Jane and would sometimes, when bored, include me in her play. One day she had a brilliant idea that would be, I was told, great fun for me. Why not! If Joan said it would be fun, it would be. What a good sister! She told me to climb into the carriage, and she would take me for a ride. I of course was too big for it, but I folded myself into it. She put her hands on the handle and started running down the sidewalk. Fun? She was having fun, and I was being terrorized. I am sure I was yelling, "stop." At my young age, what reservoir of words would I have as a retort? I might have whined about it to my mother, but angry words were not what we were used to. I was glad to get out of my carriage and resume being a mother to my doll.

My Teachers and My Mother

In the fourth grade, we had a teacher who had the reputation of being "mean." All of our teachers were what we would have called "old." Perhaps it was the figured dresses, the oxford shoes and the styleless hairdos. Maybe it was due to having a mother who took enjoyment in having her hair look pretty and wearing up-to-date though conservative dresses when out of the house. She had lovely taste in her clothing. Perhaps that was from having lived in a city, her creative nature and having seen real art in progress. Anyway, her habits and dress were not lost on her youngest daughter.

When my mother was working in the house, she wore something from her closet that was considered too old and worn to wear elsewhere. So it would be an old cotton dress or skirt and blouse. In the kitchen she wore an apron. So I was used to seeing the type of clothes my mother wore at home. If she was ironing, she might look a little nicer than, if she was cleaning the floors or bathrooms. It was enlightening to me as a child, when I visited the home of my friend Charlotte, to see her mother was wearing what she called her "house dress," a clean, simple, cotton dress. It was what she wore in the house. Why put on something that was good enough for outdoor use, when people had to save and make do.

My mother's fall and winter dresses and suits, of fine quality, few in number, were either navy or black with long sleeves. I remember, however, a red silk or rayon dress that she purchased for a special occasion; red went well with her dark hair. She seldom veered from "basic" clothes, as she felt that "they were always good." Knowing she was going out for the evening with my father, I would walk into her bedroom and sit on the bed, as she was getting ready. She would take her dress from the closet, and we would chat. Maybe she would say, "I am running late; Daddy wants me to be ready in half an hour." I would see her slip her dress on, then put a piece of jewelry on. She did not wear chains, only a string of pearls or a pin. I would tell her she looked pretty. And she did.

Looking into the Eighth Grade Classroom

Usually I was able to walk home from school with my sister Joan, and sometimes I would leave my classroom and go upstairs and wait outside Miss McEnroe's eighth-grade classroom. One day as I was waiting, looking through the glass in the door and seeing familiar faces, I watched as Miss McEnroe put her fingers through Dick Donley's hair and held on. She then rapped his forehead against the blackboard several times. I don't know what he had done or said, but she had her way of dealing with it. Dick was the son of the principal, Herman Donley. Dick was a popular boy, but he and his buddies were hell-raisers.

One day my fourth-grade teacher's eyeglasses became broken when she was out of the room. When she returned to her desk, she discovered the broken spectacles, and she turned on one of the girls a few desks from the front. She blamed this girl for breaking her glasses, and I can remember wondering why she singled her out. I was appalled and more than a little frightened by the teacher's anger and lack of compassion. Of course, now I can empathize with the teacher's concern about the cost of replacement.

I can still picture the horizontal lines drawn on the blackboard by my teacher and the alphabet carefully and precisely drawn. This was the case with numerals as well, written with such perfection. She then went on to script. It was called penmanship, and the slow motion writing of the teacher was quite beautiful. We had to practice to make our writing readable. When the penmanship classes were over, we were on our own, and our writing became distinctly ours.

I started the fifth grade in 1936, and my teacher was Mrs. Sadie Nagle. She was very kind and likeable, and indeed of all the teachers in my early years, she was my favorite. There was no art department in the school then, but we had art class perhaps twice a week, and I liked that. I remember particularly the day we were given drawing paper, a pencil and chalk and told to draw pussy willows. I was so thrilled with the results, to see that what I had drawn really looked like pussy willows, several on a stem with white fuzz above the brown cap. I put my name in the lower corner and took it home with the anticipation of giving it to my mother. She put it in a black frame. I wonder if she reminisced about the pussy willows stuffed into my nose. The daily work given us was enjoyable, I did well ending the year ranking third—credit goes to my teacher's kindness.

Daddy

My dad learned to hunt as a young man and enjoyed shooting game birds that my mother cooked. He also hunted for deer. From those few deer hunting trips he had the skins made into gloves for those they would fit as well as a deerskin rug. One of the late hunting trips was to Pennsylvania, where he hunted for bear. He shot one and brought the meat home for my mother to cook. He was disappointed that the meat was tough and stringy, whereas venison was tender and palatable.

He also loved nature and knew the names of most trees. While he was driving to jobs around Putnam County, he would sometimes spot a hickory or black walnut tree. Sunday mornings were for Sunday school at St. Andrew's Church on Prospect Street, but in the afternoon we would all pile into the car. He would have picked out a hickory tree under which we were to pick up the nuts from the ground. He always asked the owner, often a farmer, for permission to do this. I can remember that on the workbench in our garage were numerous untouched black walnuts. It was a challenge to touch these rough shells, and they were extremely difficult to crack open. Even so, I can remember the distinct flavor of the black walnut in candy. On future winter Sundays, we would sit at the kitchen table and pick the meats from the nuts, and my dad would take great joy in making black walnut penuche. There were also a few times when we all made popcorn balls.

On work days my father would return home for dinner at about six o'clock and we would start dinner at half past six. Before six o'clock we three girls would start asking my mother if Daddy would come home soon. As soon as one of us noticed his car coming in the driveway we would run for the back door, each of us trying to reach him first. The first two would take one of his hands and the third child would gleefully grasp the end of his jacket and bring up the rear as we headed for the back door. It must have been very satisfying for him to have three daughters who loved him that much.

The Fourth of July

The Fourth of July was always greatly anticipated, as my father would bring home boxes of fireworks. There were little red "half-inchers" which were for the children, and my father taught us how to light them with a lighted punk. Sometimes we would light them singly and sometimes a string of a dozen. We were careful, but it was only luck that kept one of us from serious injury. When I was in high school, my friend Louise Vanderburgh told me that her father, Dr. Alexander Vanderburgh treated many children with burns, eye injuries and blown off fingers each Fourth of July. It made a lasting impression on me.

One year we were waiting for the annual nighttime display put on by my dad on the square wooden float in front of our cottage. Our large family group was sitting on the shoreline watching with enjoyment, when we saw my father suddenly push the entire box of fireworks into the lake with his foot. He had accidentally dropped a lighted cigarette or punk into the box and did not take time to look for it, as he knew what the consequences might be. Thus, the Fourth of July ended without a bang and with great disappointment and relief on the part of the adults.

Operator, Operator!

My father made and received business calls at home. Our telephone number was 5-2, my Uncle Phil's number was 4-2 and my grandfather's number had three digits, 3-1-4. In order to make a local call, it was necessary to pick up the receiver and wait for the operator to say "number please," and the caller would say, "4-2 please." In order to make a long distance call, the operator had to be called, and the caller would state the number. The operator would say, "Just a moment, please," and she would make the connection.

When the dial telephone came in, we could dial a local number. To make a long distance call, one would dial "0" and the operator would ask for the desired number. She would then connect the two parties.

Table Manners

At dinnertime, we sat at a long rectangular table that seemed very large, when I was small. My two sisters sat on one side with my mother at one end and my father at the other. I sat to my father's right. When we had mashed potatoes, he would make a hole in the mound, put a piece of butter in it, and then cover it with the potatoes. When I dipped into the mashed potatoes, the butter would run out. He enjoyed meals and wanted us to, also.

My mother had her way of handling a problem like "talking back" or disobeying a request at the table. I can hear my mother say, "Go stand in the corner until you can behave." I can see Joan standing facing the corner of the room shifting her weight from one foot to the other. I never wanted to have to do that, but I believe it happened once, when I did not stop "chattering" with my sisters when requested. Joan had a way of egging me on,

Occasionally on Sunday morning there were orange slices to begin our breakfast. I became concerned, when I swallowed a pit and said to my father, "Daddy, I swallowed a pit!" His answer with a twinkle was, "It may sprout a tree." Was he kidding? I was imagining tree leaves coming out of my mouth. Of course, he had to be kidding. He must be kidding.

If we wanted to leave the table after having eaten or for some reason during the meal, we were taught to ask, "May I be excused?" When receiving the answer "yes," we were permitted to leave the table. If one of us left the table without permission, my mother would say, "You did not ask to be excused." It meant returning to the seat and asking to be excused. It was done pleasantly, and we responded. Children do forget. When asking for a dish to be passed at the table, we were expected to ask, "May I please have the peas?," or "Please pass the peas?" My mother would also tell us not to interrupt our father when he was talking. Polite and respectful children make for polite and respectful adults. We accepted the lessons and never argued with our parents about what they expected of us on the subject of courtesy, known as "common courtesy." Such courtesies were taught at an early age and were woven into the fabric of our lives.

When entering the house, my father always removed his hat. This was done by men and boys when going into anyone's home or church, and a hat or cap was never worn at a table while having a meal. It was also the gentlemanly act to hold a door open if accompanied by a woman. One cannot assume then that a woman would not hold a door for a man passing close behind her going through a door. The key word was courtesy by either sex. When a man saw another man or woman coming his way on the sidewalk, he tipped his hat, meaning he put his fingers to the edge of the brim as a greeting.

Guests Arrive

When my mother was in her thirties, she played bridge once a week in the afternoon with three other women. She and my father belonged to a couples club that met on Friday evenings once a month. When it was my parents' turn to have the club members, I would sometimes help her make sandwiches made of cream cheese and pineapple as well as chopped olives and cream cheese. By enlisting my help it kept me from "getting in her way." I am sure my sisters were nowhere to be found. Any place but working in the kitchen! The sandwiches were made of white bread and wheat bread with the crusts cut off. These were served with coffee and cake part way through the bridge games or at the end of the evening. There were also special buttery, white, flat mint candies.

My two sisters and I would be in our pajamas ready for bed sitting near the top of the stairs and watching people come in through the front door. Then as they got down to serious playing, we would hear the words "trump," "eight of spades," "nine of diamonds," "rubber," and we didn't have the least idea of why these words were being spoken. We would hear my aunt laugh, and we would say, "That's Aunt Helen." Then we would hear a man speak or laugh, and we asked each other who that was. It was all great fun, but we were not allowed to go downstairs while the party was in progress. We knew what was expected of us. Usually my mother would excuse herself to check on her children and would sometimes find us sitting on the stairs. She would then hustle us into our beds and kiss us goodnight again.

What Fun We Had!

I had my own tricycle, but looked forward to being grown up enough to ride a bicycle. Though a new bicycle was expensive, used bikes seemed to be everywhere. Boys found a bicycle handy to get to an after-school or Saturday job. Later learning to jump rope, play hopscotch, running, skipping, playing tag and laughing kept us busy and happy. To be out of doors playing was so exhilarating! As little kids we played "Who's Got the Button," where one person would touch the closed fist of each child standing in a circle saying "button, button, who's got the button?" One person had a button in her fist. If that person were touched, she would be "it." A similar game children played was "One potato, two potato, three potato, four." While making a fist one child would tap the two fists of each other child. At the end of the rhyme, the last person tapped would be out of the game. It would then become someone else's turn.

"Jacks" is the name of the game played with two children. The set included about six jacks; metal, almost star-shaped, with metal prongs. The set of jacks was taken in one hand, tossed into the air, and they fell scattered. The little ball was tossed into the air high enough that it gave time to gather as many jacks as possible before the ball came down to be caught. How many throws it took to capture all the jacks was the idea of the game. "Hide and Seek" and "Tag" were very popular games enjoyed with friends on lawns and on the nearby streets. No one would be hurt, except by skidding or slipping on gravel or grass. Boys played marble games to pass the time. I learned to shoot marbles, and on rainy evenings I would use a circular pattern in the old oriental rug as the pot. I'm sure my cousin Malcolm taught me how to play marbles, or I learned by watching him. Our games did not require any costly toys. I had a collection of numerous marbles, a collection to be admired. (When I outgrew the interest in playing the game, I saved them and eventually gave them to my little brother). Marbles varied in colors and striations, but there were also clear marbles and larger ones with an animal standing within them. These were rare and collectors' marbles.

Until bicycles became preferred, we spent many summer days roller skating on the sidewalks of Putnam Terrace. To put the skates on, they were slid onto the underside of the shoe's sole. When it was in place, a skate key had to be used to tighten the metal pieces close to the leather sole. Having the leather sole gripped in such a fashion hastened the demise of the shoes, as eventually the stitching would give way, and the sole would loosen. Therefore, we were advised to wear old shoes while skating. The heel of the shoe was kept in place, because there was a raised lip at the back of the skate. A leather strap buckled over the instep held the skate in place. Outdoor skates did not roll smoothly as did indoor skates.

In the fall of the year our large oak tree would drop its plentiful leaves, and this was the sign that we should find the rakes and put the leaves in the largest pile we could make. The pile would be placed a few feet from where we would drop from our swing. We did this each year somehow expecting that this high pile of leaves would cushion us from the ground beneath. It did not. We all got covered with broken dried leaves and dust ending up needing a bath and tired enough to sleep well that night.

As we grew bigger, friends from Putnam Terrace and Putnam Avenue spent summer evenings playing "Kick the Can." The Blaney boys and the Durkin girls were some of the players. We kept playing as darkness approached and eventually had to give up and go home. I was always expected to be home before darkness set in. One summer evening I was having so much fun playing Hide and Seek, I ignored the approaching dusk. My mother always clapped her hands, when she wanted our attention—and it could be heard all the way down the street. I was running across the street and stubbed my toe on the curb of the sidewalk, falling on my chin. I had an inch cut that was bleeding, so I left for home arriving after my deadline. Of course

I received a scolding but was also patched up with care. When I was told to be home at a certain time, I was to be home at that time. I believe my mother might have said. "If you had minded me, you wouldn't have fallen."

When springtime came, we started looking forward to Decoration Day on May 30. The members of the American Legion and the Auxiliary started their annual sale of poppies made by the World War I veterans at Castle Point Hospital. Originally made of cloth, they are now made of paper by the veterans in the veterans hospitals as a fund-raiser. When I put a dollar in the box and walk away wearing the poppy in my lapel, I feel that I have done a small thing for the veterans.

The Great Depression

The Great Depression

There was talk about our country being in a Great Depression, and I learned that a family of good friends had lost a large amount of money in the stock market crash. Being personal friends, my parents were quite naturally concerned for them. We children were once included in an invitation to their home for an Italian dinner. Perhaps that is where I learned to enjoy Italian food. One evening, after dinner, our hostess wanted to pass around her Jordan almonds, nuts with a thin coating of pastel colored hard candy. She had forgotten her hiding place, but her son always found it, usually behind the books in the library, and he would help himself to the nuts. She would have to consult him, but when she found the box, there were usually only a few nuts left, leaving his mother annoyed and embarrassed.

At my young age I noticed the Italian influence in the décor (although this word was not part of my vocabulary then) of their home, or at least I knew it was different. Their enclosed porch was sunny, and there was a baby grand piano finished in an antiqued medium green Italianate. By then I loved piano music, and I remember my sister's friend playing "La Paloma." I admired anyone who had studied and played the piano.

The Great Depression of 1929 put many people out of work. Industries closed down, and men could not feed their families. Many families across the country had to make the heartbreaking decision that the man of the family must leave his wife and children, so that there would be one less mouth to feed. Thousands of men and many women, black, white and others took to the freight lines, crisscrossing the country in search of work or a handout. Conditions during this time were put to music and words in the song, "Brother Can You Spare a Dime," heard on the record sung by Bing Crosby, one of the most popular "crooners" of the time. I do not know of a person in Brewster who had to do this, but I also do not remember that there were free meals at churches or collections of food for any needy families. But I was very young. Another song that was heard often was, "In a Shanty in Old Shanty Town," that was referring to the encampments made by hoboes. These people were not only blue-collar workers from the closed factories, but educated professional lawyers, doctors and engineers. The domino effect was working from top to bottom. Businesses closed or found it difficult to pay workers.

The Depression was felt in our town as well. Children wore hand-me-down clothes, and men went without a new suit or tie. Women running a household kept close watch on their budget to make sure they could get through the next week or month on what money was coming in. People who had gardens were fortunate, as they could can what they produced, and they ate quite well throughout the winter.

Some bartering took place. Doctors were paid in food instead of money. My father was owed money by a man who had a water system installed at his summer home in Putnam County. He owned a garment business in Manhattan, New York.

Instead of being paid in money he asked my father, if he would accept a winter coat for my mother as payment. It was a very nice green winter coat with a fox fur collar, and she of course was thrilled to have a new coat of very good quality. At another time a similar situation took place. In payment for work done my mother received a stone martin fur piece. They were fashionable at the time, and my mother looked stunning wearing a suit with this fur piece over her shoulders. For the younger generations, it may seem that the wearing of a beautiful fur piece would be ostentatious, but one has to know that in the 1930s, dressing "from head to toe" was the accepted style of the times. Ladies enjoyed looking their best, and others enjoyed observing them. Such a payment of course did not help the budget. After a few years the fur piece was put away, perhaps as styles changed or war clouds loomed.

Having been in the Navy in World War I, my father was a member of the American Legion. My mother was a member of the auxiliary, and because of this, she also walked in the parade wearing the navy blue auxiliary uniform. My two sisters were members of the girls' auxiliary and they wore navy blue capes and hats. I was too young for the auxiliary, and I walked along in the parade holding my mother's hand. The bands from Danbury, Connecticut, and other towns played and a drum and fife corps lent a dramatic sense to the happenings of the day. From the time I joined the Brewster High School band in the sixth grade, I never missed a Decoration Day parade (since 1976 called Memorial Day), nor have I missed many times when I could wear a red poppy made by hospitalized veterans.

Perhaps it was later that my mother conveyed some experiences that she and my father had, things they did together that were fun and memorable. It was during the period of

Prohibition, between 1920 and 1933 when it was forbidden by law to manufacture, sell or transport alcoholic beverages. Bars had been closed and restaurants could not legally serve liquor. They visited a "speak-easy," one of those places where, with the right code word said at the door to the establishment, one would be permitted entrance. Inside would be served drinks to paying customers. It was a daredevil kind of thing to do, and not done regularly.

Another experience was on a motor trip to Sault Sainte Marie on the Michigan/Canadian border. At that time simply driving that distance was an experience not to be forgotten. But that was superseded by their first ride in an aeroplane and their last for a very long time. How very exciting that must have been.

Hoboes Ride the Rails; Coal Car Spills

The New Haven and Hartford Railroad ran along the edge of the village of Brewster. In fact school children could look out the school windows and see a section of it. Hoboes appeared along the tracks and riding the freight cars, and there was a hobo encampment within view of the school. There was also one between the railroad tracks and the shoreline of Tonetta Lake.

Schoolboys who could not afford the ten-cent fee at the Tonetta pavilion used to swim at Brown's dock at the north end of the lake. They used to talk with these hoboes and hear their stories. One of these boys was William C. Pitkat, Jr. who contributed his story to *Those Who Served/Those Who Waited*. They saw the shoes with holes in the bottom and cardboard placed inside. They saw them wash their clothes in the lake and hang them on a line strung between bushes. I used to look over from our cottage and see boys swimming there, not knowing that they could not afford to do otherwise. But they were having great fun.

At one location the New Haven Railroad, north of Brewster, ran parallel to the tracks at the New York Central roundhouse. Before this point was reached there was a curve. Coming from Connecticut fully loaded with coal in the coal cars and going too fast for the curve, one day the train jumped the tracks, turning the cars over and spilling the coal. The people in the neighborhood of North Brewster could hear the accident occurring and went to look. They soon filled bushel baskets and bags with the precious blue coal that they could use for their furnaces. The coal lay there for a long time, and several years later when taking a short cut walking to Tonetta Lake, we would see pieces of coal near the tracks. This was undoubtedly where Santa Claus found the coal to put in children's Christmas stockings!

Vreeland's Pond

Occasionally my father took us on a Sunday to Vreeland's Pond on Turk Hill, a private pond on which the owners allowed Brewster people the privilege of skating. Mr. Herbert H. Vreeland, the owner, rose from humble beginnings to become a financier and chairman of the board of the Royal Typewriter Company. He was known by people in the village, but I was small and did not become acquainted with that family until after I had graduated from high school. Mr. Vreeland's grandson, Donald von Gal's story was given to me by his widow, Lizette, and is in *Those Who Served/Those Who Waited*. Don came to our house several times when he returned from the war.

The Vreeland Pond was two miles out of Brewster, and most kids did not have the means of getting there. We went to

Vreeland's Pond before I had learned to skate, and so I had double runner skates that buckled over my galoshes. They were good for beginners but were very dull and did not glide at all.

My dad loved to ice skate, and I can remember him putting on his racing skates and quickly taking off across the pond with long gliding motions. He had learned at a young age and was quite a good skater. My sisters had single runner skates. When I first started to imitate my father and my sisters, I took about four steps and fell down. I started again determined to skate, but fell again. Of course my dad had his movie camera and took pictures of his youngest daughter trying but falling. I wasn't happy with my performance and especially having it on film. I do believe I could have started with single runner skates as it seems that double runners were only good for standing still or falling down.

At an older age when viewing the film and seeing the sad expression on my face, I wondered if my family knew that it really wasn't being filmed that bothered me, but my great disappointment at not knowing how to skate.

My Sister Joan

One day we were in our home and Joan was near the kitchen doorway. She called me, and naturally I responded. The closet door next to the kitchen where coats were kept was open, and she coaxed me or pushed me inside. It was my second experience with a dark closet. She either locked the door or held it closed. She knew very well it would frighten me. It was great fun for her to do something to her younger sister.

Joan also did amusing things for the benefit of someone else. My cousin Phil recalled watching Joan as she took balls of dough in our kitchen, tossing one and then another to the ceiling. Each hit made a ring and then fell to the floor. When asked what she was doing, she said that she was trying to get one to stick. If this was my mother's pie dough, I can only imagine her response. Or when finished, did Joan mix the dough together and put it where my mother would complete our dessert pie? And when did my mother discover the rings on the ceiling?

Phil had another experience with Joan that was memorable. They were on the tracks below the bridge over which we frequently walked. He watched as a train approached, and Joan stood on the tracks waving her arms toward the engine. She jumped away from the tracks, as the engine came close. I remember hearing my mother threatening Joan about being on the tracks, but I am not sure whether it was said as a warning or as a scolding. She knew well that these actions were forbidden.

Besides sliding down the banister when my mother was out of sight, there was another activity that was to be great fun. Joan took one of my parents' card tables and brought it to the top of the stairway. The stairs were carpeted with a thick wool nap. This was exciting. Knowing I was smaller in size she said, "Get on, Dodie and you can ride down the stairs." The table was folded of course, and the top of the table was put next to the carpet so it would slide. She gave me a push, and like a shot I was at the landing below, and the table crashed into the wall. When Joan tried to ride on it with me, it didn't slide as well. And I had had enough.

She was always thinking of something to do. This time it was also on the stairs. We learned that we could actually sit on the edge of one step and bump ourselves down a few steps. That wasn't enough fun, so she would tell me to hold her feet and back down the stairs pulling her along. Then it was her turn to pull me. Being bigger and with more guile, she pulled me farther and faster. The fun was over. It amazes me that the trust of a younger sister is so strong. It did not last forever.

Cunningham's Swamp

It wasn't long before I was joining my sisters when they went ice-skating at Cunningham's swamp. Charlotte Tuttle and I often went together or met there. It was a wonderful place for us, because it contained bogs around which we would skate, but had a large enough space to play "Red Rover," ("Red Rover, Come Over, Come Over") and to play "Snap the Whip." Very often several strong high school boys led the line and at the end of the line was the smallest and weakest skater. I made sure that I was somewhere in the middle of the line. When the leaders got the line going fast enough, they would head in the opposite direction, and the ones at the end of the line, being unable to hold on, would go sailing across the ice. I remember a young boy I often saw at the end of the line. He seemed to like the challenge and the thrill.

One day my sister Joan arrived home from skating at Cunningham's swamp, and her clothes were wet. She had fallen through the ice. She told us she had broken through ice near the shoreline. She must have deviated from the usual spot where most of us left the ice, and I suspect she was testing thin ice.

There actually were not many of the bigger boys, the juniors and seniors who skated on Cunningham's swamp, as they were either skating elsewhere or working. Boys or girls who could find a job after school or Saturdays gladly did so.

We always waited too long before leaving, whether it was ice skating or sledding, and by the time we reached home we were in misery. My hands and feet would actually hurt, as I took off my gloves and galoshes that were only rubber or rubberized canvas. The gloves or mittens were woolen. When the woolen gloves became wet from falling on the ice or in the snow, they were quite useless. I would stay out longer than I should have, all the while having painfully cold hands and feet. The wet clothes were put over the radiators to dry. Getting nearly frozen digits or being chilled through did not prevent us from going through it all again.

There was another pond that was about the size of Cunningham's but without the bogs. It was located just below the school and was owned by Mr. Harry Wells and thus was called Wells' Pond. It was fed by a stream and had a small spillway or dam. Until I was older I did not use this pond. Those who lived close to the school found it a convenient walk. I can remember one day when the ice there was very clear, looking down and seeing a large goldfish. A goldfish! So they can live through the winter!

During the winter when there was snow on the ground, it was practically a routine to head for the snowy hill of Putnam Avenue with my sled. I wore a pair of snow pants that were lined with cotton flannel. They felt very good, when they were new. From pulling them on without removing my shoes the lining became torn, but I wore them regardless. After being outdoors for hours, my thighs became chapped from rubbing against the rough woolen material. As I headed home, I hurt and found it painful to walk. When I opened the kitchen door my mother could see misery written on my face. She would see the red, chafed area, and I would say, "Don't touch it. It hurts." She always applied zinc ointment and told me that it would feel better soon. And in time it healed. She always had a remedy for my hurts.

Classical Piano

Norma MacLean spent three years at Marshall College, now Marshall University in Morgantown, West Virginia, and was very happy there. She had good friends and one especially good friend with whom she kept in contact her entire life. She was also engaged to a young man who lived there. This engagement was doomed, as during a summer vacation the young man who lived next door to us would sit on the porch with his mother listening to my aunt playing the piano. The compositions were always classical, and he enjoyed her music. One day his mother suggested that he cross the lawn to our house and introduce himself. He did that, and they started dating. He was a good tennis player, and my aunt knew very little about tennis. She did however play with him during their courting days.

I grew to love classical piano music because of my aunt. Her Steinway piano was in our house, and she practiced several hours a day. She was a lovely, generous person who treated us with kindness and love. She loved my mother and father, as they loved her.

When she was at home I would inevitably ask her to play for us after dinner. There were certain pieces I became fond of and would at times ask her to play Chopin's Minute Waltz. I loved to sit next to her on the piano bench and became used to following the music, as she played. I learned to read music that way and in time was able to turn the pages of the music for her. When it became bed time, my mother made the announcement, and my aunt would begin playing a march. At this time we three would line up, usually in our pajamas and start marching through the rooms on the first floor. One of the marches was the Marshall College song, and we would sing it, as we marched.

Soon my mother would say, "Up the stairs," and we headed for the stairs and bed.

Instead of finishing her fourth year at Marshall she transferred to Julliard School of Music in New York City. By doing this she and her new "love" could see more of one another and enjoy many cultural events there. They became engaged at the end of the school year and were married October 6, 1934. After the small wedding and reception, they were ready to leave the house for a honeymoon. I was standing amidst those family members who were wishing her well and waiting my turn to be kissed. Before I knew it she was running down the steps, and she hadn't kissed me. I started crying and saying, "Aunt Norma didn't kiss me!" My mother told me that she would return, and I got over it.

During the year of her marriage, my mother took me to Scarsdale where my aunt had invited us for lunch in her new apartment. At some point I went into the bathroom, and after closing the door I locked it. When it was time for me to leave the bathroom, I could not unlock the door. I was trapped, and called out to my mother and aunt to get their attention. Realizing that I simply could not open the door myself, they started talking to me. My aunt had to call the superintendent of the building and explain what was happening, all the time my mother continuing a conversation with me. I suspect she was afraid I would try to open the window, but that was not something I would do. After about a half hour a man came and was able to unlock the door at which time, I was released from my entrapment. I remember a bit of anxiety during that time, but was comforted to keep hearing my mother's voice on the other side of the door.

By then my Grandmother MacLean was divorced and was living with us. However, after several months, she would decide to go to her sister's family in Fishkill. Ed and Edith Kennedy had three daughters, and when she returned to our house we would hear about that family, as I am sure they heard about ours. I did not see that family often, but I got along well with their youngest daughter, Nancy. In later years, she became a fine artist and we communicate quite often, though she and her husband Rober Searles live in Arizona. My grandmother could only take so much from one family and their children, before moving on for a while. There were her other sisters in New Jersey, and she enjoyed getting back to them and reminiscing. We were always glad to have her return. Every once in a while my mother's family would have a reunion either in Fishkill or Brewster.

Charles A. Lindbergh's Baby Kidnapped

In 1932, news spread across the country about the kidnapping of Charles A. and Anne Morrow Lindbergh's baby boy from his home near Hopewell, New Jersey. Charles Lindbergh was an American hero who had made the first nonstop solo flight from New York to Paris in 1927, the year of my birth. Someone had used a ladder to gain entrance to the house, and the baby was taken away and killed. Bruno Hauptmann was the chief suspect, and his name was in the newspapers. I also remember hearing something about their baby's nurse. Everyone knew the names Lindbergh and Hauptmann. The latter was tried and convicted of kidnapping and murder and put to death in 1936.

When we were at home in Brewster, there were times when we would see a hobo walking up our driveway always at dinner time. We children would get excited, as we knew they were strangers. The Lindbergh baby's kidnapping was not far from most mothers' minds, and so it seemed reasonable to keep us girls safely indoors. Mother dished out some dinner from our pots to give to the hobo, as he sat on the back porch. The sidewalks were marked with chalk by hoboes who were treated well at a particular house. Surely there were some homemakers who were too afraid to answer the door to a hobo.

Later Lindbergh was a moving force in early aeronautics, and his interest took him to Germany to look at the advances made there. After being decorated by the German government and advocating American neutrality in WWII, he was criticized by President Roosevelt. He had admired what the Germans were doing but surely was not shown the entire story of Hitler's military buildup. He resigned his Air Corps Reserve commission in 1941, and many people questioned his patriotism. However, he flew fifty missions in the Pacific during World War II. In 1954 President Dwight David Eisenhower appointed him Brigadier General in the Air Force Reserve. His early misfortunes created a dark period for the American people.

An event took place over Brewster of which I was unaware and did not learn anything about it until I was doing interviews for *Those Who Served/Those Who Waited* many years later. In 1933 two people, Wiletta O'Brien Bruen and her cousin Robert Palmer both living on Peaceable Hill Road looked east over Hine's Ridge, where they saw a formation of twenty-three silver seaplanes that were the Italian Air Force. Twenty-five was the original number, two having been lost. They had come over for the Exposition in Chicago having stopped along the way to refuel. General Italo Balbo, a pioneering aviator, was Air Minister under Mussolini, and they were using this display of their airplanes to impress the people of the United States. These Brewster people who were older than I had learned more details about it in the magazines and newspapers, as it was talked about around the country. It must have been a strange and exciting event, and I feel as though I missed something spectacular in that year.

1936 was the year of the Olympics in Germany and the year Adolf Hitler had consolidated power, was building an army and an air force, called the Luftwaffe. He did not allow any German Jewish athletes to participate in the Olympics, but put two token Jews somewhere on the teams. Hitler turned his back on the great African American track and field athlete, Jesse Owens, after he won four gold medals.

Sonja Henie, the beautiful Norwegian figure skater, came to our attention that same year, when she won the figure skating championship at the Winter Olympic Games in Germany at the age of twenty-four. She had won the world amateur championship for women ten consecutive years previously, once in Lake Placid, New York. We thrilled to see her starring in movies from 1937 to 1945. Her graceful moves coming from her early training in ballet along with her lovely costumes transfixed us young people as it did all who watched.

Hitler was deviously concealing his true intent from the allies of WWI. That was the year his army crossed the Rhine to test the resolve of those countries against the agreement made after the First World War. Germany received no help in recovering from war and in fact, it was left destitute without moral leadership. Events were occurring that were not reaching the American public, or if they did, our citizens were too concerned with providing for their own families to have interest in the strife of the German people and to learn that Adolf Hitler was addressing this issue with action and promises. I would hear bits of news on our radio or from discussions at our dinner table and could often sense concern.

Crime Not Far from Home

My cousin, Philip F. Beal III related a story at about the time of the writing of this memoir. It took place, as he remembered about 1936 in Katonah, New York. The police around the country were on the lookout for the notorious bank robber, "Baby Face" Nelson. At the time Phil was working with Tommy Hughes as his assistant serviceman with P. F. Beal & Sons, and they were driving a black Chrysler coupe like the one that "Baby Face" was allegedly driving. The police stopped them, as they looked suspicious. In the car they found metal boxes, the same type box that the criminals apparently were carrying. The police thought they had captured the crooks. Alas, the police had stopped two innocent workmen carrying their tools in boxes in their black car.

Grandma and Grandpa Beal

During our summer days at Tonetta Lake, we would often wear printed rompers that my Grandmother MacLean had made for us. They were short, sleeveless, loose fitting one-piece playsuits with elasticized legs. Perhaps it was on a Sunday when I was wearing a cotton dress that my father sensed I was distressed, picked up his 16mm movie camera, and focused it on me. I was walking between my Grandfather Beal's cottage and our cottage, with an unhappy expression, back and forth with my hand in my pocket and looking on the ground. My father asked me what I was looking for, and I told him that I had a nickel in my pocket, and I must have lost it in the grass. Then to top it off my grandfather, who was standing at his bathroom window, called out to me, "What is the matter, Lucy?" I know I felt hurt. MY NAME IS DODIE. On top of losing a whole nickel, I was being called Lucy! It was later that I appreciated my grandfather's sense of humor, but I was easily hurt.

Another example of it was a few years later when he wrote me a check for Christmas and wrote my name "DeLoris" instead of "Dolores." He said, with a twinkle in his eye, that it should be spelled that way, as it looked French.

When summer was ending, my mother, often with my Grandmother MacLean's help would go each morning to our house in Brewster where preparation of the summer's bounty from my Grandfather Beal's garden would take place. They canned the multitude of vegetables and fruits. It meant washing them, packing in sterilized jars and hot-packing them. Or it was washing grapes, cooking, straining and pouring into sterilized jars, topping with melted paraffin. During the coming winter, we would eat tomatoes, string beans, peaches, pears, grape jelly and peach jam. The root vegetables like potatoes, carrots and parsnips were kept in a dirt cellar, and there were times when my grandfather would say, "Dodie, go out to the dirt cellar and take some carrots home to your mother." I can remember the odor of that dirt cellar to this day; an earthy, moldy smell that eventually permeated the vegetables. No one complained. But perhaps that is why my mother prepared carrots using butter and brown sugar.

During the fall days when I stopped to visit with my grandmother and grandfather, he would always tell me to help myself to some apples. These, upon being picked were stored in bushel baskets at the back of the house. I would be told which baskets had open lids, and I could choose from them. Amongst the varieties of apples were Rome, Macintosh and green pie apples. My favorite apple became the Pig Nose that was red and had the basic shape of the Delicious apple, but it had a distinctive flavor that appealed to me. Perhaps that was my grandfather's name for it, because I never heard of an apple with that name since. I would leave their home biting into the apple, as I made my way up the hill to our house, skipping and happy with life. Once in a while when I was on my way walking into Brewster, my grandfather would ask me to buy him a can of pipe tobacco, and for that he gave me a nickel. I would have done it for him without the five cents but of course I could buy a little bag of penny candy with it in Mr. Millar's store, or I could put it in my little bank.

My home on Putnam Avenue was about a half-mile walk into the village, crossing the bridge over the railroad tracks. Walking into town was always a happy occasion. With a friend, we would pass private homes all the way to the Baptist Church. One of the first businesses we would pass would be Tony's barbershop where my mother would take me to have my blonde hair cut even with my earlobes and straight bangs. I remember when first having the narrow paper wrapped around my throat, I felt uncomfortable, even frightened by the experience. In fact I have never liked to wear an elasticized turtleneck.

Fires and Gossip

Our house on Putnam Avenue was not very far from either the old fire house that was across from the Baptist Church or the new fire house next to the new bridge. So, when there was a fire at night, especially in the winter when the leaves had fallen, we could clearly hear the siren. There were two fires that I remember as a child. One was on Turk Hill, and it was the fire that destroyed the house of the Von Gal family. I remember sitting with my mother in the darkness on the window seat on the second floor, both of us facing the village and trying to see where the fire was. The other fire was beyond North Main Street on the Tonetta Lake Road. It was a two-story house. The day after the fire, when we drove past the house, we could see mattresses on the ground, where they had pulled them out during the fire. The house was not destroyed, but the inside must have had considerable damage.

When I was a child the fire chief was Mr. John Morehouse, and he held that position for thirty years. He drove a 1931 or 1932 Model A Ford, but I used to see him walking from the village. His business was about a mile from town on the way to Tonetta Lake, a lumber mill that was situated quite close to the New Haven Railroad tracks. During his tenure the village people were talking about a member of the fire department who had been arrested for tapping into the electrical system at the home of Doctor Douglas Richie on Oak Street, leaving him with exorbitantly high electric bills while the perpetrator was not paying for his use of electricity. He went to prison for several years. It was a sad experience for the family members while it gave the people of Brewster something to talk about.

Sickness

This was to become the last decade that disease could not be treated with antibiotics or vaccines, those wonder drugs that could either prevent or cure a disease. It was a time when parents could expect their children to come down with mumps, measles and chicken pox, as they were contagious, and therefore the siblings were kept out of the room. Most children survived these diseases and mothers had remedies to ease the discomfort.

When these diseases occurred, the shades on the windows were pulled to keep the light out of the room in order to protect the eyes. When the young patient developed enlarged glands on the neck, the mother knew her child had the mumps; when red spots occurred, she knew it was the measles. Another type of spots that itched meant chicken pox, and the doctor would make a house call. There was little he could do except leave a small envelope of aspirin and comfort the child. We three girls all came down with these diseases.

It was in late January or February of 1936, that I became ill with a sinus infection and a fever. Our local general practitioner, Dr. Robert Cleaver was called. There were no antibiotics, but I was given some pills to take every few hours. Since I was not improving, it was recommended that I see a "specialist" in Connecticut, not far away.

The doctor examined me and told my mother that it was necessary to irrigate my nasal passages. I was taken to the sink, and he placed a shiny metal object attached to a tube in one nostril. He proceeded to run water into my nose, first one side then the other, the water exiting through my mouth. I can remember the pain that it caused, and I cried out. His response was that all children cry, even when it doesn't hurt. It was a frightful experience, and I did not like his response. Subsequent to this I developed an ear infection and was in bed with a fever. In the morning I felt quite normal, but in the afternoon my temperature would rise. I became delirious, an unpleasant condition, and my mother would put cold compresses on my forehead to cool me down. The attention my mother and father gave me was comforting, but I did not like being sick in bed.

When lung congestion occurred, my mother went to the kitchen and mixed a paste of powdered mustard, called a mustard plaster. She spread this mixture on a soft piece of flannel cloth and placed it caringly on my chest. It became very warm and was supposed to loosen the congestion. At other times, Vick's Vapo Rub was spread on my chest, and a clean cloth covered it. It smelled as though it would cure me, and it felt good. My light meals were brought up to me on a tray, as I sat up in bed.

In desperation, I was put in Danbury Hospital for tests to try to find the cause of my illness. My head is very clear about the experience. One of the first things that was done after being registered and shown to my room was to be taken from the room to have X-rays taken. I was in a private room, and my parents, knowing of my fears of the unknown and of being separated from them, hired a private nurse for the times my parents were not with me at night. Having my parents say good-bye to me if only for the night was excruciatingly, emotionally painful. They were my only world, my safe harbor, my complete comfort zone.

The nurse was probably around forty years old and a kind person. She was dressed in the nurses' garb of that period: white from head to toe. Her shoes were white, her stockings, crisp white dress and starched cotton cap with the turned back cuff having a narrow black velvet ribbon attached running from one side to the other. I learned from seeing many styles of nurses' caps, that every nursing school had as its distinguishing mark, its own style, and they went from being plain to intricately pleated. She had a chair diagonally facing my bed. A medication was prescribed that looked vaguely like coffee with cream and was put in a glass for me to drink. It was very distasteful, and I could hardly get it down without retching. I do not know that any diagnosis was made.

When I was ready to go home, and feeling that I had made a friend in my nurse, I asked her if she would give me a nurse's cap. She graciously gave me one; she had helped me through what seemed like a threatening ordeal, the worst part being away from home and my family.

The illness went on for several months. My father and mother were quite concerned, and asked Dr. Donald Richie, a young doctor from Croton Falls, who had also been called to see me, to recommend a specialist. He called a friend and colleague from Philadelphia to make a trip to see me. My father would do anything for his girls, and the specialist was called without questioning the cost. I can remember seeing three men over by the window in consultation.

The next thing I knew a doctor was by the bedside, and my dad was nearby. The doctor started to insert what looked like a wire into my ear. As it went in I yelled and pulled away. At that point I heard the doctor tell my father to hold me down, or he would have to put a straight jacket on me. I understood that, but I was rigid with fear. So, my father held me with all his strength. They must have felt that my eardrum must be punctured. As I was recovering from that, I have a vague remembrance of something being wrong in the lower part of my body that made me feel ill. Summer came and I was allowed on the porch outdoors, but I still wasn't allowed to run around. In time I gained my strength back. It seems that I had some virus or bacteria in the upper part of my body that made its way through my body. Without antibiotics there wasn't a great deal the medical profession could do except to let my body heal itself, which in time it did.

My cousin Phip usually called me Dolores rather than Dodie. I was surprised and hurt on occasion when he would greet me by calling me "Delirious" as I knew what delirious meant. He enjoyed the play on my name. His parents must have talked about my illness, and he heard the word used. However, that did not last long, and he went back to calling me Dolores.

During this time away from my classes, my friend Charlotte, whom I now called Cha, would bring me work from the teacher, some arithmetic and some reading and questions. I looked forward to having this work sent to me. I wonder if I ever thanked her for doing this. I also enjoyed having her company. It was a short summer, and I was able to go on to the next school year.

Forward March!

Gym classes in the early grades were two times a week, as I recall. Our teacher was Mr. Sterling Geesman, the coach of all the girls' and boys' sports. He was a tall, well-built man who could instill fear into one, if he so chose. During the winter our classes were held in the gymnasium/auditorium. He would line up the girls and teach them what was to be done, when he gave out an order; very much military style. It would be "forward march," "to the left march," "to the rear march," and so on. I shall never forget how distraught he would become, if a girl would turn left, when he called "right." He would take her out of the line and go over "left" and "right." It was embarrassing for her. But then he was a boy's teacher to the core and really didn't know how to deal with girls. I was glad that I knew left from right.

During one gym class we were playing dodge ball or basketball, when I turned my right ankle and fell down, not being able to put weight on it. Coach Geesman picked me up in his arms and carried me out of the gymnasium. I didn't know whether to be embarrassed or thrilled. I had sprained my ankle and had it wrapped for several weeks.

During the winter months when gym classes were held indoors, we had "tumbling" classes. They included forward summersaults, headstands, cartwheels and a feat of resting the arm from hand to elbow on the mat, then pushing with the feet to raise the body to an arm stand. I used to like to kneel on the mat, arch my back, and then roll my body down on the mat using the body as a rocking chair, rocking from knees to chin.

These classes were ones I looked forward to. I did a reasonably good headstand, until one day, when I had a sharp pain go up the back of my neck. I stopped abruptly. That did not stop me from continuing to do acrobatics, but it would occasionally recur with pain as a consequence. My mother took me to Dr. Donald Richie in Croton Falls, and I gave him the history of this pain. Of course he had me stand on my head in his office to see if the pain recurred. It did not. He had no answers, and I stopped standing on my head as a preventive measure.

A Taste of Culture

Wednesdays were "assembly" days, when the entire student body took their places on the dark brown, wooden, double chairs set up in the gymnasium with the youngest children in the front rows. Our principal, Mr. Herman H. Donley would walk onto the stage holding his Bible and start the program by reading a favorite passage from it. We would often hear the 23rd Psalm, the 18th Psalm and others. While standing, this would be followed by the salute to our flag with right hands over our hearts. As we said, "I pledge allegiance to the flag," our arms went outstretched to the flag at the front of the auditorium, and it stayed in that position until we finished with the words: "with liberty and justice for all." This was followed by the singing of our national anthem, "The Star-Spangled Banner," written by Francis Scott Key. We were beginning to learn that there was something unique about our country.

Mr. Harold Knapp would lead the student body in singing from our Little Brown Books, so familiar to people from our generation. The songs we sang were from another generation, some of them very old, others from the World War I period. We sang, "Pack up Your Troubles" (WWI), "Flow Gently Sweet Afton," "Funiculi, Funicula," "America the Beautiful" and so many others. Mr. Knapp liked to direct us in singing "rounds," such as "I've Been Working on the Railroad," all the while pointing to various sections of the student body. Announcements were made about upcoming events, and occasionally there would be a guest.

One of our guests was the nationally known operatic singer, Marion Anderson, who lived outside the village on Federal Hill Road. The mother of a young Brewster student worked in her home, and one way or another an invitation went out to her to sing to our student body at our Wednesday assembly. She graciously accepted and came with her male accompanist. Miss Anderson had a beautiful, strong contralto voice. The accompanist started to play, and she began to sing, her voice filling the auditorium and echoing back. She abruptly stopped singing, apologized and explained that she would have to reduce her usual volume, as it was too much for the room. Softening her voice to just the right volume, she continued her mid-morning concert. It was ever so beautiful.

This was the same talented singer who was denied appearing on the Mall in Washington, D.C., by the Daughters of the American Revolution, because she was black. (Later when I was about twenty years old, I was encouraged to become a member of this organization through my grandmother Nellie Wilcox Beal and her ancestor, Lieutenant Wilcox. After I was married and learned about this un-American denial to sing in public, I felt I had to resign from the D.A.R. I have since forgiven them, as I believe they have learned their lesson, but I did not rejoin.)

Another guest who came to entertain the students was a locally well-known soprano who also taught voice. She was tall, large, and round in physical stature. Her gown was long, frothy, perhaps chiffon, and she had in her right hand a chiffon handkerchief. Her songs were not familiar to us. Opera was something for the future perhaps, but for some of us young children in our town at that time, it struck at least a few of us as silly. As this guest was singing, she raised her chiffon handkerchief in the air and let it float down before she raised it again and let it float down. This was all my friends and I sitting together needed. We had an uncontrollable urge to laugh but controlled it as best we could, not wanting to be obnoxious or to be noticed. Unappreciative brats!

Work, Work, Work

My mother spent the morning cleaning the breakfast dishes, doing some housework and making preparations for dinner. Laundering was a big production. On Mondays the clothes and bedding used by the five members of our family were washed. Tuesday was ironing day using a heavy electric iron, as there were no steam irons. The washing machines were electric but not automatic. When the machine was full of water the agitator started. There were no intermediate cycles. The hot and cold water had to be regulated at the faucet where the hose was connected. When the water drained from the tank, the clothes were very wet and had to be put through a wringer one at a time to squeeze out the water that drained into the nearby sink. There were no dryers or fast drying fabrics, and the clothes had to be hung outdoors on the clotheslines to dry whether in frigid weather or on warm days.

There were fall house cleaning days and spring house cleaning days, about six months apart. The rugs were taken outdoors, thrown over the clotheslines and beaten with a rug beater. Now only seen in home front museums such as the WWII Wright Museum in Wolfeboro, N.H., these antiquated tools had a wood handle, about a foot of twisted stiff wire and at the end the wire was twisted into an open work of about twelve inches by eighteen inches. The rugs were beaten by hand, and the dust would fly. They were turned over and the process repeated.

First one floor was cleaned, then the next. All the curtains were removed, washed and ironed, and if they were a type of net or lace, they were put outdoors on a sunny day stretched across wooden curtain frames, so that they dried evenly. The windows were washed and the curtains put back in place. The parquet wood floors were cleaned, paste polish added and buffed by hand. The final buffing was done using a heavy weight wrapped with a soft cloth attached to a wood handle. These tools are now museum artifacts.

We had a Hoover vacuum cleaner for weekly use on the rugs, but the floors were dusted with a dry cotton mop. Woodwork around the doors, windows and the baseboard were washed with a solution of ammonia and very hot water. In the spring the storm windows were removed and the cleaned screens put in place. Come fall the process was reversed. My father let one of his strong young workers, Tommy Hughes, lift the storm windows, but many times my mother lifted them and the screens. She kept the house clean by herself, until there were three children to care for. At that point she had a woman from town help her, and she was much appreciated. They worked together and ate lunch together. I would join them when I returned from school at lunch hour.

This same routine took place in many homes. Those whose homes did not have finished wood floors often had linoleum covered with rugs. In that case the linoleum could be washed with a cleaning solution. The rugs would be shaken or beaten.

On these busy days the family did not expect the usual dessert after dinner, but there was always something. Canned fruit and a cookie sufficed. Our usual desserts were rice pudding, custard, apple brown Betty, bread pudding or chocolate pudding. My mother made the best coconut three layer cake and orange cake with fresh orange frosting. There were many good cooks in Brewster. Years later my husband, Mallory, would say that his mother made wonderful desserts and very much the same as those made by my mother. He is certain that recipes were passed from one woman to another in our small village.

There was a girl in my class whom I did not know very well. When her birthday was coming, she invited me to her birthday party. She lived in the area of the Storm house near Route 22 and the reservoir. Her friends were there but my friends were not, so I was rather tentative as I approached her home and the gathering. When it came time for the birthday cake to be cut, I could see a dark, glistening chocolate. I had never seen a cake like that before. My mother did not make dark chocolate cakes. When I took a bite, it seemed strange, and I wasn't sure that I could eat it. I don't know whether I did eat it or not. (I would not hesitate a moment to eat it today!) I was so accustomed to certain things in my life, and this was a moment in my history of something new. I did not know then that life would be presenting me with many new situations, as each year passed.

Learning from My Mother

In the afternoon my mother would bathe and dress, so that she would look nice at dinner time when my father came home from work. When I was eight or nine years old, I sat with my mother on the window seat in the second floor bedroom while she was crocheting. Her project was an afghan made of colorful squares. I became interested in learning to crochet, and she taught me, as she worked.

One day I started to make a chain. When it was long enough and after putting it around my waist, I connected it with the thought that I might make a skirt. I worked in a single crochet stitch, round and round, a few rows in brown, then a few rows in yellow. When it was about to my hips, I started with my mother's instruction to increase the stitches every now and then to make the skirt flare. This part became all brown and was in a double crochet stitch. When I was finished, I had made a skirt that fit. Then I decided to crochet narrow straps to go over my shoulders. My mother taught me how to attach the straps to the skirt.

When it was finished I proudly showed it to my father. He smiled and asked, "You'll be wearing it to school, won't you?"

"Oh no," I said.

"Oh, you have to wear it to school after making such a nice skirt. Dodie, if you will wear it to school, I will give your mother money for a yellow blouse, and you can both go shopping for one." He wanted me to be proud of my work.

"Uh, uh!"

My dad did convince me that now I would have a nice outfit, and I had made it myself. So, my mother took me to a shop that sold girls' clothes, and we picked out a yellow cotton blouse. I really was proud of my accomplishment, and I did wear it to school, but only one or two times. It wasn't exactly what the other kids were wearing. I guess I didn't want to stand out.

Music and Dance

A tap dancing class was started in Brewster taught by Mr. Newman of Danbury, Connecticut, a large and very graceful man. The class met downstairs in the town hall on Main Street on Saturday mornings. He had a piano accompanist who knew exactly what tempo to play, and each Saturday the same pieces were played, so that we became familiar with the music and the steps. The only other person whom I remember taking lessons was Rita O'Hara. She was an advanced dancer, and one day wearing a colorful costume she performed a tap routine for us. Wearing black patent leather tap shoes with the grosgrain ties was in my mind, the ultimate in shoes. I loved taking lessons, but I don't think I had the persistence to learn more and more steps and eventually gave it up. I did ballroom dancing however, for many years. I watched the movies with singing and dancing, and whatever type of dancing, tap or ballroom was great fun for me.

I was a kid who loved music and rhythm. I knew the words to songs and loved to entertain my family by singing a song being played on the radio, all the while acting out the words and dancing. Sometimes I would don a hat or grab a scarf to put around my neck. There was a melodic song with catchy words about a little old lady. With my long bathrobe on, the scarf would go over my head, and I would bend over using a cane from my father's collection, acting the way I thought it was to be old, all the while singing. It was my great pleasure, and my grandmother, sisters and my parents were laughing and enjoying my performance. This was more my style.

Clothes and Shoes

I was beginning to care about the clothes I wore, but I was still taken shopping by my mother, and she guided me as to colors, style and fit. Girls and women did not wear slacks except in the case of small girls who sometimes wore overalls of varying materials for play clothes, and denim blue jeans were unheard of. They were the farmers' work clothes. Eventually glamorous women would be seen wearing slacks in movies and slowly this fashion became available for young women. During the 1940s slacks became popular but were worn outside the school. Women found them practical working in factories, and the school administration gave in to requests of students and designated Friday as "slacks day."

For us girls it was dresses that had to be laundered and ironed. I thrilled at acquiring a new dress or two. School shoes and Sunday shoes were purchased each fall at a shoe store not far from the dress shop for young girls in White Plains, New York, about thirty miles from Brewster. My feet would be measured on a metal plate by the owner of the shop who would bring out the proper size shoes in brown leather for school and patent leather for Sundays. With the shoes on my feet he would put his finger and thumb on either side of my foot at the widest place, squeeze a little, then put his thumb in front of my big toes and press on the leather. Then he would declare the shoes to be the proper fit. My mother depended on this man, and he had a good customer in her.

There were many children not as fortunate as I. They did not have new shoes very often, but I was not aware of those circumstances at a young age. I could see that some girls and boys did not have new looking shoes, but that did not faze me. I was not comparing. It was only as an adult and learning about the conditions during the Depression years that I appreciated my family's situation. I also did not appreciate how well my mother managed the family finances and how hard my father worked.

It was always a rule that we girls upon arriving home from school were to change our school clothes and hang them in the closet for another day; no throwing them on the bed and certainly not on the floor. Too much work went into having clean and ironed dresses to have them worn only one day. We had school clothes and play clothes for after-school activities. Our good leather shoes were occasionally polished. As I had seen my father polish his shoes, a habit started while in the Navy in WWI, I eventually did the same. For play we put on old shoes. The clothes and shoes purchased in the fall were to last until they were outgrown. My sister Joan had a twin sweater set that was woolen knit. Being older than I, her clothes were a different style than mine. When this sweater set had been washed several times, it shrank as all woolens did. That meant it would be passed down to me. By then the fibers had pulled together as they shrank, so that I did not have the sweaters very long.

We were very fortunate children. I was not aware that families across our country were suffering from lack of food, because their fathers were out of work. I heard these things on the radio occasionally but could not really appreciate it all.

What Is a Barricade?

There were times I would accompany my parents when they drove to New Hampshire to take my two sisters to Sargent Camp in Peterborough, although many times I stayed at home with my grandmother. In 1935 or 1936 there were no superhighways or even highways, as we know them now. And many times the road's surface would be of packed dirt. On one stretch of winding road we were driving straight ahead, when all of a sudden there loomed just ahead of our headlights a wooden sawhorse barricade with some sort of small sign. My father crashed through the barricade, then came to a stop. The road was under construction, and we should have made a sharp left. He backed the car, and we continued on our way.

I was sitting in the back seat, my parents in the front seats. There were no seat belts. No one was hurt as we slammed to a stop, but I was very frightened by the whole ordeal. There were several years that while sitting in the back seat, I would lean forward, and ask my father, "Are there any barricades?" or "Is that a barricade?" In fact, for quite a while I didn't sit back on the seat, but would be perched on the edge, watching. My vocabulary was increased in an unexpected way.

A younger cousin lived ten miles away in Danbury, Connecticut. We got along well, and he asked me if I wanted to go to his house and stay overnight. My parents drove me there, kissed me and said goodbye. When it came bedtime, I put on my pajamas, bathrobe and slippers. I wasn't in my own home, and I was uncomfortable. It became that time to climb into bed in their spare bedroom holding my cuddly, brown bear (one on four legs made of reversed sheepskin), and I became very homesick. I started to cry, and my aunt and uncle could not console me. I am not sure how much they tried; my Aunt Aileen

Hawley was my father's sister, but I did not feel close to her. They called my parents and to my relief, it wasn't long before they arrived. We said our goodbyes and probably apologies, and we were off to Brewster. It was a great relief to be sitting with my mom and dad and my brown bear.

Oh Heck!

In the springtime I spent much time with my friends, roller skating on Putnam Terrace all the while trying to avoid the cracks in the sidewalk. But on rainy days, it was a challenge to have some fun. We had the perfect situation in our basement to roller skate there. It had a painted concrete floor, and being small I thought the open space was large. At one end was the door to the laundry room, and the furnace did not seem to take up too much space. On one side there was a rise that was actually a huge boulder covered with cement. It had apparently been too large to remove when the house was built, and so it was simply covered. I would climb this "hill" and have a good ride, until I reached the wall across the room.

I was not permitted to walk up the steps and skate in the kitchen. But it was so tempting to skate around the table on the linoleum floor. I tried it a couple of times, but when I was caught by my mother, her admonishment cleared up any doubt that I was only to skate in the cellar. Oh, heck!

From the time my grandmother and aunt came to live with us, there was always an old trunk full of costumes. It was placed at the base of the "hill" I skated down and so had to be avoided. These costumes had been my aunt's as well as my sisters' who needed them for their ballet dance class performances. I made use of them many times either for Halloween or for the parades that we children organized. If someone couldn't come up with a costume I would dig one out of the trunk. There were usually two of each costume, because my two sisters took lessons and used them. There were ducks, pirates and my favorite, a princess's dress, of course.

Winter's Joys and Other Things

We had three Flexible Flyers in our family. My sisters each had a long one, and mine was short and easy for me to handle. When I grew bigger, I would use one of the larger sleds that would accommodate a friend. Friends would gather on a snowy day, when there was no school, and we would "sleigh ride" down Putnam Avenue toward Carmel Avenue. We also found that the dirt road leading in the opposite direction down to Cunningham's swamp was a good ride—longer and with a nice bump half way down the hill. Some of the bigger boys would appear and looking for more excitement would hitch a ride on the back of a car going up the hill.

There were many memorable winters, when the snow would become so deep that after the sidewalk was shoveled, it was like walking through a canyon. Going outdoors in the morning after a deep snow fall, it was quiet, nothing moving, no sounds. When it had snowed hard all night, it was obvious that there would be no school. However, snow coming down did not necessarily mean that school would be cancelled. The phrase "snow day" had not as yet been coined. A Danbury radio station might have had announcements about school closing. Having an unexpected day off with lots of snow made many children happy, and as soon as breakfast was eaten, boys were out earning some money shoveling the snow. When I was old enough, I looked forward to shoveling the snow off our sidewalk.

Sledding was best when the cars had packed down the snow and before any plowing truck came through. Every kid in town it seemed was out with his or her sled having a wonderful time. Sometimes one boy would hitch a ride on the back of a friend's sled kneeling between the legs of the one steering or actually lying on top of him to keep from falling off. When a car came into view, the sledders headed for the side of the road sometimes turning over or coming to an abrupt stop in a snow bank.

If the snow was wet rather than powdery, it was good for making a snowman. I would start with a large snowball and start rolling it across the front lawn exposing the grass beneath, turning it so that it would remain round. Every now and then I would pack it down to keep it hard and from breaking apart. Eventually it became too heavy for me to push, and that would be the size of the bottom half of the snow man. I would do the same for the head but had to keep it small enough to lift onto the body. From there I could add the wet snow patting it all around.

It was then ready to have two pieces of coal placed for the eyes, shaped snow for the nose and a stick for the mouth. I could usually find the coal in our basement, as the remainder of the coal pile was still there.

At times when we had six inches or more of snow, conditions were just right for a hard crust to form on top of the snow. We could actually walk on this crust. Behind my friends' house was the slope that in summer was my Grandfather Beal's garden. We discovered that we could have some good thrills by sliding on the crust using whatever flat object we could find. It might be the lid of an old garbage can without its handle, a piece of wood and sometimes even riding on a snow shovel, feet in the air, holding onto the wood shaft. Some even used a sled, until it broke through the crust. On one occasion one of the girls used her sled. The steel runners of our sleds had straight, rough, even rusted, blunt ends. She tumbled off her sled on the ride, and the end of the runner pierced her abdomen. She went to the doctor or to the hospital and survived. It was a good reminder to be careful on these sleds. It was years later that the open-ended runners of sleds were replaced with the safer curved ends. The plastic disks that came along years later would have been perfect for those conditions—and much safer.

There was another measure of winter and nights with temperatures below zero. Our milk was delivered to our back porch by Rider's Dairy from Danbury, Connecticut. By the time the glass bottles had been on the porch since the delivery, the milk was pretty much frozen, and the cream had been pushed up and out of the bottle in the frozen state with the paper cap resting on the uppermost surface. The bottle would then have to be left to thaw.

The bottles were constructed so that there was a neck a few inches from the top of the bottle. The milk was not homogenized as it later became, and when the cream rose to the top just above the neck, a special bent spoon was used. It fit through the top hole and came to rest above the neck. It was then possible to invert the bottle and remove some or all of the cream into a pitcher. If the customer wanted cream other than what came to the top of the bottle, the milkman would find a note in the milk box with a request for whatever was needed.

Occasionally a boy would pass a house and see the frozen cream on top of the bottle. Unable to resist the temptation, he would break off the cream-ice and have himself an early morning iced cream.

The Danbury Fair

Every fall we school children looked forward to learning the dates of the Danbury Fair, as our school was closed for two days so that everyone could attend this great event. As a child I would attend with my parents. As a teenager, a friend or two were included. It was great fun. There were the animal barns where the animals were judged, contests for the best vegetables and preserves and stands where one could buy trinkets and souvenirs and of course cotton candy. One of my souvenirs was a pin made of gold-colored wire fashioned into my name, Dolores in script. The man selling them had all sorts of names made up, or a name could be ordered, and it would be made on the spot.

The racetrack was a big attraction where there were car races. I attended at least one of these events. It was noisy and exciting. In later years stock car races were held on that race track, and Lucky Teeter the extraordinary trick driver who drove his car up a ramp and over several automobiles came one year, and I attended that show.

In my book, *Those Who Served/Those Who Waited*, Virginia Dutcher Ward tells about going to the races at Danbury Fair, and when her niece "found out that Elizabeth Taylor, the actress, was there in a box seat, she bought two box seat tickets for us. We sat right behind her."

Automobiles and Snow Chains

Automobiles in the 1930s and 1940s were a blessing but very unlike the engineering of the future. At that time, it was possible with some knowledge of what was under the hood of the car, to make repairs, replace spark plugs and add engine oil or whatever was needed. There were windshield wipers but no anti-freeze liquid to be squirted on them in winter, and so in freezing temperatures the ice would gather along the blade.

These old cars could be difficult to start in summer or winter necessitating using the choke, pulling it out and pushing it in as the foot was applied to the accelerator hoping it would stop coughing and sputtering and start moving ahead while in first gear. After the car started, it often took one hundred to three hundred yards before the engine was firing on all cylinders, whether the car had four, six or eight cylinders. In cold weather it was a good idea when starting the car to let the engine "warm up" before shifting to first gear. Any young man who had an old car would spend hours tuning the engine to his satisfaction.

The automobiles had stick shifts from the floor on the right side of the driver. The earlier cars had the ignition button under the accelerator pedal, so that to start the car one had to depress the accelerator with the right foot, until the engine turned over. Later cars had the gear stick to the right of the steering wheel connected to the main shaft. It worked more smoothly and was more accessible when shifting gears.

Still later the ignition button was on the dash board, and as that was pushed, the driver's foot was ready to push the accelerator pedal, all the while the shift stick was in neutral. Once the car started, the left foot had to depress the clutch pedal on the left and be held while the stick shift was moved into first gear at the lower left of the "H." As the car moved ahead the left foot went to the floor again as the stick shift was moved to second gear on the upper right of the "H," and the car accelerated. This was repeated until the car was shifted into third gear at the lower right moving smoothly and gaining speed. The "reverse" position was on the upper left of the "H" and was accomplished the same way from a stop position.

In all weather conditions when making a turn, every driver had to use hand signals with the left arm outside the driver's windows. For a left-hand turn the arm was stretched out straight at a ninety degree angle to the car. For a right-hand turn, the elbow was bent with the hand pointing upward.

The hand brake was on the left side to be used with the left hand. It was for use in an emergency and after the engine had been turned off. The hand brake was the last act before leaving the car. In later years when I was driving, I was happy to learn of the necessity to leave the hand brake off in freezing temperatures, when the car was parked in the garage for the night, otherwise the brake would be frozen the next morning. It was my Uncle Phil who gave me that important advice. When the automatic transmission was developed years later, it was a welcomed advancement, but the stick shift remained popular for sports car lovers.

Before "snow tires" with large treads were made and long before studded tires were available, winter driving on snow covered roads around town was very difficult. Many times a driver became stuck, unable to go forward or backward. Often a couple of men or boys would come to the aid of the driver giving him a push to get him on his way. Going up a hill would be impossible. Putting a set of chains on the two back tires was the answer. If the snow was deep and conditions poor, four tires could have chains. The chains were put over the tire as far as one could reach. Then the automobile had to be moved ahead a foot or so in order to attach one end of the chains to the other.

Chains were not perfect but a necessity nevertheless. After they had been used a certain period of time or were run where the snow was gone, a link in one of the chains would break. The "clink-clink" sound of a broken chain, as it hit the fender again and again became a familiar one. That had to be repaired before more damage was done. For this reason alone women drivers were seldom out when snow was on the roads.

It was not unusual to see a car with a flat tire and the driver removing it to put on the spare. The car could then be driven home or to a service station. The tires had inner tubes, and when the tire was punctured, it was necessary to remove the inner tube, find the hole and apply a patch before inserting it back in the tire. Upon repairing the tire, it could then replace the spare. It was a last resort to buy a new tire, and it often put a strain on the family budget.

As with the doors of houses, the cars were seldom locked. No one in our town was going to vandalize or steal a car, nor would anyone walk into a villager's home.

New Experiences: The *Hindenburg* Overhead

One warm summer week in 1936 we were taken to a luxurious hotel at Seagirt on the New Jersey shore. My mother and a friend spent the week, and their husbands came down for the weekend. This hotel had a special dining room for children who ate early, but I only remember eating in the dining room with my mother and sisters. Having been on the sandy beach much of the day, we had to nap and then bathe and put on our pretty dresses for dinner. There was a young bellhop with whom my fourteen-year-old sister fell immediately in love. He was a handsome boy. Even I could see that.

During our stay at the hotel when we were on the beach, we looked overhead and had the thrill of seeing a large dirigible following the coastline. It went back and forth several times not far overhead, as it drew great interest from those of us on the ground. Mallory Stephens remembers seeing this dirigible over Brewster during one of its trips from Germany to New Jersey. The pilots were unable to land it, and were waiting for the wind to subside. This was one of the problems dirigibles had, and the following May we learned that the German hydrogen gas filled *Hindenburg* exploded over Lakehurst, New Jersey, while trying to land just down the coast from where we had vacationed. Old movies of this disaster show passengers and crew jumping, trying to survive the inevitable. Some did survive, but most lost their lives in the conflagration.

This disaster was considered caused by an electrical storm or a problem with the electrical wiring, but it was also thought to be a possible act of espionage. Years before WWII Hitler had great hopes that this magnificent airship would put him in high esteem in the world community. The airship had made many trips, and it must have been a quiet and comfortable mode of travel.

My mother spent many summers of her younger years at saltwater beaches and really preferred the ocean to lakes. I however was cautious, when I waded into the lapping waves. I could feel the undertow as it swept back from the beach pulling at my feet, and I did not like the feeling of what I perceived as imminent danger. I was used to the calm reassuring fresh lake water. Yet, it was not much later that Tonetta Lake was being dragged for the body of someone who had drowned. That was the year I acquired two new words: "grappling hooks."

The sun was hot and people lay in the sun or sat talking for hours. My mother was thoroughly enjoying the relaxation and warmth. She may have applied a "sun lotion" but there was no sunscreen at that time. One afternoon she went into the hotel room with a red body and not feeling well. She had a case of sun poisoning and stayed on her bed in misery for the rest of the day and night.

One day my sisters and I were digging in the sandy beach, and they decided it would be fun to bury me in the sand. Enjoying the attention and wanting to be a part of the adventure, I went along. My sisters were my world, and I believed in them. The hole was dug deep enough for me to go in to my armpits. As they filled in the sand around me, I found it harder and harder to breathe with each inhalation, as the sand fell in around my body. I found it difficult to speak. Perhaps it was my older sister, Jane who could read my distress and initiated my rescue. It was a frightening experience. Late in her life my sister, Jane, confessed to carrying guilt of participating in this act with her all her life, but when I learned of this, I reassured her that we were all kids, and she should not think of it further.

Oh, So Homesick; Pigtails

When my hair was long enough to braid, my mother braided it each morning after I was dressed. Then I learned to first part my hair in the middle from the bangs across the top and down the back to my neck. It wasn't long before I could feel the center and accomplish it quickly. Eventually before bedtime I put two aluminum curlers below the rubber band so that I had some curls at the end of my braids. My mother let me buy ribbons about one half inch wide to match my clothes. I had solid colors, Roman stripes and plaids, and they would be tied in a bow at the end of the braid. I hung them neatly on a hanger in my closet.

At our fiftieth high school reunion I was reminded by a classmate that when we were in the fifth grade, he tried to dip my pigtails in his inkwell, as he sat behind me.

In 1937 when I was ten years old, I said yes when my mother asked if I would like to go to Sargent Camp in Peterborough, New Hampshire, where my two sisters had attended for several years. They were enthusiastic campers learning to canoe, play tennis, horseback ride and arch, then coming home and singing camp songs. My mother ordered the necessary cotton uniforms. The Sunday uniform was a clean white shirt with collar and short sleeves. The navy blue shorts were made of a fine woolen serge with elastic around the leg, so that they bloused at the bottom. The rest of the clothes consisted of cotton shorts and shirt, sweatshirts, sneakers, socks, sole-less oiled moccasins, shoes and sneakers. I had never seen so many new things. She sewed my name tapes on every piece of clothing as well as the necessary cot-size sheets and gray woolen camp blankets, so that they would not get mixed up with the other children's laundry. Every Sunday night I would write out the list of clothes going to the laundry. I remember enjoying the return of my clean and folded clothes. It was like getting a present, and clean clothes felt good. Sunday was also the day we wrote a letter to our parents.

Before going to camp we found out that I had to be vaccinated, and it was done only a couple of weeks before leaving home. I also found out that with the recent vaccination I could not go swimming. I had to wait for the scab to fall off, and this could not have been worse news. While at camp my father took a picture of me looking so sad, and my fingers were holding the edge of my shorts up so that my bandage would show. So there! It wasn't fair.

Dodie, unhappy about vaccination and no swimming

At that time my hair was to my shoulders, and I asked my mother how I was going to dry my hair and get it braided, when I had to go to another sport. If I left my hair wet in braids, it very soon became sour smelling. So it had to be dried, but there were no electric hairdryers. It was my dilemma to solve. Children had haircuts, and the air and sun dried their hair. I had to undo the braids, comb them out to let the hair dry in the air. I had no choice, but I felt self-conscious about it.

When I was a few years older I would stand in front of the mirror brushing my long hair thinking about being glamorous as in the current movies. The fantasy of simply wearing my hair down my back would come, but I knew my mother would never allow that. The Victorian response would come over me. It was well engrained so much so that my own response to seeing my hair unbraided was to feel uneasy and not as attractive as with the usual braids. This continued to be my reaction as long as I had long hair—and it did become longer. (At 21 years old I had my hair cut short in the latest style.)

It wasn't long before I experienced terrible homesickness. My sisters were much more adventurous and independent than I and loved every minute of camp life. Fortunately, Jane, then age 16 and Joan, age 14 were on the senior campus, while I was on the junior campus. One group had nothing to do with the other group. Sundays were the worst days, but Jane would come over and visit me, and that was comforting. Sunday was also the day we could go to the camp store and buy postal cards, but my main interest was a long, inch-thick lime lollypop, my favorite flavor. It was the most long-lasting candy I could buy, and it cost five cents. It also later cost me some cavities in my teeth. A new experience was finding two dishes on a table in the main camp building, one full of dried prunes and one with dried apricots to which we could help ourselves. But I really wanted to be home with my mommy and daddy.

When parents' weekend came my parents visited. They knew how homesick I was, and they received permission to let me stay overnight with them at the inn in Peterborough where they were staying. I had forgotten to bring my soft stuffed bear, one they had brought me from Vermont. I took it to bed every night, but I didn't have it with me. So my mother bought me a teddy bear. It was rough and not cuddly. It was no substitute for my sheepskin bear. I can remember trying to like it, but it did not work. My bear was a comfort to me.

When we were at the inn, I somehow discovered that my mother was going to have a baby and asked her about it. It was too much for me to fathom, added to my homesickness. She did talk to me about it, but I do not remember how the conversation went. The new baby brother or sister was to arrive in February, 1938.

During the week, I was kept busy with all kinds of activities: improving at swimming, learning to horseback ride, archery and crafts. I liked it all. Horseback riding made me feel like a big girl, but I was somewhat fearful of horses, whereas my sisters were good riders. Of course I was a beginner. All the other camp activities were great fun. It was my first experience with archery and crafts like basket making and sculpting. I made a dog and a sugar and creamer set and had them fired and glazed a teal shade, a favorite color much of my life. This set was heavy and bulky, but I was proud to give it to my mother.

One day we went on a walk in the New Hampshire woods. It smelled so good. We sat under a tree and found there were little chameleons running around on the forest floor. This was a new experience, and the smell of the New Hampshire woods stayed with me for a long time. Deer ticks were not a concern at that time.

Annually at the end of August all the campers participated in a pageant. There were rehearsals, and each group was assigned a spot in the pageant. That year it was Robin Hood and His Merry Men. My sister, Jane, being an excellent archer was one of Robin's men, dressed in costume. During the pageant there was an archery demonstration in which she participated. I was dressed in a simple green tunic with a hat that had a feather. The main roles were given to the senior campers, and we acted as the back-up chorus. This was my first and only experience participating in such a pageant.

Joan spent eight years at summer camp and Jane twelve. Jane became a Counselor in Training but did not return to be a counselor. It was a high point in their year.

The Fall of 1937

Having finished camp, I went back to school in the fall of 1937 starting the sixth grade at the age of ten. My camping experience was over, and I was happy it was. The year brought growth, learning, and change; with some moments of discomfort in my up-to-then comfortable life. My mother was expecting a baby, which I did not fully understand, but I listened to conversations trying to digest the fact that I would soon be an older sister. My new teacher had a reputation of being strict, even mean. She was a tall, stern-looking woman who was not married, at that time called a maiden lady. My friend Charlotte was her neighbor, and she tried to reassure me that she was "nice." That did not help.

A few months into my sixth-grade year a girl who sat next to me rose from her seat, and I could see blood on her dress. I was embarrassed for her, as she must have been on discovering that this time in her life had come—and in the classroom. My mother had prepared me about the female cycle, but no one could predict when it would occur. The larger subject of sexuality was not discussed in many families, and I would never have brought up the subject.

I was having difficulty with arithmetic. I can remember when the teacher was adding up long columns of figures, I was doing as expected, but as the columns became longer, she was getting ahead of me. It was an inadequacy that nagged at me, and in subsequent years, I taught myself to see the tens or fives, adding two or three or by subtracting to reach the total. It felt good that I had mastered my problem. (During the 1960s when my children were in grade school, I learned that a new system of math was being implemented in the Chappaqua school. It had to do with using the tens and fives in elementary mathematics. Was this really a new system?) Once I figured this out it didn't take me long to implement my system, and I became proficient at columns of figures. High School Geometry was clear to me, but advanced math was never to be my subject.

Each day I experienced a great need to stay at home. With a sick feeling in the pit of my stomach, I found it difficult to wrench myself from the house. I wanted to be home with my mother. I felt a terrible sadness, and within a half hour of being in my classroom, I started to cry or wanted to cry, and the feeling continued throughout most of that year. At first my mother was called to school. She did not understand what was happening, and although she was compassionate, there was not much she could do. Today a perceptive teacher or parent would see that I would benefit by talking about why I felt as I did.

It wasn't possible for this young girl to put her life's happenings into perspective, to figure out why it felt as if a rug had been pulled out from under her. The house she had grown up in was no longer the same, she was no longer the youngest child, but was assumed to be capable of learning to care for a baby brother, her pre-adolescence was upon her, and she did not like her teacher—and yet there was fun to be had.

Not all students disliked their teachers, though. Winton Tolles, Hamilton College Class of 1928, started his teaching career at Brewster High School, for several years boarding at the Stephens home on Garden Street. I did not know him, as I was a child. He later became Dean at Hamilton. William Yeomans, Hamilton class of 1955, described this man as follows: "He kept order with a firm but gentle hand, understanding us better than we understood ourselves. Classmates described his patience, kindness, faith in us, humor and his huge heart." When I read that, I could not help but wish I had thought of my teachers as they thought of Winton Tolles.

One of the activities to which I looked forward was weekly roller skating that was held in the school's auditorium. Every Wednesday a large truck pulled up near the front door, and roller skates for indoor use were unloaded. The record player was set up, and the students were fitted to a pair of skates. This lasted several hours, as we went round and round, listening to the music, talking and laughing. Before I was in high school the auditorium/gym floor had deteriorated and was replaced with a shiny, new wood floor. Our roller skating fun was over, but we had a beautiful floor for basketball and other sports.

My sister, Jane had attended the Oakwood School in Poughkeepsie, New York, for one year, but my mother was not pleased with what she saw when visiting the room that belonged to her daughter and her roommate. I was with my mother during her visit, and I can remember the comments about seeing dirty clothing scattered around the room, and my mother knew that her daughter was not accustomed to these conditions at home. Of course, at home my mother was always around to say, "Pick up your clothes." Jane finished that year, but in the fall of 1937 she transferred to the Knox School in Cooperstown, New York. This was a "finishing school" where the daughters of very wealthy families attended. I can remember my mother worrying about how she and my father were going to pay the tuition.

The headmistress paid a visit to our home to discuss the matter, and a payment schedule was arranged. Then of course there were school uniforms consisting of navy blue caps, skirts and blazers, cotton lisle stockings and oxford shoes as well as white vespers dresses, shoes and other items. The school was in the cold climate of upper New York State, and that meant the uniform polo coat and other warm clothing.

My other sister Joan finished her sophomore year in Brewster High School. My parents had a lot on their minds, and it was made no easier by this teenage girl. Squeezed between a sister two years her elder, and a younger sister who was deemed to be the one who received all the attention, Joan did not make it smooth running for our parents. Of course my mother was not prepared to handle her teenage daughter no matter how normal her interest in boys was. My mother was also displeased when visiting her after an appendectomy in Mount Kisco Hospital and finding her friends there who had brought her a pack of cigarettes. She was fourteen years old at the time. That is when Joan was sent to the Knox School for her junior year. Jane and Joan were now in the same class.

Norma Jane Beal.   Joan Ross Beal.
The Knox School Graduation, 1940.

While they were at school in Cooperstown, my mother wanted to visit my sisters during their winter carnival. We looked forward to seeing the ice sculptures that were made for that week in February. My mother drove her automobile, and I accompanied her. This was great fun, but the roads were slippery in places especially in upstate New York. When we reached Cherry Valley, we had a very difficult time making the hill, as cars were sliding off the road ahead of us. My mother must have been a good driver.

It was my second experience of being at a private school, the first school having been the Oakwood School. The month of February was bitter cold, and the girls were outdoors wearing warm snowsuits while working on their ice sculptures. My sister Joan constructed a beautiful polar bear that stood four to five feet high. They would put snow, then water that would freeze overnight, and keep building, until it was completed. It was strong enough for me to climb up and sit on it.

Jane was excited about taking figure skating lessons at school. When she was at home during the winter vacation, and we were skating at Tonetta Lake, she would practice a figure eight in a slow and calculated manner. She worked at it and enjoyed it, but not having started at a very young age, figure skating was a pleasant experience for her but a fleeting one.

In springtime it was the custom for the girls to gather on the dock on the shore of Lake Oswego and give a choral concert when warm weather reached Cooperstown. During a practice session the weight of all the students caused the dock to give way, and most of the students went into the water. My sisters called to tell us about it.

Apparently the school food contained many carbohydrates and was plentiful. Even though both sisters were active in sports, they both gained many pounds before graduation. Good eating habits were not part of the curriculum.

Runaway Caught

One afternoon while my mother was not at home, I answered the telephone and found my sister, Joan, was making a collect call. I told her that our mother was not at home. She said, "Dodie, I am at the train station, and I am coming home." I was only eleven or twelve years old, but I told her that she should "go back to school, mother will be upset." She said, "No" and having delivered the message to me we ended the conversation.

Someone at the railroad station noticed a girl who was obviously from the school waiting for the train, and this most certainly was an unusual sight. It wasn't long before an adult from the school arrived, and Joan was driven back to school. Of course when my mother returned home, she immediately got in touch with the headmistress and also talked with my sister.

Joan was a good student, was on the swim team and played squash, but her grades were erratic. My mother said she had good grades when she wanted to. As a present to my mother when baby Ross was born, she received all A's. I don't think she liked the regimentation. She also missed her family. I missed my sisters, but I enjoyed being an only child the months they were away. Occasionally my father took my mother and me to a movie either in Brewster or Danbury. I loved walking and holding their hands.

My cousin, Malcolm, and I were pals. Sometimes, when his father brought him into town for Sunday school, he would come to our house and stay until it was time to walk into the village where the Methodist Church was located. We would walk together, until I had to walk up the hill to St. Andrew's Church. We often saw each other, when we were at my grandfather's house, and he was waiting to be taken home by his dad. We would visit our Grandmother Beal while both of our fathers were still working in the P. F. Beal & Sons office at the rear of our grandparents' house.

Dodie.   Malcolm.

Malcolm was on the Brewster High School baseball team, and as an older student was a very good pitcher. When I saw him in the yard at the business, he usually had a baseball and mitt in this hand. One day we were standing under the apple trees, and he was having me throw the ball to him, he having a glove and I having none. He threw the ball one time, and it hit me in the eye. The next day I had a black eye. I never held it against him—in fact I believe I was proud that I had a black eye given to me by my favorite cousin and the pitcher for the team.

Malcolm and I found out that corn silk, when it dried at the end of the cob, could be put in a corn cob pipe or rolled in cigarette papers. Somehow we obtained paper and rolled the corn silk in it, or did we find a pipe? We both smoked and coughed. After all we had seen both our fathers smoking cigarettes, and this was our opportunity to try it.

Fear of the Dentist

Most people will agree that one of the occurrences that can ruin your day (or week) is finding out that a tooth must be extracted. This was a necessity for me and was a scary thought. Knowing how I felt, my mother suggested that we go to Bridgeport, Connecticut, where a dentist would administer gas that would "put me to sleep." That was somewhat reassuring, and arrangements were made.

I sat in the dentist's chair. The nurse in her white dress and shoes and doctor in his white jacket were busy with instruments. Then a hand-size mask was brought to me by the nurse. That was frightening enough. I was told that the gas was a pleasant smell of orange, and I was allowed to smell it. I cannot really call it a fragrance. Indeed, there was a hint of orange mixed with the gas, but as the mask approached my face, I was very apprehensive. As I took ten deep breaths the fear lasted, but at about eight I was "going off." As I came to in another room I was nauseated. But that too passed. The orange gas smell stayed with me for a long time. Whenever I thought of the experience, I could smell the orange—I would relive it. It finally faded.

This Dog Bites

My father came home one day after going on a business appointment at a house in Tilly Foster. (As Brewster people know, Tilly Foster is an area on the west side of the village, named after the man who had a farm there and also mined the Tilly Foster Mine). He described walking toward the house and up the stairs toward the door, when a German Shepherd sprang through the screened door and bit my dad in the groin. The wound could not have been too bad, and it healed. The story itself was so frightening to me that I was afraid of German Shepherds for years, and I was always on the lookout for the breed of an approaching dog.

From Thirteen Rooms to Six

In 1937 my mother was very excited about plans that had been drawn for renovating our mid-Victorian house. She wanted three modern apartments with the first floor reserved for us. With the two older girls away at school, the idea of having only one floor to clean and a small, efficient kitchen was appealing to her. There was to be a modest size master bedroom near the rear of the house and a bedroom for me near the front. My mother enjoyed going over the plans the architect had drawn.

While the plans were being made, my father decided to build a cottage at Tonetta Lake where we could live during the renovations. The cottage we had always used at the juncture of the upper and lower roads and next door to my grandfather's cottage was not winterized, and therefore could not possibly be lived in during the winter. So he bought a lot closer to the pavilion than the other cottages and had the new cottage built on that lot. Although we were not directly on the lake, we looked across the road to the water, and it would be only a short walk to the beach. It was a small bungalow with two bedrooms, a bath between, a fair sized living room and a small kitchen. The living room also served as our dining area, as it had a long, narrow table built under the windows that was hinged to the wall facing the lake. It could be raised or lowered as needed. We sat on benches.

This little house was warmed by a one-pipe furnace located in the garage below the living room. There were no automatic garage door openers, and most garages had doors that swung open to the side on hinges, the door handles being where the two doors met when closed. The cottage was quite comfortable, and we were there for about two years. Each day I would ride to school with my father as he went to work. The plans for completing the house at 12 Putnam Avenue went on until the three apartments were finished, painted, and the first floor was ready for us to move into it.

One summer when we were at this new cottage my mother had set up her wooden-legged ironing board in the very small kitchen. When the board was set up there was no room to by-pass it. One day the little Gorman boy from the bungalow next door came to visit, as he sometimes did. He got past the wooden icebox, ducked under the ironing board catching the cord, and the hot iron fell on his tender arm. He received a very bad and painful burn from it, and we all felt very badly about it. How could we have known that he and his brothers and sister would become outstanding athletes, Frank becoming a Silver Medalist in the 1964 Tokyo Olympics. And he learned to swim and dive at Tonetta Lake.

At Putnam Avenue the curved portion of the front porch and the back porch, kitchen and dining room had all been torn away. A three-story enclosed back stairway was built, and what had been the front part of the wrap-around porch became what we called the sunroom. It had three windows across the front and one on the side. A door at one end led to the new patio of blue stone edged with young Taxus yews. The granite steps were recycled from those at the front of the house to the patio. The front door was built into the driveway side of the house and led to the original stairway, but the stairs now passed the closed doors to three apartments.

Everything was new: an inlaid blue linoleum floor, a blue pull-out sofa and a unique square table that opened to double its size was placed under the middle window. It became my place for doing homework. It would not be many years before a blue military service star would be hung in that window. The furniture was blonde wood—very "modern." On either side of the door to the patio were bookshelves painted white and nearby a low, comfortable leather chair with beige corduroy on the back cushion and the seat cushion. The square design of this chair was very modern for its time. For reading there was a table on which was placed a large lamp fashioned in hammered antiqued copper. My parents were very happy with this new bright and up-to-date room. However, the small living room, at the suggestion of a decorator/friend, was done in a dark red. Everything from the paint on the walls to the new draperies and the two reupholstered chairs were all red and set off by the white woodwork—supposedly the latest thing in home décor. I had no particular liking for it, but my mother was enjoying something new. After all, she had lived with old furniture for a long time.

Not everyone was happy about the changes. If my sisters were kept up to date on the renovations, they couldn't really visualize the changes taking place at home. When they came home from school, my sister Jane stepped from the car, looked at the rear of the changed house and wept. What she saw was a complete shock to her. She soon learned to accept and like the "new" house. It was a busy family, and my sisters were excited about having a baby come into the family. And of course they also hoped for a baby brother.

Now a Member of the Brewster High School Band

Starting sixth grade in 1937, I had been invited to join the Brewster High School band. (All grades from Kindergarten through high school attended classes in the same building, and the High School Band drew students from the lower grades to help fill out the band.) I was learning to play the trumpet my father had purchased second-hand for my sister Jane. Reading music came easily to me. However, the band needed an alto horn player and not a trumpet player at that time. They had an excellent trumpet section with Charlie Stefanic, Leslie Garnsey and Betty Cleaver. Mr. Knapp asked me if I would like to join the band playing the alto horn that has the same fingering as the trumpet. Naturally, I was thrilled to be asked and found it fun to play the "oom-pah-pahs" and harmony required of the alto horn player. Of course I continued to learn the trumpet. In my spare time at home I sometimes played simple tunes on the harmonica. My father had brought me an ocarina (sweet potato) from New York City, and I worked at that for a while. To me it was such a beautiful little instrument, made of fired clay with a teal-color glaze. Those two instruments disappeared along with other mementos of that time.

For the next several years the BHS band was outstanding. Besides the trumpet players there were other instrumentalists who stood out, such as Wilbur Nagle on the clarinet, Ruth Nagle playing the French horn, Ray Shalvoy on the baritone, Rita O'Hara on the saxophone, Henry Truran on the tuba and Gabriel Blockley our drummer. Except for Ruth Nagle, these players were older, and as they graduated, others moved up to take their places. But during those years of the early 1940s, the band under the direction of Mr. Harold Knapp was excellent.

Dodie in Brewster High School Band Uniform.

The Fun of Being a Kid

Norman Donley, the principal's son, was in my grade, and I remember that he had difficulty learning to read. There were one or two others who found it difficult to read as well. But it was Norm who was kept back one year because of this problem. It was probably thought that he was not applying himself. Norm was a nice boy who had a good sense of humor. Only a few years later Norm lost the sight in one eye. It was because of this that he would not be accepted into the major military services. He was however taken into the Merchant Marine and served his country well. In a few years he lost the sight of his second eye and had to rely on a seeing-eye dog.

We had been friends a long time. Except for one or two other times when we crossed paths, I did not see him again. I learned that he opened a bar and grill called Norm's on the edge of Brewster very close to the old Borden milk factory. Norm died at an early age. The establishment is still flourishing, serves good meals and is a popular gathering place.

So, I was in the sixth grade, my two sisters were away at school and there was excitement about a new baby. This was my time of pre-puberty, and the hormones were acting up, not that I knew about those things. I had a boyfriend of sorts. We started noticing each other the year before, and my cousin Malcolm would tell me that his friend Eddie Collins liked me. The attraction was mutual. I can remember in the sixth grade, looking through the window of the classroom door and seeing him walk by. HE was LOOKING at ME!

Eddie and his fraternal twin brother Jimmy lived on Center Street with their father and older brother Robert, not far from my friend Muriel Pinckney. Eddie's hair was dark while Jimmy's was red, and they had opposite dispositions. Bob was a handsome boy who became president of his class of 1939. He was very good to his brothers, seeing to it that they attended Mass and taking them to buy new clothes when needed. Passing his house to visit my friend, I would sometimes say hello to Mr. Collins, as he was polishing his dark green Buick. The boys' mother had died when the twins were very young.

On a dark night with much snow on the ground, a group of boys and girls went out to sleigh ride. We each had a sled and pulled it to a favorite hill. We were headed somewhere between Center Street and Prospect Street pulling our sleds, talking and having fun. On Friday nights in winter we frequently went sledding.

I was developing good friendships, and we had good times. Our seventh-grade teacher, who was younger than our previous teachers, was pretty with dark hair, but the students could not resist in testing her. One of the girls started loosening the bolts that held her seat in place. Of course as she worked on it over the course of many days, our attention would be drawn to her work. What fun we were all having. Eventually all the bolts were loose and the seat nearly toppled over with her in it. The teacher did see what had taken place, but I do not remember any consequences except that she was told to replace the bolts. A classroom of kids needs a good laugh once in a while.

One day when the teacher was out of the room, my friend Eddie who was a year ahead of me walked into the room and up to the teacher's desk. She had been his teacher the previous year. He had a bottle in his hand and tossed the contents across her papers. She came back to her desk and saw this inky liquid that had apparently ruined her work. She was aghast and let out a yelp. But just as soon as she did all that ink disappeared. He had spilled disappearing ink. She did not appreciate his joke.

It was about that time that ballroom dancing classes were held in the auditorium every Wednesday afternoon. I could not wait for that class each week. I loved learning all the steps, and I liked the music and the rhythm. Mr. Newman sometimes asked me to demonstrate steps with him and he danced very smoothly. It seems that all the girls loved this class, and the boys either hated it or would not admit that it was fun. One of the dances we were taught was "The Lambeth Walk." It had its own song, "… doing the Lambeth Walk," and the couples walked in a large circle stopping occasionally and changing partners. It was a British favorite, but never caught on in this country.

At the end of the class a dance was held, when we would all be dressed in our "Sunday best," boys in shirts, ties and jackets, girls in dresses and their best shoes. There was a Junior Prom and a Senior Ball that I attended. At the time I did not know that when I became a junior, the proms and balls would be eliminated. So, I was very happy to have been asked to attend these dances with the decorations made by the students. At one of the proms there was a decorated bridge that we walked over to reach the dance floor. I can remember at one dance, my cousin Malcolm was not dancing, and I asked him to dance. We danced, but he was unhappy about the whole thing, shaking his head and saying, "I don't like this," or something to that effect. I smile as I think of it. His date of course was Marjorie Lane, and I can remember admiring the formal dress she wore. Her mother had made it, and it was more sophisticated than dresses sold for young teenagers.

1938: A Turning Point

As far as educating young boys and girls, there was seldom, more likely never, discussion of sex or childbirth, and the coming birth in the family was handled with excitement and comments about the hope of the baby being a boy. I heard it said that the pregnancy was unexpected and even a disappointment. My mother was thirty-seven years old and was considered old to be expecting a baby. It also seemed that a happy life was dependent upon a boy being born.

The day came in February of 1938 when my mother was leaving our home, and my father was carrying her overnight bag for use in the hospital. Grandmother MacLean was with me, and my two sisters Joan and Jane were at the Knox School in Cooperstown, New York. They waited for news of whether they had a new sister or brother. Word was spread around the school of their expected sibling, and on February 22—George Washington's birthday—after learning they now had a brother, William Ross Beal, Jr., the entire dining room of girls sang

"Happy Birthday" to Ross and George. Everyone was ecstatic, and from then on life changed for everyone in the Beal family.

Dodie holding baby brother, Ross Jr.

In our house a small baby crib borrowed from my Aunt Norma had been readied. When the house had been remodeled, a new family member was not anticipated, and the second and third floors were not available to the family, as they were now rented apartments. After graduation, my two sisters attended different schools, and when they came home, Joan slept with me in the double bed on the first floor. Jane slept on the new enclosed porch in the new pullout sofa bed. This arrangement was definitely makeshift, but my mother felt it worked, because her two daughters were not at home on a permanent basis. However, that did not turn out to be the case. They were home a great deal, and the double bed was not large enough for Joan and me.

My parents had a bedroom in what had been the dining room, and a bathroom had been added that served the family.

For the second bedroom my mother let me choose a new bed, chest of drawers and a dressing table of blonde wood at Goossen's Furniture Store in Brewster. The dressing table had a very large round mirror, and we could have used the space it occupied. Before the house had been renovated this room was part of the entrance foyer. And so where the front door had been, there was now a window in the wall between the bedroom and the new enclosed porch—now called the sunroom. The baby's crib was placed next to this window. When a friend came, my mother would escort this visitor to the sunroom, and they would peer through the window at the sleeping baby. My parents had purchased a baby monitor so that they could hear in the kitchen any waking sound baby Ross made in the bedroom. It worked so well that one could clearly hear the sounds of his breathing.

As soon as my baby brother entered our home, I was taught how to hold and feed him his bottle of milk. I also learned how to change his diapers and help to bathe him. What a mind expanding experience it was for a soon-to-be twelve-year-old. When my parents wanted to go out for the evening they could rely on my grandmother to care for the baby, but I was soon given the responsibility of taking him for a walk in the stroller. Ross was a happy, good-natured child, and I did not mind taking care of him. We had good times together playing in the snow in winter and swimming in summer. It was often said in jest that he had four mothers. Actually my two older sisters were working after graduating, and my mother, Ross and I spent a good deal of time together.

On a Saturday I met my friends to walk "downtown" or "down street." We were all thrilled to be walking my baby brother in a stroller. On our way home, having crossed Oak

Street, we saw some boy friends approaching. They stopped and cooed at the baby or more likely stared in curiosity. One of them picked him up from the stroller while another boy backed up a distance of maybe five feet. One tossed baby Ross in the air to the other, and he was not unhappy about it—unless it registered in his unconscious! I was concerned about what was taking place, but it happened so quickly and I was glad to have Ross back in his stroller. It wasn't the soundest thing to do, and so much for being responsible. As time went by, I think that all my friends watched my brother's growing up.

Often my friend Charlotte would come over on a weekend to spend the evening when my parents went out. We would talk or play a game. Sometimes I went to her home on Carmel Avenue. Either way, one of us would have to go through "the woods" next to the Fowler's house, and when it was dark, it was a little scary walking amongst the pine trees. We usually made it a habit to walk to the edge of "the woods" and watch our friend safely to the other side, then wave. These trees are no longer there.

B-R-E-W-S-T-E-R!
Brewster! Brewster! Brewster!

In 1938 our school had dedicated an addition that was eagerly anticipated, as it meant that we would have a new music room with Mr. Harold Knapp heading the Music Department. The boys were very happy to have an Industrial Arts Department whose first teacher was Mr. Donald Graham. There was the new Home Economics Department that consisted of a large room divided between the kitchens and the sewing area. That meant another addition to the teaching staff with a new home economics teacher.

At about that time another big change was made with the addition of a girls' athletic coach whom we referred to as our gym teacher. The earliest coach whom I remember was Miss Florence Truberg. In my junior and senior years our teacher was Miss Ellene Edmond. They were both very good as well as likeable coaches. That meant we could concentrate on girls' intramural and extramural sports. Our school developed excellent girls' teams in field hockey, basketball, softball and volleyball. I eventually played right wing in field hockey, center in basketball and often first base in softball. Softball was my least favorite sport. When we played basketball at Purdys' High School, we found that the gym was not of standard dimensions, as there was no alley and little room beyond the boundary line of the court. As a result, if one was running toward the side court, she usually ended up slamming into the wall of the gymnasium. We became used to it and were prepared when a game was coming up.

Brewster High School had an excellent football team for many years under the direction of Coach Sterling Geesman. Students and townspeople turned out for the Saturday games, and the competitive spirit was intense with an air of anticipation and excitement. We played the schools in Putnam County: Carmel High School, Mahopac High School, Haldane High School in Cold Spring; and Danbury High School in Danbury, Connecticut. Our greatest competitor was Carmel High School. Danbury High School, a city school was in another league, always being considered a stronger team than Brewster. However, there were years that the BHS Bears beat Danbury, and that year the bonfire at season's end was bigger than ever. Our school spirit soared.

The band, dressed in green and white uniforms, played at all our school football games and at some of the away games. When there was a time-out or at quarter time, Mr. Knapp would strike up the band with a march. At half-time we marched on the field led by our drum majorette, the first being Margaret Bradbury, followed by Marjorie Lane and later Wilma Truesdale. The members wore white pants, green capes with braid and a military type hat. Well-tailored pants were not readily available for girls, so my mother made mine with fine wale white corduroy. They worked well for a few years, and then I was able to buy a pair. The boys' pants were probably of white cotton duck, and I am certain for some families, buying white trousers was considered a luxury. Most band members used the instruments provided by the music department, but a few students had their own instruments.

We had untied, undefeated and unscored-upon teams with players like "Bunky" O'Brien, "Red" Von Iderstein, Lucian Styne, Eddie Brady, Tom Lottrechiano, Ferd Vetare, Malcolm Beal, Henry Alfke and many others. They played as Coach Geesman sat on the bench smoking and piling up a mound of cigarette butts in front of him. He would sometimes stand and yell an order to his players. The school support was strong as the students cheered them on to victory. Brewster! Brewster! Rah! Rah! Rah!

We watched every play and noted every player. Coach Geesman, though a very tough disciplinarian, was an excellent football coach. One of the plays that he used gained the team more than one touchdown. It was called the "sleeper play." As the team lined up and started the play, the "end" would lie down unnoticed on the field near the sideline. When play started, the quarterback or the fullback would get ready to throw the ball, the end would stand up, start running for the goal line and catch the ball as he went. It was very thrilling, as the Brewster spectators could see the "sleeper." At times students would try to block him from view, standing between him and the players so that the "sleeper play" would succeed. Of course this wasn't sanctioned by the coach, but the kids had to get in on the fun. When it became known that Brewster used the "sleeper play," the team had to discontinue its use.

There was an annual Thanksgiving Day game between the Brewster High team and the alumni team. The students enjoyed watching the men who had graduated play against the current varsity team. It was always cold, and sometimes it was snowing, but that only made for more excitement. My sisters and I wouldn't miss this traditional event. My mother and grandmother were at home preparing Thanksgiving Dinner. My Aunt Norma and Uncle Elbert White would arrive for dinner with my little cousins Jim and Susan, and it was a wonderful day always ending with some music on the piano played by my aunt.

1939

WAR

The name Adolph Hitler was on people's lips—my Grandfather Beal called him "Schicklegruber." Reports came about this leader of Germany who had gained power, and governments were taking sides. Mussolini, who had invaded and conquered Ethiopia in 1935, eventually became allied with Hitler. The Nazi leader kept his secrets to conquer Poland after occupying Austria and Czechoslovakia even from him. I especially remember learning about the invasion of Ethiopia, but it did not mean much to me when I was eight years old.

Building up his following and strengthening his power, Hitler used his trained troops along the Austrian border to intimidate that government into handing over the Sudetanland with its German population. This Anschloss took place in 1938 without a battle. He then moved on to Czechoslovakia after annexing a port city in Lithuania. Hitler became known as a great orator, whipping up enthusiasm and excitement of the German people for his lies. It sounds simplistic to say he lied, but he was able to mollify, or more correctly, bluff the leaders of Great Britain, France and the United States by telling them that he had no designs on other countries. All this time he was secretly building his army, air force and navy against the agreement made in the Treaty of Versailles.

At the end of WWI the German people were treated badly by this treaty, not being given any help in the way of rebuilding the country, nor a way to come out of the economic depression into which it sank. Money became worthless, there was no work and the people needed food. Along came Adolf Hitler, a man full of hate and having written the book, *Mein Kamph*, while in prison as a youth. This hatred spilled over to most of the people in Germany against any who were not pure Germans, i.e. Aryans.

The Jewish people of Germany as well as Christians were being targeted as part of Hitler's goal of having a pure Aryan state. The notorious *Krystal Nacht* or Night of the Broken Glass instigated by Hitler's party chiefs resulted in the destruction of hundreds of shops and banks. Synagogues and Jewish homes were destroyed. Shops and banks were looted, banks closed, murders and rapes took place. All sorts of reasons were used, or no reason at all to put the Jews in box cars and transport them to Poland. Indignities were heaped upon them as they were carted away to concentration camps. This was only the beginning as Hitler's power aided by the Gestapo and his S.S. troops grew.

From then on these countries had to endure the savagery of the Nazi S.S. and imprisonment in concentration camps. It was the goal of Hitler to actually exterminate the Jews for what he considered a people lower than animals. He also took as prisoners anyone who spoke up against his policies, had some Jewish blood or were married to a Jewish person. He had the maniacal idea that the earth could be inhabited by a blonde, blue-eyed population. The leaders under him, Heinrich Himmler, Adolf Eichmann, Hermann Goering, Albert Speer and Karl Doenitz and others carried out Hitler's plans to conquer the world. He and the Nazi leaders had the majority of the German people either fooled or seduced.

The Nazi Germans were sinking our ships, and the British and American governments were watching these events. But at that time the United States was an isolationist country and did not want to prepare for a war with a foreign country. World War I had ended only twenty years earlier. As President Roosevelt and his close associates learned of the terrible events being carried on abroad, he knew we must prepare for war.

In the fall of 1939 Hitler carried out his plans to attack and occupy Poland thereafter terrorizing and killing Poles and Jews. Those who were not sent out of the country to concentration camps were used as slave labor within and outside the country.

In his book, *The Rise and Fall of the Third Reich*, William L. Shirer wrote, "the writer soon was being overwhelmed with reports of Nazi massacres. So were the generals. On September 10 with the Polish campaign in full swing, (Gen.) Halder noted in his diary an example which soon became widely known in Berlin. Some toughs belonging to an SS artillery regiment, having worked fifty Jews all day on a job of bridge repairing, herded them into a synagogue and, as Halder put it, 'massacred them.'"

The S.S. were given more and more broad powers to mete out atrocities to suit Hitler's goals of elimination of all but the Aryan race. William L. Shirer did an incredible job of reporting from Europe the day-to-day operations of the Nazis, until it was no longer safe for him to live and travel there. He was heard on the radio occasionally from London, as were the other correspondents during the attacks on London.

I clearly remember learning about the Japanese invasion of China and the Russian invasion of the Baltic states, the attack on Finland and seeing in the black and white newsreels the courageous Finnish ski troops in their white uniforms dashing through the woodlands trying to protect their country. We would watch the unfolding of events, rooting for the Finns in the newsreels as intently as we did the weekly serial movies, *Flash Gordon* and *Buck Rogers of the 21st Century*. This lasted several months, but then the news came that the Russians had won the contest and occupied parts of Finland. By then I was twelve years old, and our village life continued.

Later we learned that Nazi troops seized Denmark, Norway was being invaded and occupied by the Germans followed by the invasion of Belgium, Luxembourg and the Netherlands with their Queen Wilhelmina and family fleeing to England. Sweden declared itself a neutral country as did Switzerland. King Leopold surrendered while the allied forces of England, Belgium and France were pushed to the English Channel. The heroic retreat at Dunkerque, using thousands of boats and ships, saved a multitude of lives. A young person could not fully appreciate the constant sickening news.

The Vichy French were in North Africa under Marshal Philippe Petain while General Charles de Gaulle went to London to lead the Free French and the French resistance in his occupied country.

Bad news seemed to be coming so quickly. When we learned that Paris was being bombed, and the German army was invading France, it was shocking. But could we actually grasp this unfolding of events? And so much more was to come. But day followed day in the life of us teenagers with our activities and studies.

Be Polite

Everyone looked forward to the coming movie, "Gone With The Wind," starring Clark Gable and Vivian Leigh. My friend Charlotte Tuttle and I planned to see the movie. It was the same week that she and I had been invited by the elderly couple, Mr. and Mrs. Armstrong, who lived in our second floor apartment to have dinner with them. It was a very nice gesture for them to have two young girls as dinner guests. The table was set with linens and silverware. We were on our best behavior with the table manners we had been taught: Sit up straight. Do not talk with a full mouth. Chew with your mouth closed. Do not stuff your mouth while eating. Be polite. Say please and thank you. This did not cover instructions for boys, which would have included: take your hat off when entering a home, and clean your hands and fingernails. It was one of our first social occasions without parents, and I believe, though somewhat tentative, we behaved as expected.

We both remember that we were served a first course of broiled grapefruit. My mother had prepared grapefruit this way for special family dinners, but it was a first for Charlotte, and she enjoyed it. I believe we both wondered, "Why did they invite us for dinner?" They had no children, and it must have been a pleasure to be with young people. I do not remember writing a thank you note, but I suspect that my mother used this occasion to teach me to do so.

The New York World's Fair, 1939

Everyone followed with great anticipation the coming of the New York World's Fair in 1939 at Flushing Meadows, Long Island, New York. We followed the newsreels as the Trilon and

Perisphere were being constructed. They appeared on all the advertisements for the fair and on the souvenirs that people brought home. The school band was informed one day that it was to play at the World's Fair. What exciting news this was, and we started rehearsing marches for the occasion. All the schools in New York State were invited to have their day at the fair and to play on a raised platform on the promenade. We went there by bus and had a memorable experience playing and then walking around and viewing exhibits of the world to come—the world we now live in.

My good friends were in the band as well. Muriel Pinckney played the cymbals, Charlotte Tuttle the clarinet and Louise Vanderburgh sat next to me in the trumpet section. Until 1944 Mallory Stephens was in the band playing his cornet. He sat in the row behind Louise and me, and we would sometimes kid about the short cornet. Many years later he told me that he tried his darnedest to sit next to me, but that I wanted my friend Louise there. Louise and I had been good friends for a long time and having her next to me gave me confidence. I don't remember anything about Mallory wanting to sit next to me, but that is his story. I have since admitted that his cornet was a beautiful instrument, far better than my trumpet in quality. Mine, in fact, was difficult to play, possibly, because it had a dent on one of the small tubes. This trumpet now resides on loan at the Wright Museum in Wolfeboro, New Hampshire.

On the Second Floor with the High School Students

Miss McEnroe was my homeroom teacher in the eighth grade. She was not young at the time, as she had taught my father and his siblings. She was however bright and full of spirit. Her white hair was cut quite short, and she wore a hair comb in it. Often standing facing the class with her back to the windows, she would reach for her comb and run the comb through her hair then place it into her hair again.

One day when our class entered the room we found that Miss McEnroe's hair had a green tinge to it. Other alumnae remember other colors showing up at class time. We students agreed that she must have made an error in her hair dye chemicals. With thirty students and one teacher, the teacher could not get away with a thing. Nevertheless, we all liked her. She even gave me a ride home one day in her gray Terraplane, and of course my friends all noticed. She lived on Putnam Terrace and was related to the Smiths who lived not far away. I didn't know of the relationship at that time.

Yes, we liked her but at the same time with some trepidation, as she could come down on a student who did not keep to her standards. One day I was in my seat, second from the front. When she called on me, I did not give the answer, as she wanted it. Carrying a ruler in her hand, she came up the isle and slammed the ruler on my desk scaring me. She wanted my attention and the correct answer. Another time a girl sitting nearby gave the wrong answer, and Miss McEnroe walked toward her, took her hand and slapped it with the ruler. I was lucky. If that had happened to me, not only would my hand have stung, but I would have felt humiliated as the unlucky student must have.

One winter day with fresh snow on the ground I was in my history class. It came time to turn in our homework papers, and I realized I had left mine at home. Miss McEnroe's response was that I should leave then and there for my home and bring the papers back to school. So, off I went running most of the way home and back to school on the snowy sidewalks. I suppose I learned some responsibility from this.

At the end of one school day a few of us students stood at the back of Miss McEnroe's classroom. One of my classmates had a cousin who had recently come from Italy, and this cousin who had not mastered the English language was also in my class. One of my classmates started "joking around" and looking at me, suggested that I say a few words in Italian to him. I listened to the words he gave me, stepped over to the new student and said those few words to him. This fellow pulled out a knife, and I started running down the hallway and into the balcony of the auditorium. We came face to face with one another, and at that moment he realized that I didn't know what I was saying. I was naïve and gullible. But I learned a lesson. We got along well from then on. I still cannot believe that happened, and I never knew what I had said to him.

When we children were young—probably when my grandmother was there to watch over us—my mother went to the home of Miss McEnroe, down the street to receive tutoring in mathematics. She always regretted having been unable to finish high school, as she loved to learn. It was after I married that she accomplished a long-held desire, studying and receiving her GED. Then I was proud of her when she took her first college course in Florida. It was economics, and I was surprised that she started with a difficult course, but she was very interested in the subject.

Very Small Black Population

It was not uncommon while walking on the sidewalk in the village, to see a black-skinned lady wearing dark clothing, an ankle length skirt and black, laced, high shoes. Her name was Fanny, and my father said that he had known her for a long time. I never saw her speak to anyone, or perhaps no one spoke to her. She lived somewhere near the old post office on the hill.

We had heard about the black couple, Tony and Etta, who had lived many years before on the shore of Lake Tonetta. They were freed slaves, Tony having fought in the Civil War. For many years this body of water two miles outside Brewster was called Tone's Pond but eventually was officially known as Tonetta Lake or Lake Tonetta.

Brewster at that time had a population of eighteen hundred people and had very few black families. In the 1940s there was a black family whose son was a valuable member of the football team. Later two very nice black girls, the Green sisters, joined my class of 1944.

A Disaster on Main Street

One afternoon I was walking home from school by way of the village with my friend Muriel. Sometimes we would go to Hopes Drug Store for a Coke and have a leisurely walk home carrying our books stacked on our two-ring notebooks. This day we walked down the hill of the school to Oak Street passing the rear of the Presbyterian Church. We turned and started down the old post office hill, properly called Progress Street that led to Main Street. We heard explosions.

As we started down the hill, the firemen and police had arrived at a restaurant on that street. We had not reached the middle of the hill, when we saw a most horrendous sight. A person was stumbling alone out the door of a building almost across from the old post office. It was a woman who was so badly burned that she was charred black. We learned later that she was an aunt of a friend and died at the hospital. Other students who were already on Main Street saw a man burned beyond recognition being blown out of the restaurant where the explosion occurred. This was a very sad occasion for the people of Brewster.

Dr. Alexander Vanderburgh's house and office was not far from that location on Main Street. My friend, Louise was on her way home from school cutting from Oak Street through the Presbyterian Church yard to Main Street. She felt the ground shake and when she reached Main Street, she saw people who had been burned and hurt heading for her father's office. She also saw a man black with burns staggering toward her. Louise only remembers seeing a leather belt around his waist. Only two weeks before, a salesman sold Dr. Vanderburgh a large container of burn ointment that he felt sure he would not use in two years, but he felt very fortunate to have it that day.

Louise Vanderburgh.

1940

But My Grandparents Were Always There

Nellie was about five feet tall, round with a pleasant personality. Phil was about the same height, was balding, and had a thick, short mustache. He had a container on the mantelpiece, which I was told were the stones removed in a gallbladder operation performed at the Mount Kisco Hospital. He was very proud of this operation performed by Doctor Coopernail, a highly regarded and excellent surgeon.

Nellie had an upright piano, which I often heard her playing when I stopped in to visit after school. It intrigued me that as she played, her chubby little right hand would cross over her left hand, as she played the song. Sometimes she was lying on a loveseat taking an afternoon nap, for by then she was a gray-haired lady. I didn't think about whether they were old. I just knew they were always there, and didn't consider that one day they would not be there.

One day in 1940 my mother took my Grandmother Beal to the doctor's office. She brought her back to her house after the appointment, and then she came home. She reported to my father and to us that she had seen Grandma Beal's heart on the fluoroscope machine at the doctor's office, and what she saw was an enlarged heart that spread across her chest. She died not long after that. I remember being at home, when my parents were at my grandparents' house two houses away. I knelt on the sofa facing down the hill looking through the window at their house. It was the first death that I had experienced, and I was kneeling there thinking about it. I was taken the next day to say good-bye to my grandmother.

Preventive care in dentistry and medicine was not practiced, and medications were limited. This short lady was overweight, had high blood pressure and heart disease that must have made breathing difficult. Phil must have missed Nellie very much. One half of a very good and loving team was gone.

My grandfather was living alone in his large house and eventually hired a housekeeper. It soon became evident that the interior of the house was changing. Objects had been moved, and it was not as orderly or neat. Oilcloth replaced cotton or linen tablecloths. He seemed unruffled by the changes in his living conditions, yet I feel that he was aware. He had someone to talk to, and perhaps that is what he needed. My parents however were not happy with the situation, and I am certain that they consulted with my father's brother, Phil. Watching my grandfather living alone in the big house, my parents decided to move into his home and to rent out our apartment. I believe my grandfather enjoyed the activity we brought to his house, and he ate well.

Emma Jane and Alexander Lobdell and their daughter Jane were happy to move into our apartment. I found out that Jane was being teased by children on the way to school, and she was frightened and worried by this. I told Mrs. Lobdell that Jane could walk with me—that way no one would tease her, or I would tell them to stop. She was a nice little girl.

When Jane finished her education, she became employed at *Guideposts* magazine in Carmel, New York, where she spent many happy years. Norman Vincent Peale, who started that popular magazine, lived with his wife in Pawling, New York.

I was given the bedroom on the third floor. My two sisters shared a room on the second floor, and my parents used the master bedroom, formerly my grandparents' room. It contained a handsome wood wardrobe for clothing and a dressing table. My mother wasn't used to having this bit of luxury. My grandfather took a smaller room at the top of the stairs. I noticed that in his bedroom and others, the closets were built into the wall where the roof slanted. Because of this, one had to lean down to hang clothes. The house itself was lovely, well designed and nicely decorated.

My grandfather was not interested in men's fashions. He would rather be in his old clothes working in his garden. It was my grandmother who made sure that he was nicely dressed for church. In summer his outfit would be a Panama hat, dark jacket, white trousers and shined shoes. Knowing my grandfather, I don't believe he enjoyed wearing these clothes and probably did not very often—just to please Nellie. But who knows, perhaps he enjoyed playing the squire to his lady.

While in this house, I wanted to take piano lessons, and it was arranged with a local teacher. One day, as I glanced at my teacher as I was playing, I saw that her head was down and her eyes closed. That should have told me something!

My grandfather was receiving the Sears and Roebuck catalog, and I found it fascinating to see the multitude of products they were selling by mail. Leafing through the pages I came upon the section of girls clothing and specifically focused on an item that appealed to me. In fact it excited me that I might be able to order something that I had never had. It was a long, cotton housecoat with matching slippers. The material had a floral design, and had a long zipper down the front. I went to my mother and asked her if I might order it. She agreed, and it wasn't long before a box arrived for me from Sears and Roebuck.

I opened the box with excitement and could not wait to wear it. In time it became necessary to launder it, and my mother included it with the family laundry, but it was my job to iron it. I didn't really mind, until I found that the skirt of the housecoat had yards and yards of material. This was my first experience with catalog ordering and the last for a very long time. I could not know that down the road many years, homes would be flooded with catalogs of clothing, shoes, tools, household items, sports equipment, etc. Our family remained at 4 Putnam Avenue about two years.

My sisters Joan and Jane had spent two years at the Knox School, and they graduated together in 1940. Jane then studied at Paine Hall to become a dental assistant, and Joan, being seriously interested in becoming a nurse, registered at the Danbury Hospital School of Nursing. She had often sat in on conversations about nursing experiences between our mother and grandmother, who was a graduate nurse. One of her classmates was Elizabeth Buckstine, a Brewster girl who became a very fine nurse. She was with me the day before my second baby was born. Joan was so enthusiastic about her studies that she quickly learned her assignment of knowing the blood circulatory system. When asked in the classroom if anyone could recite the lesson, Joan without hesitating stood up and went through what she had learned. No one was expected to know this so well and so early. (Her fourth-grade teacher convinced my mother that Joan should skip a grade, because she did her lessons so fast it gave her time to get into mischief.) Her nursing school teacher for some reason resented the fact that she seemed to be showing up the other students, which was not her intention, and she was told to sit down. From then on she seemed to be the object of scorn. After a few months Joan was eliminated from the program, undoubtedly more to do with her way of responding to the instructors than her abilities or intelligence. As a first year nursing student, punishments were meted out, and one given to Joan was polishing other students' shoes with whitening liquid.

Joan then went to the Katherine Gibbs School, a secretarial school in Manhattan, following which she obtained a very good position at General Motors in Manhattan.

My Mother's Cancelled Project

My mother had an ambitious and beautiful dream that she acted upon. She had found twenty-eight acres at the corner of Route 6 and the Peach Lake Road, not far from Starr Ridge Road. She was very excited about purchasing this acreage. She took us there, and we hiked around until we found the brook in the woods below a ravine that had been eroded by the water over the years. We made several trips to the property, sometimes having picnics overlooking the running water. There were few people on the road, life was simple, and her dream was to build about eight houses on this property, one of them being a house for us. She hired an architect by the name of William Sunderland from Danbury, Connecticut, and after looking at the property, he drew plans on paper. There was great potential for my mother to accomplish her vision.

Everything was worked out with the bank so that my parents could pay for it, but this was her project. War was just around the corner, and the business slowed down due to the priority system instituted by the government. It became more and more difficult to make payments on the property, and with much disappointment it was necessary to cancel her plans to develop this land. The houses would have been beautiful, as I saw them on paper. She was ahead of her time.

The year 1940 was a pivotal year on the world scene. President Roosevelt in response to the British loss of "eleven destroyers in ten days and urgently requested help" sent "fifty United States destroyers to hard-pressed Britain." Our neutrality was not only being tested but was collapsing under the threat of totalitarianism, and our need to participate in its demise became clear. Nineteen-forty was also the year that synthetic rubber became a reality and replaced real rubber for automobile tires.[3]

That same year the draft was instituted affecting the lives of all United States citizens. But by now America understood the Nazi menace and its implications. Besides the enactment of the draft, Congress passed the Lend-Lease act that allowed American equipment, mostly old army vehicles and guns, to be sent immediately to Britain. At the same time convoys of ships being escorted were leaving American ports headed for England. From then on thousands of ships left in convoys only to have wolf packs of German U-boats waiting to torpedo them, when they reached a few miles off shore. (I learned many years later from several different people who had been teenagers in Maine that bright lights could be seen at night several miles out into the Atlantic. They would watch nightly as ships were struck

---

[3] C. L. Sulzberger, *World War II*, 59.

throwing up bright flames, and then the light would disappear as the ship sank below the surface and crewmembers were lost. (Living where I did in New York State I was spared this frightening experience.)

At the time I was not fully aware of what was taking place along the eastern coast of North America. Off the shore of Long Island German U-Boats rose to the surface to allow two or three men to board a skiff and row to shore. The story goes that they would go to a bar at 2 a.m. and sit there drinking. Then they would return to the U-Boat that was waiting for them. There were many men brought in this way to do espionage work. They would listen to citizens talking and try to obtain important information about shipping and destinations, so that they could relay it back to their Nazi superiors. Many of these men were reported and arrested for espionage from the coast of Canada to Florida and beyond. News of these situations did get around, but I wasn't aware of the extent of this threat. I do recall conversations about espionage agents in our country and about the German American Bund, the association of American Nazis.

The Dreaded Disease, Poliomyelitis

It was about this time that there was a poliomyelitis scare in the country—better known as polio. There was no vaccine for this dreaded disease, and people were contracting it with crippling effects. There was a girl named Penny living on Carmel Avenue who had contracted polio, and although she lived, she walked with a limp. This was the same disease that struck Franklin Delano Roosevelt, when he was assistant Secretary of State and before he became governor of New York State. When he became the President of the United States, he was often seen in pictures or in newsreels sitting as he spoke, or he spoke for a short time standing behind a podium making his useless legs unnoticed.

It was President Franklin D. Roosevelt who created the National Foundation for Infantile Paralysis. School children were asked to send a dime to the White House, and the mails were inundated. This organization became The March of Dimes.

My cousin Philip F. Beal III, who lived in Kalamazoo, Michigan, was on a camping trip quite a few years later with his young family, when he became very ill. He was diagnosed with poliomyelitis, and his recollection is that of feeling very ill and miserable. Fortunately he was not left with any disability.

A woman by the name of Sister Kenney developed a treatment for polio, and many women across the country attended classes to learn how to administer the Sister Kenney Treatment. They were frightened for their children. My mother took the course, and I remember being told that it involved heating woolen blankets in hot water, squeezing out the water and applying the blankets on the legs of the patient to relieve the muscle contractions. She actually practiced in the basement, putting the blanket in the washing machine with very hot water, then squeezing it through the wringer. It was hard work, but the mothers wanted to be prepared in the event a family member came down with the disease.

The Poor Chinese People... But That Was Far Away

The citizens of our country were well aware of the aggression of the Japanese into Manchuria and then into China. We felt a kinship with the Chinese people, and when the China Relief program was begun, Americans gave generously believing that the people of China were benefiting. Wellesley College-educated

Madame Chiang Kai-shek, a beautiful and striking figure, visited the United States raising money for her cause. In fact, she was a guest at an estate a few miles north of Brewster. However, instead of going to the needy Chinese people, our money, we later learned, went into the personal treasury of Madame Chiang Kai-shek.

One place they put their money was in a very beautiful residential compound on the shore of Lake Winnipesaukee in New Hampshire. It eventually passed to new owners.

Another way the Americans were helping China was the volunteering of men serving under General Clair Chenault who was in China. It was a rag-tag group of flyers intent upon causing trouble for the Japanese. Some were killed. They flew P-40 airplanes that were colorfully painted on the front with an open jaw showing vicious teeth. They were the heroic Flying Tigers. Reading about the Flying Tigers gave romance and excitement to the war we knew was going on in China. These flyers were excellent pilots, courageous and looking for excitement as they trained and fought against the Japanese before the United States was committed to war. They were later integrated into the Army Air Force.

1941

High School Years, Friends and Activities

By now it was 1941. I started my sophomore year in Brewster High School that fall. I was one of the many children who lived in the village and walked to school. There were those in the Brewster School District who lived several miles from the school, in north Brewster, Towners, and Dykemans, to name a few communities, and rode the buses to school. Prisco Brothers operated these buses for many years as well as their taxi service that operated from the Brewster station.

The walk home for lunch was always a hurried one. Sometimes I would see Tommy Lottrechiano or Eddie Vichi, upperclassmen on their way home for lunch as well. They lived on Carmel Avenue and had a bit farther to go than I. So, very often we would run together. This gave us more time at home before going back to school for the afternoon session. Despite the rush to get home and back to school, I always appreciated the fact that I could do that.

When I had been in the early grades there were rare days when I had to take my lunch. I had a rectangular lunch basket woven in wood strips that my parents had purchased in Vermont. It opened at the top, and my father had burned my name and the year 1935 on the lid. I graduated to a green tin lunch box, or to be more exact, I felt I stood out using my basket lunch box, when other students used a tin lunch box or brown paper bag. I didn't like having lunch in the school lunch room—partly because it smelled like a mixture of mustard, pickles and bologna, and partly because I didn't know the girls who came by bus very well. I would look around to see, if there was someone with whom I felt comfortable. The only foods sold in the cafeteria at least in the early years were tomato soup and hot cocoa ladled from two large, heavy aluminum urns.

One day I did not bring my lunch and had to go up to the ladies who stood at one end of the lunchroom ladling out the tomato soup and cocoa. I paid them five cents for each cup of liquid lunch, and I thought they were quite good. The cocoa was smooth and sweet, and I believe it contained evaporated milk and possibly condensed milk, Borden's condensed milk. Every new experience, even seemingly insignificant ones were challenges to my self-confidence.

My mother made memorable lunches. On rainy days she often made fresh tomato soup or vegetable soup that would be augmented by a sandwich. My favorite soup was cream of spinach. Thanks, Mom. I was so lucky to be able to go home for my lunch. Of course I always felt rushed and kept an eye on the time, so that I would have plenty of time to walk back to school and still have time to stand in the school yard with friends for a few minutes. I allowed at least twenty minutes for return time and often met Charlotte or someone else on the way back as well.

My Grandmother MacLean had a couple of favorite soap operas on the radio that came on at twelve noon and half past twelve. She really got into the story and did not want to miss the next episode. If a character in the story was going through a sad situation, tears would come to her eyes. She could easily relate the sadness in the story to the sadness experienced in her life. Sometimes, I would feel sympathy for her, and other times I would "kid" her. Either way I might say, "Grandma, you're crying," and she would smile as she stepped away from the emotional scene. I enjoyed spending those few moments with her.

For the most part I did not disobey my parent's wishes. If something questionable came up, I didn't have to ask for I knew right from wrong, and I usually used common sense. There was one time when I knowingly disobeyed my mother. The movie, "The Hunchback of Notre Dame," was at the theatre, and my friends and I planned to go to attend. When I told my mother I wanted to see this particular movie, she told me she did not approve my seeing it. I don't believe that she knew the story—it was the "hunchback" in the title that made her think that it was not an appropriate movie for me.

I disagreed with her decision and wanted very much to see that movie. There was a small, oval, metal bank that I would sometimes put a nickel or dime in. It was one that the Putnam County Savings Bank had given my mother, and I believe my sisters also had one, although I think by then my parents had forgotten that I had it. There was a slot in the top that was long enough to push in a folded bill. There was some change in it, and a bill that I could see. Using a folded piece of paper I tried to ease out some coins between the teeth in the slot, but nothing would come out. It was impossible to remove a bill that way, so I decided I must pry open the bottom that had a key hole in it. Eventually I was able to grasp the paper bill and ease it out. Now I was sitting with a five dollar bill, more money than I had ever had to spend as I wished. I actually wished it was only one dollar.

I felt so sure that this movie was a perfectly fine movie, that I used the money from the bank for the ticket. I never told my mother, as I was sure it would upset her, and I always felt that my decision was right—and my mother did not understand about the movie that turned out to be a lesson in human kindness. I did have a twinge of guilt in defying my mother, as defy was her word, as in "don't defy me." Whether she was right about the movie or whether my position was a correct one, I should have honored her wishes and given up the movie.

There was a movie that gave me nightmares. The title escapes me, but it took place in the south. The scene that was so unnerving was when someone was running away and unexpectedly ran into quick sand. He struggled and struggled, slowly being sucked down into the goopy sand. The character looked terrified, and I was drawn into his struggle. Did I realize that the movie makers did not sacrifice an actor for that scene?

On Saturday nights the Main Street of Brewster was buzzing with activity with more people than on other nights. That was the night that the farmers from outlying areas came to town to do their shopping or to simply sit in their trucks or cars and watch the people walking by.

In high school very often I would go to the movies on Sundays with a friend or two. Several people my age were not permitted to attend the movies on a Sunday, a hold over from puritanical beliefs as with card playing and dancing. There were Saturday matinees and Sunday matinees, sometimes double features and always with a black and white newsreel and a Looney Tunes or Dick Tracy comic strip. If there was a football game at the high school on Saturday, the football game took precedence over the movie, and Sunday would be the movie day.

My Grandmother MacLean enjoyed going to the movies which she referred to either as "the pictures" or "a picture show." I suspect that this came from her earlier days when the movie industry was in its infancy with black and white silent films. The films would show actors and actresses in the fashions of the early 1920s and the dialogue would be at the bottom of the screen. Usually there would be a piano that leant drama to what was going on in the story. The silent movies were referred to as "silent pictures" and this is apparently why my grandmother used the terms that she did. Sometimes we went together walking into the village for a seven o'clock show and walking home. She was a good sport.

Of course everyone in our class knew who liked whom but not everyone had a boyfriend or girlfriend. Eddie Collins was shy with me, as I was with him. He would sometimes walk me home, each of us saying very little to the other. He would not call me, because he would have to speak to my mother or father, but after a couple of years he did call. We didn't talk for very long, and I can't imagine what we had to say to one another unless it was about an upcoming basketball game or movie. When my mother answered the telephone, she would call to me and whisper, "it's Mickey Mouse," because of his deep voice. I was easily embarrassed, but she had to play with me a little. He actually did imitate Donald Duck for friends. I never told my mother that we girls would meet the boys before a movie. I did not know how to tell her. She was a worrier about such things, as I had seen regarding my sister.

Muriel Pinckney.   Charlotte (Cha) Tuttle.

Louise Vanderburgh and Muriel Pinckney and I had become friends, and sometimes we spent Saturdays together going to the movies. Often Charlotte Tuttle joined us. One day Muriel and I were looking for something to do, as we walked across the bridge and looked down and decided to make our way down the embankment. A stream of water ran parallel to the tracks. We picked up sticks and tossed them in watching them glide with the current. Concentrating on our activities, neither of us noticed a train that was slowly backing up from the Brewster station only a half-mile away. We looked up just in time to jump across the stream out of the way of the train. We both agreed that we would be in big trouble, if our mothers found out. Muriel's father worked on the railroad, and my mother's father, also a railroad man, had been killed while working. So it was our secret. As teenagers we girls were often together on Halloween dressed in some costume we had individually put together. We were out to have a good time, receive some candy and observe the demeanor of the ladies of the houses where we stopped.

Some were resentful and probably frightened. Others did their duty and handed us a bowl of candy. Most were pleasant, and we called them by name. We did not carry large bags to fill and took only a few pieces to put in our pockets or eat as we walked.

One year Muriel and I decided to go behind a house on Maple Avenue, known to us as Day's Hill, and as we walked, we saw some late cabbages still in the garden. We pulled a couple out of the ground and tossed them aside. They may have been frostbitten, and I hope they weren't edible and being counted on for dinner. But we did not think of that.

It was probably the same year on Halloween that we two reached Garden Street. We actually were good kids. It is only in retrospect that we realize we were acting in a sub-delinquent manner. There was a wire fence delineating the school property and a home on Garden Street. Down by the fence we could see a rusted drum and had to do something with it. Fortunately for us it was empty, so we lifted it up and over the fence. We watched it roll noisily down the hill to the football field. Then we departed.

Another time we were near Muriel's home where an elderly lady with white hair lived in a little house. She wasn't one of Muriel's favorite neighbors, and we picked up some gravel and tossed a handful onto her porch. We waited in the shadows, as she opened the door to see what made the noise. She then closed the door and went inside. We had had our fun. The thought crossed my mind that she would now have to sweep the porch. What was it that made us do something like that? I guess we never thought of getting old ourselves.

The act that made me feel some guilt was pulling up the cabbage. We shouldn't have done that. I was always salved by the fact that this sort of thing was not a common occurrence for me, and as I look back I am still somewhat shocked at my actions. And there was a little voice in me that was aware that I should have been elsewhere.

As a child I remember the day after Halloween, my father called our attention to the telephone pole at the end of our driveway. Up about ten feet there hung two of our wood lawn chairs. I believe my sisters knew the boys who carried out this prank. They were always doing something like this. My father was not angry about it, although he had to climb the pole to retrieve his chairs. He was probably remembering the pranks he played, when he was a boy.

My friend Muriel Pinckney grew up on Center Street, a few houses from Eddie and Jimmy Collins, "the twins" as she called them. My cousin Malcolm Beal "went steady" with Marjorie Lane who lived at Tonetta Lake Park. He and the Collins boys were good friends in those early years. Marjorie and I on a few occasions would walk to Tonetta taking a shortcut from the Brewster school, across the length of the football field. We walked under the New Haven & Hartford Railroad, walking through fields, until we reached the rear of a house on Peaceable Hill, across the road just south of the Palmer farm. Behind this house was a fenced in area where a large, black bull was kept. We had to walk fairly near the fence. I was frightened the first time, but we just kept on walking.

When we were living at Tonetta Lake Park, and I needed a ride after school, I walked to my father's office. When we were back at the house in Brewster, my friends and I would walk to Tonetta going up Railroad Avenue, crossing the railroad tracks, taking the dirt road to Tonetta Lake Road passing the O'Brien house, then up the hill to the entrance to the park. It was a two-mile walk. As a young child, I was permitted occasionally to walk from our cottage to the entrance, carrying my cat to meet my father as he was coming home. The entrance with two stone pillars, also had walls that curved from low to high with pointed stones imbedded in cement. I climbed around this wall one time and slipped, badly scratching my arms and legs. From then on I tested my physical skills elsewhere. I walked through this gate many times thereafter.

They were carefree days, usually coming home with a sunburned face, back and legs. Even though it hurt, and I needed to apply Noxema which helped for a time, I would repeat this ritual many times, for having color that turned to a tan was the goal. No one knew that early sunburns would result in later years in the development of pre-cancerous lesions or skin cancer and have to be treated medically and even surgically.

Remember Pearl Harbor

On Sunday, December 7, 1941, I was at home with the radio on. Listening to the news that came on urgently and with much emotion, we heard about the Japanese "sneak attack" on Pearl Harbor. We weren't sure where Pearl Harbor was, but we soon found out it was the United States naval base in Hawaii. There were no televisions, but the news on the radio was constant with reports. The next day newspapers were filled with the latest news about the devastation, and the American people were in shock. It wasn't long before the theatre newsreels were showing the latest about the attack.

The Japanese attack on Pearl Harbor resulted in the loss of the core of the United States Navy, and most airplanes on the ground were destroyed. Thousands of civilians, officers and enlisted men of the navy and air force died. From then on when referring to our enemy, they were called "the Japs" or "the dirty Japs."

We then heard President Franklin Delano Roosevelt address the nation via the radio telling us that our country was now at war with Japan. We learned that President Roosevelt addressed a joint session of congress and from then on his famous line, "a date that would live in infamy" referred to December 7, 1941, and would be repeated throughout the coming decades and perhaps down through history. Henceforth, the citizens of our country were "glued" to their radios even more than usual, eager for the news of what was happening day to day.

The President's radio addresses, his "fireside chats" became important to the American people. It didn't matter what political party one voted for, as he was our leader, our commander-in-chief. He knew war was coming before the American people did and was working behind the scenes to prepare the country for war. Before we were at war neither the citizens, nor many congressmen were willing to face the inevitability of our need to fight. Once the country was attacked, he was free to appoint people to build up the military and the war machinery. Defense factories proliferated and finding defense workers was no problem.

Shipbuilding was a top priority, and one of the men put in charge of overseeing design and building was Captain Richard Morgan Watt, Jr. whose daughter would soon be a classmate of mine and later a good friend. Captain Watt's specialty was the landing crafts that were to be used as invasion boats carrying men ashore under heavy fire. They were LSTs, LCTs, LCIs and more. He was insistent and persistent about the quality and safety of the ships, traveling from shipyard to shipyard for inspections during the building process. He was especially insistent that "his" ships be air conditioned, knowing what it was like to serve on one that was not.

The Higgins boats, amphibious assault vessels, sometimes called "small boats" were used in almost every beach invasion in WWII. They were small enough to be hung on either side of the transports using davits. The Marines climbed down to waiting landing craft on nets that had been thrown over the side. Landing crafts had different designations according to their use. They carried troops, tanks, and other supplies. Many of the war ships were manufactured in sections hundreds of miles inland and shipped by rail to the long assembly line on Mare Island north of San Francisco. Its naval yard repaired ships and sent them back on duty.

In *Those Who Served/Those Who Waited*, William Pitkat Jr. tells of being on Mare Island. The first time he was waiting for his ship to be completed. It was the USS *Dixie* AD14. The second time it was the USS *Brennen* DE-13. His third newly commissioned ship, the USS *Connolly* DE 306, "went to Hawaii in January 1945 and joined a large convoy for the invasion of Iwo Jima."[4] About Mare Island he said, "It was an old yard and ships became too big for the drydock there. They built good submarines and good small ships there."[5]

Bill Pitkat also told the story about the time in the summer of 1940 that his ship had moved to San Francisco "where the Japanese were still able to get oil.... I looked around and I said this place is loaded with Japanese merchant ships—oil tankers. We were moving slowly amongst these tankers.... Up on the bridge I could see two officers with white uniforms on. I thought for merchant marine they looked pretty spiffy. One guy

---

[4] Stephens, *Those Who Served*, 215.
[5] Ibid., 212.

had a pair of binoculars. They were busy…. They may have been more than merchant ships. One fellow had a big pair of binoculars and kept looking at us. The other one kept looking in the chart house bringing out an identification book. They may not have had anything about our ship, because it was brand new. They probably reported back and may have had someone else somewhere taking pictures."[6]

Bill went to Pearl Harbor, and fortunately, having left before the Japanese attack was on his way back to Mare Island in September of 1941. He subsequently saw action taking reinforcements to Okinawa. Early one morning as his ship was going north "toward Guam, headed for Okinawa" it must have been exciting to hear his "name called out over the loud speaker and to go up on the bridge and lo and behold it was my brother Bobby's ship, an APH Hospital Evacuation Ship, the USS *Rixey*. He was a radioman, and he sent a message." Another time both their ships were at anchor, and they were able to spend some time together.[7]

Henry Kaiser, a shipbuilder, started building Liberty Ships that would carry men and supplies across the Atlantic and Pacific oceans. They were constructed by the hundreds at many shipyards around the country. Some metal plates were put together by large rivets, but others were welded. Those that were welded turned out to be unsafe, many of them cracking in rough and frigid waters or when a bomb hit nearby. A teenage friend, George Hinkley who became a Naval Armed Guard tells of his difficult duties on the Murmansk Run in *Those Who Served/ Those Who Waited*. His ship, the JLM *Curry*, was one of those ships, and when on their homebound trip it fell victim to frigid waters and

---

[6] Stephens, *Those Who Served*, 213.
[7] Ibid., 215.

nearby exploding bombs, a major crack occurred that was too large to weld. George and crewmen were rescued by crewmembers of a British ship. His heroic duty and experiences are hard to imagine. During that period I never envisioned what my friends were going through.

Other ships were being built and quickly manned in order to get them to the theatre of war, where they were needed so desperately. Ships large and small were christened before entering battle. To name a few, they were destroyers, destroyer escorts, aircraft carriers, cruisers, battleships, patrol boats, amphibious assault and tracked landing craft, all given initials such as DE for destroyer escort and PT for patrol boat. Many Brewster boys became crewmembers or were transported on them throughout the war, and of those many contributed to *Those Who Served/Those Who Waited*.

Most news had been relayed by telephone, shortwave radio or Morse Code to the newspapers' home offices. There were, however, newsmen like Edward R. Murrow who had gone to London to broadcast nightly even before the London "Blitz" started there, and soon reporters were at the fighting fronts wearing Army khaki and writing about what they were witnessing. Familiar voices heard on the radio reporting were Lowell Thomas, Charles Collingwood, Gabriel Heater, H.V. Kaltenborn and others. They were not all in London, but we could depend on Edward R. Murrow who was young and dedicated. They were depended upon by millions of Americans for daily news about the war. (After the war Edward R. Murrow had a home in Pawling, New York, not far from Brewster.)

William L. Shirer in his book, *The Nightmare Years: 1930–1940,* tells about the day-to-day progression toward war, while he was a foreign correspondent in Berlin, Hamburg, Paris,

Vienna and Moscow and other cities in Europe. He tried to convey the message to the American and British people and their governments that Hitler was making plans for war. It is an enlightening, fascinating and readable book. His book, *The Rise and Fall of the Third Reich*, is a comprehensive history that should be a must for history classes studying about World War II. The history and details of those years should, in my opinion, be imprinted on every student's mind in this country, for most of those who fought in that war were students or recent graduates of high school.

Our President had been in contact with the British Prime Minister, Winston Churchill. Although the people of the United States were isolationists, President Roosevelt knew that we would become involved in the war, as the German U-boats were already attacking our shipping lanes and those of England and keeping vital supplies from reaching Great Britain. Newspapers told of the Nazi war machine and the countries it had overtaken. We read the papers and listened to the radio, learning of Nazi expansionism. It began with the occupation of the Sudentenland in 1938 while Britain and France paid little attention. Hitler went on to annex Austria in 1938; then in 1939 his troops invaded Czechoslovakia and Poland. In 1940 war came to Denmark, Norway, Holland and Belgium. Paris fell to the Nazis in 1940. The Blitzkrieg was the method—tanks rolling fast taking the people by surprise. It was only a matter of time when Hitler's appetite would be assuaged by attacking the United States. But first he had to invade and conquer Great Britain. He and Japan on the other side of the world were bent on CONQUERING THE WORLD. I remember in 1935 as a child of eight years old learning that Mussolini, dictator of fascist Italy, invaded Ethiopia. I was to learn much more in the coming years.

Of course people talked about war, but it wasn't until our country was attacked at Pearl Harbor that the American people's ire was stirred, and they were ready for war. This meant that they were willing to do almost anything required for our country, to help build factories, shipyards and expand air bases. It also meant that young men as well as women became anxious to do their part and started to "join up." Those who enlisted had a regular salary, regular meals and clothing provided by the government. This seemed better for many than their prospects in civilian life, as the country was still feeling the effects of the Depression. People wanted to work, but there were few jobs available.

By this time the Civilian Defense Corps had placed aircraft lookout towers at appropriate sites around the country. There was one on Route 22, and there was one at Brewster High School and of course others. Adults and students signed up for a turn at watching and reporting any airplane that became visible in the sky. The boys in their shop class were making models of American and enemy airplanes. They were suspended inside the lookout tower. There were also sheets of paper pinned to the wall showing silhouettes of airplanes to help in describing the planes that were being reported. When one appeared, it was the rule to use the telephone in the tower to report to the central station and describe what we had seen and at what time. The telephone company cooperated in this effort. I took my turn.

Mallory Stephens was twelve years old when he first started to volunteer to spot airplanes. His partner was Norman Donley, a young teenager. Mallory was first assigned the hours of 12 midnight to 4 a.m., because he lived across the street from the hastily constructed wood tower overlooking the school at the end of Garden Street. When it became clear that this was too much for a twelve-year-old, his hours were changed to 4 a.m. to 8 a.m. Even the very young were dedicated.

We saw mostly small civilian planes and occasionally an Army Air Force airplane. These were necessary precautions as no one knew whether an enemy plane could reach our shores—and hadn't the Italian air force flown over our country only five years earlier? After all, our Pearl Harbor had been attacked and shortly thereafter our Aleutian Islands, Atka and Siska, off Alaska, would be invaded. The Japanese, small in number, were repelled in a battle of which I have little memory.

There were some who were already in college, and they left to join the service of choice rather than wait to be drafted. Those who answered the call to work in defense factories included men who were too old to be drafted, women or men who were 4-F (rejected for health reasons). They received wages not available elsewhere—but more important, they were supporting the war effort. Every American citizen wanted to do that. Many men took jobs in the factories and were in time drafted. Some hoped that by working in defense factories they could avoid being drafted, but that proved to be a false hope. Those who by their personal beliefs were against the use of guns were called "conscientious objectors" and were allowed to work at a job related to the war effort but without being trained for combat.

Young women and housewives went to work in the factories knowing they would earn good salaries, but they also found new freedom from housekeeping and the chores therein. They also knew they were a part of the defense team of their country.

There had in fact been boys from our area who had already been conscripted into the army long before the Pearl Harbor attack. When they were inducted, they were told that their training would be for one year. They would do their duty and be back home before long. In fact with jobs being hard to find, a year in the Army with pay seemed like a good deal. Aldo Sagrati who was several years older than I, was taken into the Army under the conscription law expecting to be home by the end of December 1941. Since we were not at war and our industries were not turning out uniforms and equipment for war, these conscripts were using uniforms from World War I and in many cases trained with broom handles instead of guns.

In 1940 and 1941 a new fashion for men started appearing on city streets and in newsreels. It was called the "zoot" suit. The trousers were very full, tapering close to the ankles. The jacket had a wide collar and very broad shoulders, and the bottom edge reached the knees. There was usually a long vest as well. A large link chain could be seen hanging to the knees under the jacket. A wide-brimmed hat with a large crown and slick shoes completed the outfit.

This style might have made some inroads into the standard or conservative styling of the day, but with the demands made on the country's fabric and clothing industries by the nation's military, this "zooty" fashion had no chance of surviving. Skirts were kept at a reasonable length—to the knees—during the war, and there were no extravagances in the cut of clothing. All branches of the services called for dress uniforms, fatigues for training and daily work and working uniforms for all medical personnel. This included caps, socks and underwear. Rationing of certain items of clothing for civilians made its contribution to the war effort as well. Civilians were encouraged to conserve in every area.

In Those Who Served/Those Who Waited, Aldo Sagrati told about getting ready to go home at the end of 1941 when his year of conscripted duty would be completed. He went to the haberdasher, where he was serving in the south and ordered his "zoot suit" and expected it to be ready so that he could wear it home. When the soldiers learned about the attack on Pearl Harbor, they also learned that there would be no releases from the army, and no one would be going home. He cancelled his order for the suit he was looking forward to wearing and before long was on his way to the Pacific theatre to fight the Japanese. He also told of hitchhiking in California and being picked up by our future president, Ronald Reagan, who told Aldo that he went through Brewster on his way to visit his friend and actor, Robert Montgomery, who had a home in Towners, north of Brewster.

I was given a small allowance, but that didn't cover my teenage needs. As a small child my father gave me five cents for polishing his shoes. He always liked his shoes to shine, and sometimes there were two pairs to shine. When I was big enough to handle it, I mowed our lawn for one dollar. My grandfather soon decided I was competent enough to mow his lawn. Both these lawns were large, and our front lawn was sloping. There were no motorized mowers—it was push and pull. For my grandfather's lawn that was flat, I received one dollar and fifty cents. I enjoyed making my own money and saving it. I was a gentle spender. Since I liked having some of my earned money put away, I couldn't both spend it and save it. I was what we call "a Depression kid."

For several summers I took on a third lawn to mow, the one at the Tonetta cottage. That lawn sloped and was steep at the roadside. So now I was earning over three dollars each week.

Most weeks I was doing three lawns in one day, Saturday. I started early in the morning and hurried through one after the other. Sometimes I started after school on Friday so that I would have more of Saturday free. Someone had to drive me to Tonetta until I received my driver's license at sixteen years old. My mother usually expected me to dust furniture and vacuum the three flights of the rear stairway on Saturday mornings. I was not fond of the latter job.

Our village had a soda bottling plant owned by Mr. Fenaughty on Oak Street, and he sold root beer, orange soda, sarsaparilla and other flavors. Occasionally my father would supplement my allowance by giving me a dollar. In fact there were times, when I had no money and would ask him for enough for the movies. I learned that my father was generous, but I also knew the boundaries. I had found that "no" could come from the lips of my mother and father when they found it appropriate.

Most of my friends liked to stop at Hope's Drug Store. There were several booths in the back as well as the counter stools. Most of us didn't have the money or didn't want to spend it on the expensive items like sundaes for fifteen cents, banana splits at twenty-five cents or even an ice cream soda for fifteen cents. I allowed myself a movie for fifteen cents and a bar of candy for five cents. I usually bought a glass of Coke for five cents or an ice cream cone for the same price. Breyers' ice cream came from the large gallon containers set down below the working counter. My favorite favor was strawberry, whether a cone or in an ice cream soda.

Sometimes on a Saturday or Sunday evening my dad would drive into the village to buy us ice cream to take home. One of us would go into Hope's Drug Store and order a quart of

Breyer's that was hand scooped into a smooth surfaced, buff-colored, cylindrical cardboard container packed tightly. The family consumed the entire quart as there was no freezer to preserve any leftovers.

During the summer at the Tonetta Lake pavilion I frequently bought a bottle of Coca Cola after swimming. The Coca Cola bottle was light green and sold for five cents. When Pepsi Cola came out with the twelve-ounce bottle for five cents, the same price as the six ounce bottle of Coke, I sometimes took my second choice: "twice as much for a nickel too!" Candy bars were five cents, and I occasionally treated myself to a Milky Way, Almond Joy or a double popsicle.

My parents were members of the Kishawana Country Club located on Route 22 north of Brewster. My dad enjoyed playing tennis until the doctor told him at age 40 that he should stop. There was no reason for him to stop, because he had no heart problem, but he did desist. He then played golf, and he did have many years of enjoyment from that. My mother was left-handed and was quickly discouraged from playing golf. I was given a lesson in hitting a golf ball but did not actually play for many years. My mother did enjoy for a time being involved with activities at the club. She actively helped in the arrangements for a costume dance, where the members were to wear costumes of the 1800s, and an old surrey was borrowed, so that pictures of participants could be taken sitting in it. I was there the day before the dance and saw all the activities of decorating for the barn dance. My mother went beautifully dressed in a long black lace dress, an antique black lace bonnet, lace gloves and carried an antique black parasol. The fact that war was coming had not yet made an impact.

It was about this time that we classmates were taking Home Economics offered as a new course. Our teacher, Miss Haviland was helpful and pleasant. Muriel Pinckney and I decided to work together and to make dresses alike. We went to Mr. Susnitsky's New York Store on Main Street and picked out the yardage of material needed in navy blue. Our pattern was for a princess style dress, fitted at the waist, and with long sleeves.

Mrs. Pinckney had told Muriel that she was not to use her treadle sewing machine that stood against the wall. It was during the process of working on our dresses that we wanted to sew some seams, and Muriel suggested we go to her house after school and use her mother's machine. While I was sewing and feeding the material under the needle, the needle came down on my middle finger, going through my fingernail and out the other side of my finger. I quickly pulled my finger down from the needle, and there was very little blood. Muriel said, "Don't tell my mother, because I am not supposed to use her machine." No one ever knew. The dresses turned out well and to individualize the dresses, we each purchased sets of collars and cuffs for a finishing touch.

Most of my friends did not attend my church, which was St. Andrew's Episcopal. Muriel Pinckney and Charlotte Tuttle were Baptists. There was to be a baptism at the Baptist Church, and it was one of our friends who would be immersed in the small, baptismal pool. This was going to be an enlightening experience. I wanted to find out just how this was done, and to see the minister lower the person into the water. I was glad I had been baptized as an infant.

There was another time when Muriel and I worked in concert. We were in the next semester when we took the cooking class, and we were told that at the end of our term we would be hosting a dinner for the members of the school board. The students were paired and assigned different foods to prepare, from soup to dessert. Muriel and I were assigned an apple pie and scalloped potatoes. We were doing well and having fun, when the spontaneous thought came to us that would surely add to the fun. So, as we were preparing the potatoes and the apples, we decided to slip a few sliced potatoes into the apple pie and a few sliced apples into the scalloped potatoes.

When it came time for the auspicious occasion, the students were there, some waiting on table, others cleaning up. We were excited, watching for any expression on the faces of the guest board of which my grandfather and Mallory's Uncle George Hine were members.

We watched with great anticipation only to find that they were apparently enjoying their meals and our prank went unnoticed by all. Or did it?

By the time we were seniors we knew one another well, and sometimes we simply could not help ourselves from playing tricks or being obnoxious. On one class day one of the students brought in a film negative and lighted it setting off a great puff of black smoke. Another time a couple of students brought in pocket mirrors. The sun shone into the room, and the mirror was placed in the sun while the hand moved the reflection about the room. It was especially shone on the black board as the teacher was writing on it. The teacher turned to the class and decided that Henry Alfke was the culprit. He was sent to the principal's office, taking the blame for something he did not do. Henry was well liked by all. He was a gentleman, a good student and an excellent athlete. In a short time he would be killed in action in Europe, soon after graduation.

It was after school had let out that Muriel and I, having been working on the school newspaper and thus found our classroom and the hallways empty of people, went back to our home room. There we found that our teacher had written Shakespearian verse across the full length and width of the blackboards. We decided it would be fun for all, if we removed some of the words, just here and there, and insert an inappropriate but humorous word in their places.

The next morning, when we walked into the classroom, our teacher was carefully erasing our words and putting in their places the proper words as she had originally written them. She did not ask who did it, and we satisfied ourselves that no real harm had been done. This teacher was occasionally tested by other students. It was known it could easily be done. Scoundrels!

The Aura of War

While living in my grandfather's house, I came home from school to find a very busy group of ladies who were seated around the dining room table. On the table was a four-inch stack of very heavy fabric. When I asked my mother what they were doing she explained that they had an assembly line (my mother's idea). One woman would cut from a pattern, the next would pin seams, and another would baste the seams. The next seamstress sewed the seams on a sewing machine—on and on until the zipper was in and the hem stitched. These were women's skirts that the Red Cross would send to England for the women there. Besides a drastic shortage of food, there was also a need for warm clothing as the English people, men and women combated fire and destruction caused by the German bombing attacks during the Battle over Britain.

Also while living at my grandfather's house we would still go to our cottage at Tonetta Lake. During those couple of months, my father's sister Babe and her husband Donald and children, whose home was in Croton Falls, would come to Brewster and stay with our grandfather. Donna would have been about one or two years old and Jacquie was twelve in 1940. Jacquie recalls Grandpa Beal taking her to the train station in Brewster so that she could ride to Croton Falls where her father would meet her. It was one stop away and the cost of the ticket was ten cents.

In the fall of 1940 the Selective Service law was passed by Congress, and young men eighteen years and older could now be drafted for service in one of the military branches. The age limit for drafting at one time was thirty-eight years old. War was within view for our country. While Great Britain was being bombed, it was also sending bombers over Germany, and the United States was sending war planes to England. Our government was paying attention when Japan signed a pact with the Axis powers.

It was the time of the big bands such as Glenn Miller, Tommy Dorsey, Jimmy Dorsey, Glen Gray, Benny Goodman, Guy Lombardo, Harry James, Sammy Kaye, Kay Kaiser, Gene Krupa, the Mills Brothers and many others. It was also the period of swing music, romantic ballroom dancing and the jitterbug. Different parts of the country had their own versions of the Lindy, sometimes called the Lindy Hop. The music from these big bands was full, melodic and rhythmical. Lyrics were understandable and those to which we could relate. There were silly songs, patriotic songs and beautiful love songs. Songs were being written relating to war and teenagers had their favorite bands and singers. Movies with war themes were starting to be shown in theatres. Many Hollywood actors appeared as army fighting men, navy sailors and flyers. They boosted morale and sent the message that the allies were going to defeat Nazi Germany, Italy and Japan.

Actresses appeared as officers' wives, canteen volunteers and wives waiting for their son, husband or father to return home. It seemed that everyone was on the same page with the same pursuit: Victory!

We listened to the many recordings of Bing Crosby who had a smooth and mellow voice. At the same time Frank Sinatra was singing many favorite songs with the Tommy Dorsey band, one of my favorites being "Blueberry Hill." Some of my friends went into New York City to hear Frank Sinatra sing. I didn't ask if I could do that. I was happy to hear his recordings. The girls would scream and jump up and down at his appearances. As much as I enjoyed his voice, I was not interested in being a part of a screaming crowd. His voice was very appealing in his early recordings, but we did not know that he would become even better and have a long life of entertaining with his music, his acting and his humor.

Music was a big part of the young people's lives. Couples romantically involved would dance cheek to cheek, but romance or not, boys and girls loved to dance. As a young teenager I was learning to jitterbug, and my friend Ray Shalvoy and I found jitterbugging together was a common joy. In the summer we would dance to the juke box in the pavilion at Tonetta Lake. We would dance until the perspiration was running down our faces. That mattered not. It was endless fun. There were a few times when I had been swimming and ended up dancing in my bathing suit and bare feet, but bare feet on the old wood floor was not comfortable.

Ray invited me on a movie date a few times, and we went to the Capital Theatre in Danbury. He always greeted people with a smile and often a "wise crack." He was fun to be with. He would pick me up in his father's black Ford, and there was always an odor of engine oil, when I would step into the car. I never mentioned it to him. In those days cars often leaked oil and perhaps that was the source of the odor. The interior of the car was always clean. To have a date with a boy who could use his family's car and to be picked up at one's door was an exciting occasion. He was always cleanly shaven, dressed nicely in slacks and sport coat with saddle shoes, and I would be dressed in my cotton dress or skirt, blouse and saddle shoes.

Leich's, a "take out" place with the owners dispensing hot dogs over the outdoor counter, was a favorite place between Brewster and Danbury, where we could buy the best hot dogs with sauerkraut, mustard and relish with a dill pickle across the top. Everyone in the area knew Leich's and couldn't resist stopping there when returning from Danbury.

Ray taught me the do the "shag." This was a very energetic dance with a quick jump step. Not many kids, if any, in our area learned this dance as I remember. From watching old movies from the 1920s I believe that the "shag" came from the flapper era. It was great fun to feel that we could dance on and on with no stopping considered.

On one of our dates, Ray gave me a birthday present. His mother had made me a pair of white angora ankle socks. They were very beautiful and I wore them with pride. It was a very touching thing she had done.

On Friday nights about three or four couples would go to the Shalvoys' home, where we were welcomed to dance. The rug would be rolled up and Mr. Shalvoy, who had a small band, sometimes played the piano for us. Ray had a big collection of phonograph records with our favorite bands and singers. We both loved Glenn Miller and Harry James records. Ray would often be seen holding an imaginary saxophone and imitating one of Tex Beneke's songs, especially "In The Mood." I didn't collect records, because I didn't have a record player. I couldn't save enough money for one, and I never asked my parents if they would buy one. On Saturdays I listened to WNEW where the latest hit records were played, and they rated the songs according to the most popular for the week, "The Top Ten."

My mother having grown up in a different time did not take readily to the music she heard me listening to on the radio. She liked the melodic songs of Bing Crosby and other "crooners." But when it came to the fast, jazzy tunes, she would say, "turn that awful music down." It was a generational thing.

In the basement was an antique pump organ. We had no piano, as my Aunt Norma had taken her Steinway. Again I wanted to take piano lessons, and my mother acceded to my wishes, but reminded me that we only had the organ, and if I wanted, I could learn on it. The organ was quaint with a round shelf on each side about head high when sitting on the stool. They were for holding oil lamps. It had push/pull stops to create different nuances in the music. They were for the accomplished. Having the same teacher as previously, I took weekly lessons. When I became focused on reading the music, I would forget to pump the organ, which had to be done with the feet in order to pump air into the organ. When the feet stopped moving, there was no air and therefore no music. Learning to play was one thing, but having to move my feet at the same time was an added challenge.

Music from the pump organ was not very satisfying. Even if I didn't play well on a piano, at least it had a better sound than the old organ. So, my mother suggested that I take the twenty-five dollars from my savings account—leaving around five dollars—and buy a second-hand upright piano. Now I had my own piano—with a piano key or two that were depressed. When I played and struck one of these keys, no sound came forth. It was distracting and discouraging for this blooming piano virtuoso. My lessons did not continue long enough for me to remember when I discontinued them.

Telephone Pranks

One or two of my friends were with me at my house when one of us came up with the idea to have some fun on the telephone. This is the way it worked: We called a store in the village where we knew that tobacco was sold, and when a man answered, he was asked, "Do you have Prince Albert in the can?" (Prince Albert was a pipe tobacco). When we received the answer, "Yes," he was asked, "Why don't you let him out?" and we hung up the receiver laughing.

The other prank was to call some lady and tell her, "This is the telephone company, and we are testing your telephone. Will you please step back three feet from the telephone and whistle like a bird?" And we would wait, hang up the phone and of course we thought that was hilarious.

Brewster, being a town where many men were employed by the New York Central Railroad, it was inevitable that there would be a railroad joke. This one was passed amongst young boys, and they thought it to be bend-over funny: "Did you hear about the big fight on the train? No, what fight? The conductor punched a ticket."

The *Normandie* and "Hellz A Poppin'"

We heard the shocking news that the French luxury liner, *Normandie*, docked at a New York pier had become engulfed in flames, and everyone thought that it had been the result of espionage given the fact that we were at war, and there were espionage agents within our country. This ship had been seized by the United States Navy after the Pearl Harbor attack and had undergone conversion to a troop ship. It was renamed the USS *Lafayette*, undoubtedly in honor of the French General Lafayette who helped our country fight the English during our American Revolution.

Instead of espionage we learned that the fire was a result of an acetylene torch being used by men in the ongoing conversion of the ship. Water was poured into the ship in the hope of saving it, and because of the weight of thousands of gallons of water collecting to one side of the ship, it capsized.

It may have been the day we were on our way to see the show, "Hellz A Poppin'," starring Olsen and Johnson, that our family saw this beautiful ship lying on its side not far from our view on the lower West Side Drive. It was a sad and memorable sight.

P. F. Beal & Sons had done work on a water supply system for a farm located north of Carmel, New York. At the entrance to the farm stood two ten-feet by four-feet white milk bottles. My father was given tickets to the show by Mr. Johnson for the entire family, and when he told us about the tickets that evening we were greatly excited with anticipation.

During the show it was said that there were spiders and bugs running loose in the theatre, and this created audible excitement. Soon we began feeling creepy-crawly "things" about our ankles. They were shooting puffed rice throughout the theatre to create this effect. At the beginning of the show a deliveryman began walking up and down the isles carrying a small plant and calling out the name of a lady I'll say was Mrs. Gladmeyer to whom he wanted to deliver it. About every twenty minutes, as the show progressed we would hear him calling, "Mrs. Gladmeyer, a plant for Mrs. Gladmeyer," and as he walked the aisles we could see that the plant was larger than previously. Each time he appeared calling, "Mrs. Gladmeyer, plant for Mrs. Gladmeyer," the plant was larger until he was walking with a plant four or five feet tall. This always created laughter within the audience.

Upon leaving the theatre and heading to the door, we could see a plant that almost reached the ceiling, and the deliveryman was sitting atop the plant, still calling out the lady's name, Mrs. Gladmeyer. We all left smiling.

One of my father's customers was Rex Stout, the popular author of mystery novels. I went along one day when my dad had an appointment at his house off Milltown Road between Brewster and Connecticut. It was an unusual sight to find that one wall was made of glass bricks. They let in light without allowing anyone to see inside. I found later that glass bricks could not legally be installed, as they caused fires to start because of the sunlight hitting the glass and being magnified on the interior of the house. However they are now used commonly in the south and must be of a different composition or not used where the sunlight hits the building.

Going on another appointment with my father in Lake Carmel, we were invited into the house. As we looked ahead at the interior stone wall, a natural stream was running down and was exiting through an unseen pipe. The scene has remained with me, and I wonder who occupies the house now.

Dodie with Ross Jr. at 12 Putnam Avenue.

1942

War Comes to My Home

My dad, like other men and boys started to feel the "itch" to join one of the military branches of service. He felt that since he had been in the Navy in World War I, this was the service of choice. Now forty-five years old, he went to the Pentagon early in 1942 to offer his services to the Navy hoping to be given a commission. Upon learning about my father's business experience in the well drilling and pump business, he was directed to the army office. As soon as it was learned that he had experience in water supply, the Army took him for the North African invasion planned for November 8, 1942, not far hence.

The 401st Engineer Battalion was hastily formed as a water battalion. It meant that experienced drillers had to be recruited from around the country and drilling rigs had to be found and transported to New York City. It also meant that tools, piping, casing and pumping equipment had to be procured. My father was commissioned a captain and was told that he could take with him two of his own employees who had already been drafted into the Army. Those two men were LeRoy Barrett and Arthur Ashby. They were great assets to him, as he set out on his Army assignments. He would be responsible for a number of drilling crews who were in the process of drilling for water at different locations. In the 1940s the core drilling machines or the chop drills could take from two to six weeks to complete a well. After the war a new and faster machine was manufactured making it possible to drill a well in one or two days.

Mom and Dad, war years.

It was at the end of summer in 1942 that I was sitting on the lawn of our Tonetta Lake cottage with my friend Ray Shalvoy. We were talking about the war, about Ray going into the Navy and other friends going into service and about my father leaving in October.

I accepted the fact that he would be going, not knowing what it would be like having my father, whom I loved so much, go away. After Ray left I went into the cottage where I knew my mother and father were talking. He had been in New York City at Tripler's store all day purchasing all the uniforms, including a British Warm coat, shoes, socks, captain's bars and engineer's pins, and they were all spread across the bed. He was surely going away.

My father had to make arrangements with his partner, my Uncle Phil to run the business, and my mother was to receive a weekly check of twenty-five dollars. With the allotment that he would send home, they felt that my mother could manage the house and the finances. As it turned out, she found it difficult paying for fuel for the house, food, gas for the car, insurance bills and incidentals like doctors fees that came up. Several months after my father had left home, I believe she had to ask my uncle to increase the amount by a few dollars.

They decided to help with the water heating cost by installing a coal stove in the basement where the laundry facilities were located. It would run twenty-four hours a day and had to be fed coal and stoked before bedtime. We all learned how to keep that fire going.

School started after Labor Day, and I knew that October would soon come. I was starting my junior year in 1942. In many ways I was looking forward to it. I had a few good friends, many classmates I was fond of, and they were good people. I would miss those who had graduated the previous June: Betty Cleaver, Gabe Blockley, Tom Lottrechiano, Roy Garnsey and Eddie Vichi. Betty was always pleasant to me, and of course I idolized her for the way she played her trumpet. Gabriel Blockley who lived on Hillside Terrace always treated me like an equal, although she was two years older. We often walked to school or home together. An excellent athlete and a talented drummer, she went to Cortland State College in New York State and became a girls' athletic coach. Her parents took me with them one weekend to visit Gabe and to look at the college.

I knew most of the class of 1942, and most of the boys were already fighting in the war or would soon be doing so. The same is true of the Class of 1941 and 1943. There would be many heroes in those classes.

Late October came and the date that my dad was to report at New York Harbor where the convoy of ships was preparing to leave for the invasion of North Africa. He was under secret orders as were all service people and could not talk about what he knew. My mother was very curious about where he was heading, and they talked, my father being careful not to say too much. Somehow she deduced that it was North Africa where he was headed and started guessing where the landing would be. She decided he would be headed for Dakar on the west coast of Africa. She was not too far off.

It was about 4 a.m. when my father came into our bedrooms and kissed each one good-bye. He was in his uniform, so unlike what I was used to seeing. He hated saying good-bye, and I can only imagine his thoughts, as he was driven away in the army car to New York Harbor.

When morning came, and we girls were in the house with my mother, she tried to make it seem like any other day. But it wasn't, and we all knew it. There was an emptiness that was almost palpable. But our routines took hold, as we went through that and subsequent days.

I have lost those thoughts which must have come to me at different times, like arriving home for dinner, listening to the news on the radio or simply moments while at school. What is very clear is rushing to the door when Mr. Arthur Hanson, our mailman, arrived at the house. On school days my mother would receive the mail and probably shed tears, when a letter arrived from my dad.

There were not many Sundays that I missed going to St. Andrew's Church, often walking there with my friend, Ruth Orton, who had moved next door to us on Putnam Terrace. I had been baptized there as a baby and confirmed by the Rev. Frederick Coleman who was still the rector at that time. Prayers were said for the men who were fighting the war, and I took these very seriously. At night I would say my prayers, and my father was the one I prayed for the hardest. I cried into my pillow many nights—and not being certain that the prayers made any difference. The hymn we sang about "those in peril on the sea" made it hard for me not to cry, and I still react emotionally to those words today.

In 1942 the movie, "Casablanca," came to our local theatre starring Humphrey Bogart, Ingrid Bergman, Paul Henreid, Peter Lorre, Claude Raines, and Sidney Greenstreet. The story took place mostly in Casablanca, French Morocco. I saw the movie most likely after my father's departure for the North African invasion. There were two male movie stars that I had a crush on; one was MacDonald Carey, and the other was Humphrey Bogart. I sent for a picture of Humphrey Bogart and one day received in the mail an eight-by-ten-inch photograph. He was handsomely attired in sport coat and slacks, wearing argyle socks with loafers. The argyle socks and loafers really did it! I still like the knitted argyle pattern but never see knitted argyle socks and loafers. They are as classic as the movie, "Casablanca." As for a crush on that man, though he was not old, he was certainly well over the age for a teenager to be attracted to. (Lauren Bacall had no hesitation in that regard.)

On November 6, 1942, the Allied invasion took place along the coastline of North Africa. My father was in the convoy headed for Casablanca, but not being in a combat unit had to wait until D-3 when the area was secured, and it was safe to bring in non-combat forces. He and his battalion could then go ashore safely and from there would receive orders to proceed to sites where water was needed.

The First Christmas Without Our Father

We usually went to the Christmas Carol service held at eleven o'clock on Christmas Eve. Many times upon leaving St. Andrew's Church, it was snowing and very beautiful, as we walked home. Christmas of 1942 was very different than other Christmases, when my father was present, although we kept the custom of going to the midnight service. My father had a certain cheerfulness and excitement that made this day fun. We had all mailed gifts to him—those we thought would be useful. I had knitted and sent him a pair of khaki socks. There were presents under our tree and a box of gifts that he had mailed from "somewhere in Africa." The fact that he had gone shopping in that strange land and picked out gifts for each of us made them special.

There were several engraved silver bracelets and a special one for my mother that had pyramidal points all around with amber stones between them. It was much too elaborate, and I must say hazardous for our culture. There was a wrap-around, narrow arm bracelet in the shape of a snake with the head at one end and the tail at the other meant to be worn above the elbow—an arm bracelet. We had fun putting it on, but I do not think it was ever worn. My gift was a wide, colorful, tooled leather embroidered belt that I wore many times. There were several strings of amber beads and enough fez hats for each of us. The fez was round, flat-topped, maroon, and box-like with a long, black silk tassel that fell down the side of the hard, cloth-surfaced hat and worn by the Arabs at that time. It was seen worn in the movie, "Casablanca." My mother wore hers several times. I initiated mine by wearing it to church. I wonder what religion I offended that day.

My mother received a caftan made of a natural hand-loomed fabric. It was embroidered and crocheted in black and maroon from the mandarin type neckline down both sides of the opening about seven inches as well as at the end of the sleeves. The hemline was finished in intricate needlework the color of the caftan. It was quite a magnificent piece of work although hardly appropriate street wear for this country. I remember it being said that my father thought my mother would like it, because she had worn a similar type of dress when she was pregnant for me. I remember that caftan, because she would wear it on Sunday mornings at breakfast. I recall a certain void, something that we were all feeling being without my father that Christmas. He was missed so very much, and we knew he was missing us. But we were not alone, as all across our country fathers, brothers, sons and daughters were being missed.

One of our Brewster High School graduates was in the invasion of North Africa, landing at Fedala Beach about nine miles from Casablanca on the west coast. It was John Santorelli who was in a Higgins small boat, where the landing, as he tells it, was chaos. He went from there under great difficulty to Bizerte in preparation for the landing at Sicily. He was in the invasion at Anzio in Italy and the Normandy invasion. In *Those Who Served/Those Who Waited*, John's story is that of another Brewster hero.

1943

Rationing

It was 1943 that silver-colored pennies started to appear. They were made of steel, and I can remember thinking, "This isn't right. Our pennies are copper!" But every bit of metal including copper was going into the manufacture of war materiel—tools, ships, guns, ammunition, airplanes, jeeps, tanks and all the other vehicles needed for the war effort.

By now everyone was tearing off ration coupons for the purchase of many items. Leather, rubber, sugar, canned goods, meat, butter and petroleum products including gasoline were on the rationed list. Lumber for lumber companies and builders as well as pipe could only be obtained through the government priority system. Therefore businesses suffered. Leather shoes were rationed as well as all rubber footwear. The priority was that the fighting men would have what they needed, be it equipment, clothing or food. Rationed items were only purchased by using ration stamps for which every family applied. But few Americans complained, as we were all fighting the war.

Since breakfast sausage was scarce and rationed, my mother bought a product called "Scrapple." She sliced and fried the pieces, and maple syrup was poured over them. This was a pork product, meaning that it contained the various parts of the pig and had the pork flavor. It wasn't high on the appreciated list, but we adjusted to the change in our eating habits. This product can still be purchased.

About this time the people of the country were encouraged to use the revolutionary concept of V-mail letters when writing to servicemen and women overseas. One would buy special stationery that was to be written on only one side. It would be folded into an envelope, so that an extra envelope was unnecessary. It would be addressed with the person's name and mailed to one of many special military post offices set up across the country. For instance, there were three army post offices: APO New York, APO Chicago and APO San Francisco. When the letter reached one of the government post offices, the letter was reduced photographically and put into a small envelope that had a window for the address. When put in sacks for shipping, they saved a tremendous amount of space on a ship, space so desperately needed for equipment and troops. The government knew the importance of getting mail to our troops, even if they were in combat on an island beach.

Because my mother was working for the Red Cross in Carmel, New York, four miles away and also as a Red Cross nurse's aide fifteen miles away in Mount Kisco, Westchester County, she was given gas coupons that allowed her to buy enough gasoline for those purposes. My recollection is that we had a "B" sticker on our windshield.

It is not possible for me to say when I was first aware that occasionally my mother had serious headaches. There were times when I would come home from school and find her lying on her bed, and when I called out "Mother," as I always did, she would say, "I am lying down with a sick headache." There were other times when she would be sitting at the dining room table with her head in her hands, and she would complain of seeing stars and having a dizzy spell. Her headaches must have been very bad, and I am quite convinced that they would now be diagnosed as migraine headaches.

Picture of three daughters for Dad overseas, 1943.

Sweet Sixteen and Easily Embarrassed

A few friends were invited to my home for my 16th birthday party on March 5, 1943. I woke up that morning to freezing weather with a freezing drizzle that covered the wires and tree branches with a coating of ice. The walks and roads were ice-covered, and it was generally a nasty wintry day.

I told my mother that I thought my birthday party would have to be cancelled. There was no electricity, so I was sure my birthday cake could not be baked. My mother assured me that we would have a birthday party, and I would have a birthday cake. She had contacted our good neighbor Miss Mariah Birch who had an iron wood stove in her kitchen, and my mother had arranged to bake my birthday cake in her oven. My mother was not a person who disappointed, if she could arrange otherwise.

My friends, boys and girls came, and the party was held in the basement that had been turned into a recreation room. It was a room that was not used very much, and it certainly wasn't elaborate. It was good for a kid's party. Most of us when going to a birthday party would spend fifty cents, one dollar or maybe one-fifty for a gift. It would be a box of stationery, a pair of socks, a fountain pen (pens used liquid ink), one linen handkerchief or candy. There were games like "spin the bottle," and "post office." A girl was chosen by a boy to meet at the post office, and on that day it was the furnace room—and he would kiss her. Well, that was pretty exciting! There was also anxiety that a boy a girl didn't much like would call her name. Ooooh!

Teenage Clothing

Like all teenagers we had our preferences, when it came to school clothing. Although not all girls wore them, the favorite shoes were saddle shoes or loafers. My mother thought that loafers were not good for my feet, so I had no loafers. I did have a pair of brown leather shoes, but my favorite pair was saddle shoes. I was able to buy black or blue saddles that had sponge soles. Between the sponge sole and the upper part of the shoe was a fine layer of black or blue rubber, matching the saddle color. With them I often wore sweat socks with a ribbed top that was not turned over. They were woolen and had to be hand washed, which I did faithfully. Because they were woolen I had to use sock stretchers to keep them from shrinking. In time they shrank regardless of the care that was taken.

We wore skirts and pullover sweaters over a blouse or the sweater alone with a string of imitation pearls. It was not unusual to see a girl wearing a cardigan sweater turned around, so that the buttons went down the back. It was a way of having a pullover look from the front. When I was a sophomore and junior I had a navy blue woolen coat that came just below my knees. Because I did not like to wear a hat, in cold weather—partly because I had braids on my head, I was usually seen with a scarf over my head and ears, babushka style. In very cold weather, if it was not snowing, I wore a pair of rabbit ear muffs.

Dodie, high school senior.

As the fall of 1943 began, my mother received a telephone call from my Aunt Helen, Malcolm's mother. She wondered if I would be interested in looking at a coat and two dresses that she was no longer going to wear. I drove my mother's car to their home on Turk Hill and tried them on. They were so beautiful. The knee-length coat was overall rust color with a large muted plaid of golds and browns. One dress was a woolen jersey knit in rust color, and the other dress was a fine woolen gabardine in princess styling. Down the front were navy blue buttons, and the button holes were in kelly green appliquéd leaves. Everything fit me. My aunt and I were the same size. I wore the coat to school, but saved the dresses for a special occasion. They were a perfect gift, and I looked and felt grown up in them. She had wonderful taste.

1943

On February 10, 1943, just before Valentine's Day, General George S. Patton and General Ernest M. Harmon stopped to inspect the installation my father was working on with his men. They commended him, and that must have put a smile on his face.

Captain William Ross Beal and drilling crew
on site in North Africa, ca. 1942.

It was still while in Morocco that my dad was asked to make a reconnaissance for work at the palace of the Sultan of Morocco. This of course meant having his men drill a well and install pumping equipment. Because it was a hot climate, there would be no need to build a pump house below ground as was the custom at home. The pump was put in an enclosure above ground, large enough for the pump and storage tank and with access by means of a door. The French Consul General on March 7, 1943, was pleased with the work and told my father that the Sultan had been there already and passed approval. My father was subsequently invited to have dinner at mid-day "with one of the important ministers" and was told to bring his camera. The next day he was invited to visit the gardens at the Palace and part of the Palace itself.

He told of walking at the end of one of the balconies and believing that the next door led to the garden below, he put his hand on the knob. The Arabic First Minister said, "No! No!" Turning to the French Consul, he said in French, "That is the door of the Harem, and no one is allowed to go in there." Rotten luck, Dad!

On March 18, 1943, my father wrote a letter that told about meeting the Sultan of Morocco:

"...He told me that he appreciated very much the work I was accomplishing here as water was very important to his people...he appreciated also the prompt and efficient manner in which it was done...and said, 'In view of all this I would like to honor you by bestowing upon you this decoration.' He stood up and I walked over to him. He then pinned a medal on my blouse. The AGO Office had sent an Army photographer down. He took a flash photo of the ceremony and another examining an Arab knife and silver sheath that was given to me immediately after he pinned the medal on me...."[8]

This knife and sheath were put on a plaque by my father on his return and it will soon go to the Southeast Museum in

---

[8] Stephens, *Those Who Served*, 9.

Brewster, New York, as we siblings agreed that it is part of the history of the village.

In a letter home he asked my mother to tell my Uncle Phil (his brother) that "the ground water temperature here is 68 degrees which is the annual mean temperature. In New York it is 50-51 degrees." He was able to purchase an old coupe and sent us a snapshot of it. He had painted on the door "Dodie." I was surprised and delighted to have my name on an old olive drab car that was being driven wherever my father had to go on his jobs in North Africa.

Apparently I had voiced my concern in a letter to him about the Arabs. I don't know why I thought I should be worried about them, but he reassured me by saying, "Tell Dodie not to worry about the Arabs. I get along very well with them. They are around wherever one goes." Richard Rapp told a different story in *Those Who Served/Those Who Waited*. He said that the pilots, whether going to their planes or getting off, had to run "because the poor Arabs would kill them and take their clothes. The French treated them terribly. When we went hunting and would shoot coyotes and birds, we gave the Arabs all the game."[9]

In all cultures there are those to be avoided and those of good character. In my father's case he told of going into a rug shop in Casablanca and befriending the Arab proprietor. His business was undoubtedly a profitable one. This man, Monsieur Bouelal, and my father hit it off very well, and my father was invited to come to his home and share a meal. Being Moslem there were no women present, but there were two or three other officers, one being a Lieutenant Roosevelt, a younger man than my father. Another time there were six local Arab guests,

---

[9] Ibid., 67.

undoubtedly prosperous, dressed in their native garb and "a Sahib representing the Sultan of Morroco." It seems that they genuinely liked each other.

After the war my father arranged to have an Arabic edition of the *Reader's Digest* sent to him. There was never a response, and my father often thought of him and wondered what happened. I remember that the Sultan of Morocco went into exile after the war, and perhaps there was something political in Monsieur Bouelal's not responding.

Between my junior year and senior year I studied algebra and Latin at the White Plains High School summer school. I went there by train and found a few Brewster friends on the same train. This was a good thing, as I started my senior year having done fairly well in both subjects. Geometry being spatial in practice was understandable to me. I enjoyed English, learning to construct sentences properly. Having syntax taught us clarified structure, and lessons on grammar taught us the use of phrase and clause using correct punctuation. I also found that Latin helped my English.

A young and pretty teacher, Kathryn Hubbard, had joined the Brewster faculty teaching commercial English and other commercial subjects. She was always friendly to students, greeting us when passing. Since I took no commercial subjects, I only became acquainted with her, when as a sophomore I joined the knitting club. She often wore a beautiful yet classic sweater that she had knitted. She was younger than the other teachers except for the home economics and physical education teachers, and her clothing reflected that. It in itself made the students feel she could relate to them more so than the older teachers.

That was when I made my first pullover sweater made with navy colored yarn (I was a practical person), and it fit. As a result

I had many years when I enjoyed knitting sweaters, argyle socks and mittens. When my dad returned from the war, I took on the most challenging project, and that was a beige vest for him made from fine wool that seemed to take forever to complete. I believe he wore it once or twice for my sake, but he was not a vest person.

Later I made a special gift for my father, knitting on the instep of each black sock a gold colored maple leaf. Of course everything handmade of wool had to be carefully washed in cool water, rolled in a towel and put on sock stretchers. Somehow I never minded having to do this, but then we didn't have any choice, as easy-care materials had not been developed at that time.

Start of Senior Year and Bombs Continue to Drop, 1943

The fall of 1943 I started my senior year at Brewster High School and became fully involved in field hockey, then basketball and softball. I wanted to go to college, but hadn't learned to study. I took my books home and read and wrote assignments, but I did not know what to do to prepare or apply to colleges. Much of this was my doing, as I had a certain fear of teachers, whereas I should have looked upon them as my friends. Perhaps I did not vocalize my desires to my parents, and besides they had other things on their minds. So, not knowing the art of studying I did my homework, took the tests and studied as I knew how. I knew I was going to graduate.

It was about this time that a classmate, Ruth Orton moved to Putnam Terrace, next door to our house. We became good friends walking to school and to St. Andrew's Church together.

Many of us liked to dance, but it was Ruth who was cited in our year book as the "best dancer." She was also an excellent athlete. She was the first person I ever knew who could not wear a gold ring as it made her finger turn green.

Louise Vanderburgh, Muriel Pinckney and Dodie Beal.

The officers of our senior class were William Ives, president; John Palmer, vice president; Louise Vanderburgh, secretary; and I was treasurer. The one who didn't like mathematics was treasurer! Each Friday I stayed at my desk and sold United States war stamps to my classmates. They bought denominations of ten cents, twenty-five cents, and fifty cents. When the stamp book was filled, the student would go to the bank and turn it in for a war bond. We were helping the war effort, and we were proud to do it.

By now Louise had decided to join the Cadet Nurse Corps and planned to go to Simmons College at the beginning of the program. We were the two students whose fathers were overseas, and I know she missed her dad as much as I missed mine.

Bombing continued over Europe and fighting continued in the Pacific against the Japanese.

As soon as war had been declared by the President of the United States, Franklin Delano Roosevelt, Americans, young men and many women could not volunteer fast enough to join the Army, Marines, Army Air Force, Navy, Coast Guard and Merchant Marines. In many cases boys of seventeen years old tried to enlist but were told that they would be taken only with a parent's permission by signature. Many parents would not sign, and the boys waited until they were eighteen. Other parents did sign the paper that allowed their son's enlistment. Some went in at seventeen without parental consent, eager as they were to join the fight. They undoubtedly looked older, were convincing and lied about their age. It was evident to all that every body was needed.

There were so many friends who had family members in one of the services. Muriel Pinckney's four brothers, the eldest, Raymond, (Army) the twins, LaVerne (Navy) and Lafayette (Army) and the youngest brother, Earl (Army). Muriel was the youngest child. Rita O'Hara's only sibling, Harding, (Air Force) armorer/gunner and photographer was killed in action in November of 1943. Willis H. Stephens, (Air Force) pilot instructor, my cousin, Malcolm T. Beal (Army), my second cousin, Murray Beal (Navy), my neighbors, the Smith brothers Edward, Donald (Rooster), Robert (Snuffy), killed on the Alaskan Highway and Paul, (Army), Howard Dingee, (Marines) employee of P. F. Beal & Sons, Dr. Alexander Vanderburgh, (Army). My classmates were Henry Alfke, (Army), killed in action, William Macomber (Air Force), tail gunner, Robert

Heinchon (Navy), Farrell Reed (Navy), Harvey VanDerlyn (Navy), Peter Tavino, (Navy), Peter J. Tavino (Army) and so many more. The stories of some of the above are written in *Those Who Served/Those Who Waited*.

My friend Muriel enjoyed telling us what her brother LaVerne had written. Serving with Verne in the Navy was Victor Mature. We all knew that name from the movies. He had a smooth demeanor, broad smile and had dark hair with the greasy look. He appeared in some B movies but also some WWII movies.

A member of the class of 1943, Ray Shalvoy enlisted in the Navy after graduation from Brewster High School. Our friends gave him a party and a farewell gift of a silver identification bracelet, known as an I.D. bracelet. Besides the name that we had engraved on it, he could have his military serial number, blood type, hometown or whatever else he wanted added. These became a very popular gift to give a young man. (After the war Ray became a dentist and married. He died at a young age. I have often wished that I could have talked with him after the war, but I was not in Brewster, when he came home.)

My sister, Joan, taught me to drive in our family's 1940 Packard. She taught me how to shift gears from first to second to third and also reverse. She was a good teacher, and my lessons took place in our driveway. Back and forth, turn, reverse and out to the end of the driveway we would go, until I did it smoothly. As soon as I became sixteen I took my driver's test in Carmel, New York, my mother driving me there. It wasn't long before the Packard was traded in for a dark green Chrysler Highlander with green, wool tartan upholstery. It had the shifting stick attached to the steering shaft near the steering wheel. It also had "overdrive." It was a beautiful and comfortable automobile, and

I never minded going on an errand for my mother driving her car.

A few of my friends had after-school or Saturday jobs in the village. Muriel Pinckney took a job at Feinson's clothing store. Ray Shalvoy worked at Hope's Drug Store on Main Street behind the soda fountain making ice cream sundaes and ice cream cones. A couple of times he waved me off, when I tried to give him the nickel I owed him. He was one of those fine fellows known as a "soda jerk."

On Saturdays I worked at P.F Beal & Sons from eight-thirty to noon answering the telephone, as the secretary was off on that day. I had no intention however of working in an office in the future. I had started doing this on Saturdays during the summer before my father went into the army. I believe I made twelve dollars each Saturday. The men in the service department only worked that day, when there was an emergency, and a customer was without water. Sometimes my Grandfather Beal would walk slowly by on his way to his garden. We sometimes visited for a few minutes. My cousin Malcolm started working in the family business very early, and sometimes I saw him there. My Uncle Phil would come in and work at his desk. I tried not to bother him—only to give him messages. He was a fine, gentle and humorous man, and I am sure he missed my father. I know that my grandfather worried about him.

One day while driving on the Taconic Parkway on the way to the Saratoga Racetrack my uncle stopped to give "a lift" to a nicely dressed man who was hitchhiking north. It was not long before a New York State Trooper with his siren blaring stopped my uncle for speeding. My uncle stepped out of the car, and the trooper wrote a ticket and handed it to him. He told the hitchhiker who was seated that he had been given a ticket, and the man asked to see it. "Just a minute," he said and opened the door, then walked around to where the policeman was still standing. In a friendly manner he talked to the trooper, putting his arm around his shoulder. Soon he was back in the car and said to my uncle, "Step on it!" He then handed the trooper's book of tickets to my Uncle Phil and told him that now he would not have to pay that ticket because the policeman now had no book of tickets. Being surprised he asked, "How did you get that?" His passenger told him that he was a professional pickpocket on his way to the Saratoga Racetrack.

My uncle asked the pickpocket why he did not pick his pocket, and the reply was, "because you gave me a ride, and you're a nice guy."[10]

My Uncle Phil telephoned our house one day and asked if I would like to go along with him on an appointment in Carmel. I was very pleased, and I readily accepted. I wish I had gotten to know him better. I knew he and my father were very close.

After her graduation from BHS, Marjorie Lane who soon became engaged to my cousin Malcolm Beal worked for the OPA (Office of Price Administration) and Rationing Board in Carmel, New York. She would have to approve requests for the gasoline ration stickers that were put on the windshields of every car. People with greater needs for gasoline, like physicians or Red Cross workers, were entitled to more gasoline than a person with less urgent needs. When a serviceman came home on leave, he could go to the office in Carmel and request some extra gas for the duration of his leave. They were good to the servicemen.

Many people patronized Anderson's Drug Store, a few stores down the street from Hope's Drug Store. When the first

---

[10] This story was given to me by my cousin, Donna O. Maurice.

television sets became available, Charles Anderson bought one and had it turned on all day so that customers could take a look at this coming technological advance. There wasn't much programming, but it was intriguing. I paid little attention to it at that time.

War, Part of Our Daily Lives

Young women were not drafted, but they were allowed and even encouraged to enlist. Posters appeared all around the country encouraging them to choose the WAAC (Women's Army Auxiliary Corps became the WAC, Women's Army Corps), WAVES (Women Accepted for Volunteer Emergency Service—NAVY) or SPARS (Coast Guard Women's Reserve). In magazines and newspapers attractive young women appeared in uniform telling girls that they could wear this uniform and be patriotic too.

Norman Rockwell, an American commercial artist, painted pictures that were used on magazine covers depicting the American family in different situations. In the window there would be a flag with one or more stars showing how many members of that family were in the service of their country. A gold star hanging in the window meant that a son or father had died. He depicted American holidays such as Thanksgiving with father carving the turkey and the family around the table waiting for their plates of food.

We Liked to "Dress Up"

Hats and gloves were standard features of a woman's wardrobe. White gloves were often worn when dressed up, but kid leather gloves the color of a suit were also used and were very attractive.

Whatever one's family financial situation, hats were always worn to church. It was unthinkable to go to a church service bareheaded, except for men, who always removed hats. One felt undressed without a hat and gloves when the occasion called for them. The women were in attractive dresses and suits, stockings and pumps. Some of the styles could have had improvements, but women wanted to look neat, clean and attractive.

Seamless nylon stockings would eventually replace the silk stockings with seams that were in short supply. The stockings, of course had to be held up in some manner. They were often clipped onto girdles, whereas there were many women who chose to use a thick elastic band, put it up the leg to the top of the stocking, and roll the stocking down to above the knee. Since fabrics and fibers were in great demand by the armed forces and auxiliary branches, American ingenuity came forth with leg make-up. It became very popular for summer use, as it came in several tan shades, and when smoothed on, was very attractive. Some chose to draw a seam line down the back of the leg. Pantyhose were an innovation of the future.

It looked out of place to see a man outdoors without a hat, usually a fedora—that is a woolen felt hat with a brim and a matching grosgrain band around the hat. Some hats had narrow bands, but those were worn usually by men who wanted to stand out from the ordinary. When a man was dressed in a suit, shirt and necktie, his hat usually matched or contrasted with the suit. Those who could not afford good clothes, nevertheless were seen wearing a fedora. These were worn even in cold weather. Warm knitted hats were seen mostly on outdoor workmen, children and young people as well as on skaters and skiers.

Brewster, New York, was only ten miles from Danbury, Connecticut, the hat-making center of the country. There were several hat manufacturers there, including Lee, Stetson, Mallory and others. Stetson hats were well known, because the western cowboys and other westerners wore them. They were known by easterners as "cowboy hats." It is said that every man in Danbury wore a hat when on the street. It was a proud city.

Although slacks were not commonly worn by women, they were being sold and we found them very comfortable and "chic." Slacks did appear on movie actresses looking casual and attractive. Before I was an upperclassman, some older girls wore slacks to school only to be told that they were not to be worn in school. It wasn't long before Fridays became "slacks day." Denim was certainly the material of the farmers' overalls, but it wasn't long before blue denim jeans started to show up in ladies' wear, especially on young women. They were rolled up to just below the knees. They were not commonly worn, but throughout the next decade, they became more and more popular.

Women Serving Our Country

Women flyers were not accepted into the Army Air Force. Women who loved to fly had a difficult time convincing the Air Force brass that they were as capable of handling a fighter airplane or bomber as a male pilot. They had a lot to overcome but they started to be used to fly newly manufactured planes to where they were needed at various air bases and from one base to another. In some cases they made trans-oceanic flights to overseas bases. They piloted not only bombers but fully armed fighter airplanes.

One young female pilot, I was told by a former Air Force pilot, was what was known as a "hot shot" pilot. Knowing that her fighter airplane being ferried over the Atlantic Ocean had guns and ammunition, she sought out Nazi airplanes to shoot them down on her way to her destination, figuring why not kill a few of the enemy. They had no uniforms and were a loosely knit group. They performed their piloting duties for the love of flying and love of country. Eventually by proving themselves good pilots, they were organized, were given uniforms and became the WASP (Women's Army Service Pilots). They served our country willingly and honorably relieving the male pilots for combat or training duty. When the war was ended they were released of their duties wherever they were at the time. They were not a military entity.

The government, badly in need of nurses not only for duty overseas, but also for work in our civilian hospitals created the Cadet Nurse Corps. I joined a group of girls who were interested in becoming nurses on a tour of the hospital facilities at Wingdale Hospital north of Pawling, New York. This was a hospital for mentally ill patients that eventually became a Rest and Rehabilitation Hospital for the Army Air Force. I had no interest in joining the profession, but my good friend Louise Vanderburgh was interested and destined to become a nurse. The class she joined after high school in 1944 was the last class of the Cadet Nurse Corps.

Our Place in the World

Thousands of ships left American ports headed for England only to have wolf packs of German U-boats waiting to torpedo them, when they reached a few miles off shore. (I learned many years later from several different people who had been teenagers in Maine that bright lights could be seen at night several miles out into the Atlantic. They would watch nightly as ships were struck throwing up bright flames, and then the light would disappear as the ship sank below the surface and crewmembers were lost.)

At the time I was not fully aware of what was taking place along the eastern coast of North America. Off the shore of Long Island German U-Boats rose to the surface to allow two or three men to board a skiff and row to shore. The story goes that they would go to a bar in the early morning hours and sit there drinking. Then they would return to the U-Boat that was waiting for them. There were many men brought in this way to do espionage work. They would listen to citizens talking and try to obtain important information about shipping and destinations, so that they could relay it back to their Nazi superiors. Many of these men were reported and arrested for espionage from the coast of Canada to Florida and beyond. News of these situations did get around, but I wasn't aware of the extent of this threat. I do recall conversations about espionage agents in our country and about the German American Bund, the association of American Nazis.

When the United States entered the war, the ships would carry American troops heading for England and the North African invasion, and they too were sunk by German U-boats. This continued as the war progressed, and more men and equipment were needed for further invasions. The loss of men and materiel was extreme.

Boys one and two years older than I were now in uniform, and articles and photographs began to appear in our local newspaper, the *Brewster Standard*. It told of our local servicemen and women who were in training for the Navy at the Great Lakes Naval Training Station in New York State or at Camp Pendleton in California or one of many, many training camps, naval bases and airfields around the country. Very often someone serving in this country or overseas would write directly to Marjorie Addis, the publisher of the paper giving his or her change of address. Mothers of servicemen and women also stopped by the *Brewster Standard* office and handed Marge information about their sons or daughters serving in one of the military branches.

Every one in the country was aware of or engaged somehow in the defense or support of this mighty war effort. Posters appeared everywhere telling us that our fighting men were the best, and they needed our support—that we should grow Victory gardens so that we could feed ourselves, and the military would have all the food it needed. We were told by pictures on these posters to give blood and not talk about any information we had regarding the whereabouts of our servicemen. A poster read, "A slip of the lip can sink a ship."

There was a poster showing a map of England and the countries already occupied by Nazi Germany. It was a picture puzzle with one piece missing. That piece was England, and it was in the large hand of a Nazi wearing a ring bearing the swastika. He was about to put the puzzle part of England into place. The printing on the poster read, "Bits of careless talk are pieced together by the enemy," and "Convoy sails tonight." We understood what that meant.

Some posters told us to save metal items for the scrap drives carried out by the Boy Scouts. We were told that this scrap metal would become airplanes, tanks and guns. We were asked to conserve on everything from shoes to gasoline. For almost everything we had to apply for coupons for each member of the family. That meant some very careful planning by the head of the household. It meant standing in line, when butter was expected at the grocery store and the same for meat. It meant we took care of our shoes, because if the shoes wore out and the coupons were used up, the person wore an old spare or if possible had the shoes repaired by the cobbler in the village. It was a common practice to have new "lifts" put on the heels of men's and women's shoes when the leather became worn down from wear. People took pride in their appearance for the most part. It was also, however, a common sight to see a woman with heels that were noticeably worn down or stockings that had a run or a repaired run in them. We understood the message to save, save, save.

The government asked its citizens to buy war bonds. Many people bought them outright knowing that the money would go to finance our war effort. In ten years they would earn interest and receive either $25.00, $50.00, $100.00 or more depending on the denomination of their original purchase. Many citizens made a great effort to purchase as many bonds as they could afford. It was not a "me first" society. We were at war and protecting our freedom and liberating those not free was our priority.

Philip F. Beal, III attended Williams College majoring in chemistry and graduated in December of 1942. I was a junior in high school at that time and did not see him, nor was I aware of his plans. After having two interviews, one at the Winthrop Chemical Company in Rensselaer, New York, and one at Columbia University, he chose the job at Winthrop, because they were producing penicillin, and that interested him. What he did not know was that had he taken the job at Columbia, he would have been working on the Manhattan Project (the development of the atomic bomb). If there was any regret at this decision, he was compensated by the fact that years later having a fine intellect and interest in chemistry, he was the first to synthesize hydrocortisone at Upjohn Pharmaceutical Company. What a contribution this was to mankind! He and his wife Martha lived in Kalamazoo, Michigan, raising their family there. They had a son Philip F. Beal IV, and three daughters, Helene, Sally and Barbara.

My Summer Reality was Tonetta Lake

My friends and I spent many hours at the Tonetta Lake pavilion even on rainy days. A couple of boys from Yonkers taught us a new card game called Knuckles—and for good reason. The loser of the game would have his or her knuckles struck with the tight pack of cards for the number of points lost. There were many bloody knuckles. My interest in that game faded very quickly.

A few of the residents who had spent many summers at Tonetta and considering themselves "Tonetta people" used to play tricks on the kids who were newcomers. One boy was full of the devil and used to invite boys and girls to go out in a rowboat and go "snipe hunting." He instructed them to take a stick, because when they reached the other side of the lake, the hunting would begin. They rowed to the other shore, and he told them to get out of the boat and start beating the brush with their sticks in order to flush out the snipes, and he would return to pick them up later. Snipes were imaginary. They were never picked up and had to make their way through brush and thickets walking back to the ice house and pavilion. And so, the newcomers were duped and initiated.

We listened to the latest records of the big bands being played on the nickelodeon. It cost five cents—a nickel—for one record. We were happy just listening to our favorites, learning the words and visiting. Once in a while someone would receive a telephone call or make a call at the telephone booth at the end of the pavilion on the porch putting a nickel in the slot for a local call. If a person talked over the allotted time, the operator would come on the phone and say, "please deposit another twenty-five cents" or whatever the amount that was overdue. And it would be done. If the caller left without putting overtime money in the slot and walked away, the telephone would ring, but there would be no way to collect the overtime amount.

A Close Call for a Young Swimmer

One day Louise Vanderburgh was swimming with me at the pavilion. We were on the large wood float diving off the diving board, climbing the ladder and diving again. Sometimes we simply lay on the floor and sunbathed. There was a second level to the float that had an extension of two 2" x 4" boards reaching over the water on one side. At the end and between the wood was a pipe. Swimmers could stand on the lower level and jump, grabbing the pipe and swing before going into the water. Though there was a railing around the second level, there were swimmers who ducked under the railing, walked out a short distance on one of the wood extensions, then straddled between the two over the water. Some went all the way to the pipe and dived from there. A few would dive going under the pipe.

Louise and I were there, when a boy younger than we climbed the stairs, and we saw him walk out toward the pipe. Although we called out a word of caution, we watched anxiously as he made his dive and struck his forehead on the pipe, landing in the water unconscious and bleeding. There was never a lifeguard. Louise and I dived in and pulled him around by the ladder. It was impossible for us to pull him up, but fortunately there was another person on the float who helped. We yelled to shore for someone's attention in order to make a phone call. No one could hear, so we decided between us that I, being a good swimmer, should swim in and make a call to the Fire Department. (there was no 911 then). Louise stayed with the boy. I was able to find a rowboat and Louise and I brought him to shore. We had both received a Red Cross life saving certificate and felt confident in what we were doing. At any rate he had a large V cut into his forehead, as his scalp was torn back, and he was bleeding. The ambulance arrived and took him away.

I can remember what that boy looked like, and I knew his name at the time. His family had a cottage at Tonetta Lake Park. I saw him later and his wound had healed. I don't believe he knew anything about his rescue.

Every summer in my memory I swam at Lake Tonetta. When I was small it was at our cottage. As a teenager I spent hours with friends at the pavilion diving off the dock and swimming to the float. When I was with a friend at the cottage we would swim to our float, dive and race. As I used to like doing a surface dive going deep swimming along the bottom, one day I had a peculiar and frightening experience. When I reached the bottom of the lake, and no light was coming from above, I became disoriented and did not know where the surface of the water was. My breath was almost gone, and I had to do something immediately, so I stopped swimming, held what breath I had left and let my body rise. Once I started to rise to the surface, I swam frantically to the air above. Even good swimmers can get into trouble.

The Peach Lake Day Camp

For two summers Louise and I had jobs as counselors at the Peach Lake Day Camp sponsored by the Brewster Lions Club. The camp ran for six weeks, and the cost was minimal for the campers. With our lunches in hand, we took a bus from

Brewster, and from then on we were in charge of the campers. Mrs. Sadie Nagle was the director of the camp. Louise was given duties on the waterfront, and I was given the crafts area. At the end of the day was a general swim in which all campers and counselors were at the waterfront and swimming, the counselors keeping an eye on the young swimmers. We enjoyed the responsibility and the small monetary reward.

This was the last summer before I graduated—a busy summer socially with dancing at the pavilion, having movie dates and spending time with my friends. Some of my favorite people had graduated, and many of my male classmates were in or waiting to be called by the Army, Air Force, Marines, Navy and Merchant Marines.

I began my senior year in September 1943 just after Labor Day. My dad had been through the North African campaign and was in Sicily doing his work of supplying fresh water to airfields, hospitals and the troops.

As a senior I was playing my trumpet in the school band. I played center on the girls' varsity basketball team proudly wearing the green satin shorts and top. When springtime came, I played on the varsity softball team and took part in track running and jumping. By this time our senior Washington, D.C. trip, our junior prom and senior ball were all cancelled because of the war. This was the case with other classes as well. It was a disappointment, but who was there to have as a prom date anyway? And we all understood. Louise Vanderburgh and others set up the record player for an evening of dancing and refreshments. I was there helping too.

Betty Cleaver played taps for many years on Decoration Day, May 30 after we had paraded through Brewster. After she graduated I was asked to do the honors at the Electra Zone field where a short ceremony was held, led by Mayor Henry H. Wells, a veteran of the Spanish American War and currently the head of the Selective Service Board. That day was usually the signal for several students to take their first swim of the season at Tonetta. The water was still too cold for most of us.

It was a common sight in the 1940s to see a convoy of olive drab Army vehicles going through town. There might be one hundred vehicles, trucks with uniformed soldiers. They could be going to an army base or to a port of embarkation headed for combat. Village people would wave and they would happily wave back. There were instances where soldiers would toss out postal cards addressed to their loved ones hoping that the people catching the cards would mail them—and of course they did.

At times the lead jeep would make a wrong turn and head up the hill to a residential area with the convoy following. It would be quite a mess, as they did not know how to get to their route without turning around. It then became routine to send a soldier ahead at different intersections, so that he could wave them on in the correct direction.

My personal life was much as it had been the year before. I was on the various varsity teams and loving every minute of it. I enjoyed the activity, the accomplishment and working with my teammates in field hockey, basketball, softball and track. I worked hard at practice and at games, working with my teammates to win.

The high school band was not as good as it had been when I first joined it. Many of the fine players had graduated, and many were in the service. Louise Vanderburgh and I did our utmost to play well as first and second seat trumpeters. Charlotte Tuttle had moved up in the clarinet section and Muriel Pinckney was still counting measures until it was the time to hit her two cymbals together. I don't remember her ever missing her "moment." Ethel Jean Ekstrom had moved up in the drum section where Gabe Blockley had performed so admirably. Since soccer had replaced football, there were no football games to play at, when we would have enjoyed marching during the halftime. There was a Putnam County band competition in which several of us were selected to play. My recollection is that we went to Haldane High School in Cold Spring, New York, for this.

The Invasion of Sicily, July 1943

The following is what was going on in my forty-six-year-old father's Army life in Sicily beginning just after D-Day, but while there was still aerial fighting. (What he wrote in his diary was not written to his family.) In his diary he told of "anchoring about one mile off shore from Gela at 6 A.M." on the thirteenth of July:

> "Left ship and good food on an invasion barge at 3 P.M. Evidence of a tough time on D-day—two large ships sunk. One bomb landed in the funnel of the ship and 134 soldiers and sailors lost their lives. Marched 4 miles, full pack—air mattress and blanket. Bivouacked in an almond and olive grove…marched back to the beach to find trucks. Gela, population 20,000, had its water main broken and the city is without water. Truck and machine (drilling machine) has not been delivered on shore yet."
>
> "July 15, 1943–(diary) "Lt. Mitchell and Colonel Hurley were killed by a mine. They were in a Jeep with another officer and driver. Gunfire is almost over, but there is much aerial patrol by Spitfires…"

July 16, 1943–(diary) "left the company to put in a well at Gela, Sicily airport. About ¼ mile north of airport found a frame building used formerly for two 20 mm. Italian gun positions…cleared out the building and are using it for my crew….placed the two guns in position and have 2000 rounds of ammunition…"

July 18, 1943–(diary) "expect a big raid at the airport tonight…am running the drilling machine and 4 ton Piamont and ½ ton Dodge on Italian gas-the dump is close by-enemy left their barracks in such a hurry that spaghetti was still on their plates…"

He continued saying that a mine went off near his machine killing three boys who were shepherds. They had come to the building for clothing while he was away. A priest made one small box and two large ones for the bodies.

"Condition of ground is bad. Low on water. No food-just getting by-everybody asked for something to eat-all buildings in town shattered and a good many completely demolished."

Since arriving in Sicily he and his men could not sleep, as the lice and sand fleas were so bad. And the flea powder did not work.

Aug 18, 1943–(diary) "Tested well. Got a letter from Florence and Dodie…"

August 19, 1943–(diary) "Sent package to Florence. Had bad day. Moved machine to 59th Evac. Hospital. Gave instructions to proceed with building stone pump house…"

Then he went on to say there was a very bad air raid with flack dropping all around hospital and bivouac:

"British ship on fire and lit up harbor; then they bombed ship and sank it. Number of dead and missing 16. Wounded 46. German fliers brought in to 56 Evac. Hospital and 91st Evac. Hospital…"

August 19, 1943–(diary) "Went to 91st Evac. Hosp. to check pipeline and 56th to check pump. Turned on pump…Turbine pump—big flow. Handles satisfactorily."

August 26, 1943–(diary) Moved machine from 56th Evac. Hospital to Mondela staging area. Started drilling at 3 p.m. Drilled 20 ft. All sand and shell rock…."

August 28, 1943–(diary) "…Went to Mondella. Returned to area after having written letter home. Truck hit a shell hole and threw me out while out on job. Hurt my back. Did not do anything about it…"

August 29, 1943–(diary) "Couldn't get out of my bunk. Taken to 91st Evac. Hospital. Doctors all good to me. X-ray shows no bone broken. Very bad pain in my back. Upset stomach. In misery, trying to lie flat on my back.

August 30, 1943–(diary) "…Lt. Sheffield, Capt. Soltroff in to see me. Another X-ray picture-nothing shows broken." End of diary.

It was while my father was in Sicily that I wrote the following poem. It was printed in the school newspaper, *The Bear Facts*, probably not because it is a fine example of poetry, but because there were so many family members away in the war, and it helped that my friend Louise Vanderburgh was the editor-in-chief.

YOU LEFT

You left New York-you went to sea,
We didn't know how long you'd be
You arrived: there was no dock
You knew it had been "some hot spot"
You worked hard and had some fun
Lots of times you thought of your son
That was some very tough job, but you did your best,
And all the time you thought of the rest.
In a short while your commander said
We're moving on, so pack up your bed.
And when all this was done, again you thought of your son
And all the rest back in bed.
Then you remembered what your officer said.
That's the way it went for days and months,
You did two or three jobs in a bunch,
From Casablanca to Rabat, Fez and Oran;
You only tell us what you can.
But now that you are in Sicily
You might even get to Italy-
Maybe you'll go to France, Germany and Poland,
And by doing so, soon get to your homeland.

Father recuperating, Atlantic City Hospital, 1944.

My dad was put in a plaster cast, was in the hospital for two weeks, then sent to Africa. He was on two hospital ships, and when he returned home was in three hospitals, one in Atlantic City and the last at Fort Dix, New Jersey.

While he was in Atlantic City, my mother and my six-year-old brother and I drove down to see him. It was in February and was bitter cold. We all bundled up and sat on the benches on the boardwalk overlooking the beach and ocean. It was so good to be with him, but one could see that he was in pain and the pain was not all physical. He had witnessed some terrible sights.

When he was well enough he was given a twenty-one day leave, and subsequently he was on his way to the EORP Field Maintenance Office in Columbus, Ohio. I was preparing to take my final examinations at Brewster High School. The weather was warm and beautiful. My mother and I were starting to pack for our trip to Ohio. She was a very clever packer, knowing what would make us feel at home at our new destination.

1944

Graduation

During our graduation ceremonies my father was not present nor was my friend Louise's father, as he was still in China. She was asked to prepare a song for the occasion, and Mr. Knapp asked me to play Schubert's "Serenade" on my trumpet. I knew it well, but when I stood up in my black gown and cap and started playing, my knees began to quiver. I was certain that everyone in the audience could see my gown moving.

The morning after graduation our dark green Chrysler was pulled up to the front door in order to pack last minute items. We were headed for Ohio with my mother and me taking turns driving and my six-year-old brother a passenger. Our gas rationing coupons were safely in my mother's purse. We had driven several hours, when we came upon a uniformed boy about my age who was hitchhiking. His uniform was that of the Merchant Marine, and he was on his way home on leave. We took him as far as we could. There was no thought of whether we should be picking up a hitchhiker as one never passed up the opportunity to help out a serviceman in this manner.

We stayed at a motel in Columbus for about two weeks before moving to Marion, Ohio. While staying at a motel, my little brother was wandering around the yard and discovered a little footbridge that led to the nearby house. As he walked onto the bridge, a large Chow dog came barreling his way and bit him. He had apparently invaded the dog's space. My parents had Ross treated, and there were no ill effects.

After a month my dad was assigned to Fort Belvoir, Virginia, as Assistant Post Engineer. He found out that his responsibility was to take care of the post dump. When he inspected the area, he saw that the garbage and trash lay exposed over a wide area. He could see that it was unsanitary and began a program of having a bulldozer push all the trash to the periphery, leveling it and covering it over. His other responsibility was the swimming pools on the post, keeping them clean and properly chlorinated.

We had to find a place to live, until a house on the post became available. We were fortunate to find an apartment over a garage on the property where a major rented the main house. The apartment was on a dirt road outside Alexandria about twelve miles from Fort Belvoir. Next door was a family with two young boys who cared for their own horses and entered horse shows. This was a new experience for me, as I saw them preparing for the show and plaiting the manes of their horses. My hair was braided. I had never heard the word "plait," nor had I ever attended a horse show until that fall.

A local horse show was fun, and I had met my neighbors who were participants. I remember one female equestrian who was dressed more elaborately than the local people. There was a comment going around that this wealthy horsewoman from a prominent family did not belong in this show, as she would take prizes that the local people felt they would ordinarily win. There was a note of bitterness yet acceptance. She was an expert horsewoman.

The rest of that summer we enjoyed going to the Officers' Club pool to swim and occasionally to eat at the club on the new post. The old post was on the other side of Route One where the beautiful brick houses with white trim were the residences of the generals, colonels, lieutenant colonels and some majors. The captains were in smaller, two bedroom, wood-sided houses where the barracks and drill fields were located, mostly on the west side of Route One. The number of these houses was few. My father drove us around the area to see where we would eventually be living.

My cousin Malcolm Beal tried to enlist in the Army two times, but during the physical it was discovered that he had flat feet, and he was rejected. After his high school graduation in 1943 he volunteered again and was finally accepted but in the category they called "limited enlistment." He was in training at Fort Belvoir at the time my father was Assistant Post Engineer, and when he learned that Malcolm was there, he asked for permission to visit him. We all drove out to a wooded area in the rain, and Malcolm was advised that he had visitors. When I saw him I got out of the car and walked with my dad toward Malcolm. I think he was glad to see us—I know I was happy to see him. I reached in my pocket remembering that I had a candy bar and handed it to him. He took it without hesitation. I wish I had thought to buy a large quantity to give him.

It wasn't long before he was sent to the harsh environment of the Aleutian Islands as part of the Engineer Corps. He was stationed on Amchitka, and his work was "related to repairing and maintaining airfields on Adak and Attu"; "the airfields were used as stopping points for the Air Force airplanes on their way to the Pacific Theatre."[11]

We wrote a few letters at the time. I remember that he said the wind was so fierce and the snow so heavy that, when it was necessary to go from one building to another, one had to take hold of a rope that was strung from building to building. Not doing this could mean being lost in what we now call a "white-out," snow so heavy that the visibility was zero. Receiving a letter from him meant a great deal to me, but I wonder if I wrote to him often enough.

Before he reached the Aleutians, the Japanese had invaded and occupied the two islands, Attu and Siska, and the American soldiers who were stationed in Alaska had to fight them. Those Japanese who were not killed left and did not return. This was before the battle of Midway Island in the Pacific. After Pearl Harbor was attacked, and we were sorely unprepared to fight a war, it was not known whether the Japanese would attack the mainland of the United States. One of the soldiers from Brewster who fought to rid the Aleutians islands of the Japanese was Francis Creighton who was highly decorated for heroism during this engagement with the enemy. The people of California must have had worries about the possibility of a Japanese invasion, as there were incidences of Japanese submarines off the coastline. Anti-submarine nets were strung in some areas to keep out the enemy subs.

One day I walked down our dirt driveway to pick up our mail from the box. We always looked forward to the *Brewster Standard's* arrival where we would read about the young men and women in service. As I walked up the driveway, I would start

---

[11] Stephens, *Those Who Served*, 2.

reading the paper. It was then that I learned that Bob Collins had been killed fighting on Guam in the Pacific. I felt shocked and very sad. I thought of his younger twin brothers, wondering where they were and knowing what a loss it would be for them. In *Those Who Served/Those Who Waited*, I quoted from Jimmy's letter to Eddie saying that he hoped he could get to where Bobby was buried.

In the Town of Southeast seventeen boys perished serving our country. I knew most of them. Henry Alfke was my classmate and was only in the Army a few months before he was killed in Europe. Wilbur Nagle had played the clarinet in our school band. I knew his two sisters and of course his mother was my fifth-grade teacher. John O'Brien, Jackie or "Bunky" to his school mates was a top turret gunner on a B-24 Liberator. It was shot down over Berlin, Germany, not far from the Belgian border on April 29, 1944. He was declared killed in action. Before leaving for Europe, it was after basketball practice that "Bunky" O'Brien arrived at the gymnasium probably hoping to see some of his friends. After I had changed out of my practice clothes, he asked me, if I would like a ride home. It was not long afterward that the sad news was learned.

Harding O'Hara was several classes ahead of me, his sister Rita being one year ahead. Harding played clarinet in the high school band and also had his own orchestra. He trained as an armorer-gunner and photographer on a B-24 Liberator. Assigned to the Eighth Air Force in England he flew missions over Germany and the Ploesti oil fields in Romania. It was on a very long mission to Norway to cripple German power stations and mines hidden in the mountains that the German Luftwaffe attacked, and his plane crashed into the waters between England and Norway.

Edward Smith, his three brothers all serving our country and a sister Margaret, were neighbors whose home was on Putnam Terrace. Edward was killed on the Alaska Highway. Donald Smith found out about his brother's death, when he went to visit another brother, Robert (Snuffy) while serving in England.

Back to My Reality

Little attention was paid to what I would do—what I would pursue. I had no inkling at the time of what I was capable. I had considered physical education, as I did love the sports I had participated in. However, I was not prepared academically, nor did I know much about myself, and we had no counselors. Our lives were centered on the war and my father being away. This was the case for many girls. My high school friend who had four brothers told me that it was only important that her brothers be educated. But she was smart and after high school obtained a very good job.

My new acquaintance Lura Mae Whitfield from Iowa who lived where our apartment was located, was a student at the Saint Agnes School in Alexandria, a small Episcopal girls' school. That fall I enrolled in Saint Agnes School for a post-graduate year. There were three other post-graduate students there, and the other eight seniors had attended for numbers of years. Many of their fathers were Naval captains, admirals, generals and colonels who were professional officers, most having gone to West Point or Annapolis. But I could not have been more proud of my dad and the contribution he made. Some of these officers may have been stationed in Washington, D.C. Others may have been with their men on hazardous duty around the world. The father of my classmate, Julie Halloran, was the beach master during every island invasion in the Pacific theatre. We did not talk of these things.

The year at Saint Agnes was the only time I had ever ridden a bus except for away games at other schools. Now I walked a quarter mile to Route One at Fort Belvoir and caught the bus to Alexandria twelve miles away. In winter the weather was brutally cold and damp, and I felt it especially while waiting for the bus. Every experience is worthwhile, this one making me empathetic toward those who had to ride the buses to work.

I did not know much about racial segregation until we moved to Virginia. In Brewster we had a few black students—a girl I did not know and two sisters in my class who were well liked. There had also been one or two older football players. As far as I knew everyone got along with no problems. I was not aware of any bigotry, although I have been told that there was some. Now I was to learn that I could not go to a seat at the back of the bus. It seemed very strange. Then I could see when the bus was crowded that the black passengers had to push their way to get to the rear of the bus. It was the accepted way of doing things there, as I witnessed. Even I accepted it—but what did I know at that stage of my life, especially having come from a small town in the north.

The memory of my first day at St. Agnes School is quite vivid, as I looked around at the girls who were strangers. I felt like the small town girl that I was, and my classmates for the most part seemed so "sophisticated," although there were some who stood out as warm and friendly. I participated in the "new girls" day wearing a beanie and whatever was required. It was my classes that were of concern. In the English class taught by the headmistress, I found that the girls had read books that I had not. We read the poetry of Keats and Shelley and others. My self-confidence would come years later. I was at home on one of the school teams, and I did learn some tennis on their asphalt court.

A bad decision, well intentioned, that I made was to repeat a class in French II. I had the credits from Brewster, but I was, let's face it, a mediocre French student. Miss Kramer once said in front of our class that my French pronunciation was to be admired. That did not make me understand, nor make me fluent in the language. So I thought I would do something worthwhile for myself and improve my French.

My first day of French class was a memorable if traumatic one. The white haired French (as from France) teacher announced that upon coming through the door of the classroom, there would be no English spoken, and from then on every word was in French. I was devastated. The next day with my heart in my stomach and a lump in my throat, I went to class. After class I went to the telephone in the main building, and in tears I called my mother and told her that I would not be going back to French class. She understood. Of course I had to have an appointment with the headmistress, Mrs. Macan. She approved my decision—what could she do and what did she really care, since I was a postgraduate student.

Chemistry when I was a sophomore in Brewster High School was a course that was a disaster. My first teacher was Mr. Ralph Truran. When he left, our principal, H. H. Donley taught our class. After a month or two we had another substitute teacher. In the spring a new teacher, Mr. Podawils was hired. My final grade was not a passing mark. So at St. Agnes I decided I would rectify that. We had a female teacher who was wonderful. (She was also the athletic coach). I understood everything from day one, had about twelve experiments to do independently before the end of the year, and I did them successfully. I was proud of myself when my final grade was an eighty-five. Things were looking up.

Home at Fort Belvoir

My brother, who was six years old, received a black and white puppy for Christmas that year. He named him Poochie. He did not have him very long before the puppy ran across the lawn next door and into the main road. He was struck by a car and was killed. It would have been fun to have a dog in the family, but he was not replaced. We were more saddened for my brother than for ourselves.

A two-week holiday was coming up and another girl also attending St. Agnes and I applied for a job at the gift shop in the Pentagon. I was placed at the jewelry counter, and she worked in another department. I traveled by the bus that took me from Fort Belvoir to the underground bus stop at that huge government building. Of course I never got to see any of the building itself, but I did see many in uniform, as well as civilians who worked there.

One warm day while my father was working, my mother and I were at the swimming pool on the new post. We were permitted to swim on the old post where the high-ranking officers' families swam, but this pool was nearer our home. We were sitting on chairs on the long side of the pool, when I decided to go to the end where I could dangle my legs in the water.

My suit was still wet from having been swimming. Soon I started to feel a sensation like a bite or burning on my derriere. I went over to my mother and told her about it. After standing under the shower for a long time, the feeling continued, actually becoming worse. It was no bug bite.

When my father came home for dinner, I told him about it, and brought my bathing suit to him to examine, even showing him my burns. By then the suit had two large holes in the seat. My mother and I were informed that the chlorinator for the pool which was my father's responsibility had been out of commission for a long period of time, and he had spoken to the colonel trying to get it repaired. It was necessary, we were told, for the soldier who worked at the pool to mix a solution of chlorine by hand and toss it into the water. Drops had spilled on the edge of the pool and dried. That is where I had sat, and I had two red burns on my skin to show for it.

After looking at my suit my father said, "You are going to have to go with me and show the colonel your burns." My eyes widened and my mouth opened, but I knew my dad was kidding, and he did take my suit to show his commanding officer. This undoubtedly hastened the repair of the chlorinator. My dad said he was lucky a colonel's wife hadn't sat in the dried chlorine.

We usually went to the Sunday services at the post chapel, but one springtime Sunday we decided to drive down Route One to the historic Pohick Church, where George Washington had attended. It dated back to the 1700s and had box pews with white painted side walls that were about three to four feet high. These kept the drafts away from the parishioners, the church not being heated in those early days.

During the service my father turned and whispered in my ear, "Do you smell something?" I thought, what was he up to? Then he told me he had left the oven on at home. My mother had prepared baked beans and had turned the oven off leaving the beans in the warm oven. My father, always poking his nose in kitchen affairs, had turned the oven back on feeling the beans should be cooked a while longer. He had forgotten to turn off the stove before we left. So, now there were two of us wondering about the condition of the beans and the house.

While driving home my father informed my mother of what he had done. We all hoped the house hadn't burned down. When we entered the kitchen door, there was the smell of burned beans, and they were black.

There went our good bean supper. We then went to the Officers' Club for our meal, but as I recall they didn't offer much on Sundays. My dad was always lifting pot lids on the stove to see what was cooking. This time he really did it.

During the summer of 1944, I met a young officer, a Major Jay Thylacker from Pittsburgh who asked me out on a date and came to our house, introducing himself to my father, a captain. We went to the movies on our first date. He then took me to dinner at the Army and Navy Club in Washington, D.C., a very elegant place for officers only. He was a major at age twenty-four and an engineer. Twenty-four is young, but I was much younger (seventeen). It wasn't long before he received orders to go to China and I learned that he was in Shanghai. Although we wrote a few letters, I never heard from him again, and always hoped that he returned home safely.

1945

Life Goes On

On March 5, 1945, I turned eighteen and at times felt quite grow-up, although in reality I was still quite immature. It was the style to dress up for dates and special occasions. One outfit I remember was a black and white print dress, the black streaks resembling narrow zebra stripes, but a simple style. I also had a two-piece black faille spring suit with a bolero jacket, a popular style. With those I wore a black Milan straw picture hat, this style also being popular at the time and black fabric pumps that did not require ration stamps to purchase them. I enjoyed wearing attractive clothes, yet I did not spend great amounts, nor did I have a large selection at one time. My mother was more an influence on me than on my sisters as regards clothes. I knew that what she told me made sense, and I saw that she knew how to dress with style. The styles of the day were attractive, simple and in good taste if one shopped in the right department stores.

Our little white house was on a side road with only four houses. Across the street were a captain and his wife. As I recall he had been on the faculty of Carver Military Academy, and now he was in the Provost Marshal's office at Fort Belvoir. That was the summer I first learned about ticks, as another neighbor would take her baby indoors after being in a playpen and check his body for this annoying insect. Undoubtedly it was a dog tick. It would be many years later before the deer ticks became a serious problem in the northeast. Lyme Disease was discovered in Lyme Connecticut, and it was found to be caused by a spirochete and was spread by the deer tick carried on mice and deer. It caused various symptoms including arthritis. Usually after being bitten by the tick a large round rash would appear at the sight of the bite. The disease continued to spread into other states, and fortunately it was found that antibiotics could be used for treatment.

The road we lived on ended at the drill field. It was a short distance from the barracks in the opposite direction. Every day it seemed columns of uniformed soldiers were marched by our house on the way to being drilled on the field. One day my mother looked out watching the soldiers marching by, and at the end of the column of men was a little, short fellow in uniform with his wooden gun. It was my brother, and it was quite a sight. He said he had friends in the barracks, and he visited them. As Aleksandr I. Solzhenitsyn said in one of several books about the Russian labor camps, *The Gulag Archipelago: Three, Katorga Exile*, "As the fathers live so the children play."

One day when my father was in Washington, he ran into Tommy Lottreciano who was from Brewster. He was with a buddy, and my dad invited them to have Sunday dinner with us at our house at Fort Belvoir. Tom was in the Navy and had been one of our star football players. After the war Tommy was encouraged by Coach Sterling Geesman, who became a coach at Ohio Wesleyan College, to transfer there, where Tom would be on their football team. He did transfer from Columbia University and played on the Ohio Wesleyan team.

My Sister Joins the WAVES

Joan left her job in New York City and took a job at the Sikorsky War factory in Bridgeport, carpooling each day. She enjoyed her work there, as she was biding her time until my father returned. One day she came home and was describing a sight from her office window. It was a secret experimental plane that, as she described it, was like a large wing. It must have been a prototype of the airplane built in the 1990s—the Stealth Bomber. It did not go any further, as the factories were turning out fighter planes and bombers, the B-17, the B-24 and later the B-29.

Joan in her WAVE uniform, 1944-45.

The WAVES was Joan's goal, having waited at my father's request until he reached home. She took her Naval basic training at the Sampson Naval Base and became a corpsman. While in training she and seventeen-year-old James Terwilliger of Brewster crossed paths. She loved nursing work and made a proud WAVE. Her first station was at St. Albans Naval

Hospital. One day while on duty a young Coast Guardsman from Brewster noticed her walking by not being quite sure it was my sister. He called out "Joanie" and she went to him. It was John (Butch) Santorelli who had been seriously injured at Normandy while on his LST. He was very happy to see her, and she could not do enough for him. He said that she was very busy at the hospital where the seriously injured battle victims were treated.

Jane was working at the J. P. Stevens fabric laboratory in Manhattan, testing nylon for parachutes. While working there, she told us of the new material for ladies' stockings (pantyhose were not made) called nylon. One day she brought a pair of nylon hose home. They were beautiful and were silkier than silk, and they dried in a few hours, whereas the silk stocking we were used to took a couple of days. They also lasted longer.

She enjoyed this important defense work. While there she met a young man who was waiting to go into the Army Air Force. We were at Fort Belvoir, when they decided to marry, and the wedding and reception were arranged to be held at the Officers' Club. The day of the wedding we were waiting for Joan to arrive from California, where by then, she was stationed at the Alameda Naval Hospital. When she reached our home at Fort Belvoir she was very ill with a viral infection. She said she couldn't miss the wedding and came all the way by train. She had to leave the next day in order to get to her duties on time. One cannot imagine greater family loyalty.

While my father was not yet discharged from the Army but was anticipating getting back to Brewster, he had been thinking about having an automobile to drive when the time came. He asked me when home on an earlier trip to go to the Plymouth dealership and pick out a car for him. I believe he wanted a four-door car but said order whatever I could, as cars were still not readily available. So, I did just that. I was able to get a black two-door coupe which was very satisfactory to him. I appreciated the responsibility he bestowed upon me.

In the spring of 1945 my father went back to civilian life. Before leaving our little house on the post at Fort Belvoir, we were all instructed to check the rooms to make sure we were not leaving anything behind. My sister Jane was with us, and when we were all ready to leave the house, Jane went into the attic. There she found stuffed into the rafters, the brace that my father had been given to wear for his recovering back. He told my sister not to say anything about it. Perhaps he was leaving his memories behind as well, those experiences in Sicily after the Germans bombed.

My father had arranged with a civilian worker at Fort Belvoir for me to board with his family for the last two months before graduation at St. Agnes School. There were three girls, the youngest a few years older than I. I had my own bedroom, and I ate my breakfast and dinner with them. They could not have been a nicer family, treating me as one of their own.

I graduated with ten classmates (including four post-graduate students) from the St. Agnes School wearing our own white dresses and holding a bouquet of red roses. I was happy that day. My parents drove down to the graduation ceremonies and to drive me home. I would not see any of my classmates for fifty years, when Mallory and I went to Alexandria for the 50th reunion in 1995. Julie Halloran Rush and her husband Richard were very generous in paying for one night for every classmate at one of the finer hotels there. We enjoyed that weekend, and in the years to follow we met with several members of the class both in Florida and New Hampshire.

End of World War II

On May 7, 1945, the formal surrender of Nazi Germany took place—VE Day. On September 2—VJ Day—Japan formally surrendered aboard the USS *Missouri* in Tokyo Bay. Our country went wild in celebration. My cousin came from Danbury in his open convertible car, and my friends and I rode around town in a parade of cars celebrating with horns honking. We went to the Busy Bee (now the VFW building) on Peaceable Hill Road known mostly as a bar. But that day they were serving food, and I ordered spaghetti. As the waitress reached our table and was about to put the plate at my place, the plate was tilted, and the spaghetti slowly ran off the plate and grazed the side of my white skirt. It mattered little. Perhaps she was doing some celebrating as well. We were all so happy. The war was over!

Post-War Days

The Heroes Return

Our Brewster boys would slowly make it home. So much had happened, yet I knew so little of what our servicemen and women had done for our country. Many years later, in fact it was during the presidency of Ronald Reagan, the old veterans would be formally thanked at Normandy, France. From then on many books were published about their experiences, the battles and the U.S. at war. In 2004 my book, *Those Who Served/Those Who Waited*, told the stories of Brewster veterans and the people who were at home waiting for the war to end. There were many not included in the book. I was privileged to have been given these stories.

In January of 1946 after serving in the Engineer Corps in the Aleutians Islands, Malcolm Beal returned home. Philip Jr., his father, was terminally ill, and Malcolm was glad to have returned home to be with his dad. We grieved his loss. From then Ross and Malcolm ran the business as partners. In March of 1946 Malcolm married his childhood sweetheart, Marjorie Lane. They had four children, Phyllis, Malcolm Jr., Perry, and Faith. The business continues to be run by the Beals, now in the fifth generation.

Another Kind of War Casualty

Jane spent some time with her new husband in Florida while he was training, and then he went to England to fly missions over Europe. On his return Jane wore a beautiful new red suit with a fur collar for which she had saved. She was very happy. My father let them spend time at our cottage at Tonetta Lake. While there her husband told Jane that he had fallen in love with an English girl. She went to Brewster and told my father. He told her to go to the bank and withdraw all the money she had been saving, as it was hers. In the meantime, her husband was at the cottage, intending to finish his leave there.

My father had to tell him to leave, as he was no longer welcome. She went to Reno for her divorce spending six weeks, and while in Reno she obtained a job selling flowers on the steps of the court house. This gave her some spending money and helped to pass the time. It was so very devastating that she came close to having a nervous breakdown. I was at Blackstone Junior College in Virginia when my mother called to tell me the story. I broke down and cried, as it was heartbreaking news, and I felt so sad for my sister.

From 1945 through 1947, I attended Blackstone College in Virginia, a small girls' school. I met girls from many states and a few from Cuba. These Cuban girls were from wealthy families, nicely dressed, friendly and had a sense of humor. Just before leaving for a Christmas holiday, we had a light snow that absolutely thrilled these girls who had never seen or felt snow. They were out on the grass tossing the snow in the air in great delight. Having lost track of them, I wonder what happened to them when Fidel Castro came to power. Perhaps they are in this country.

At the beginning of the first semester, I decided that I wanted to study piano again. The first year I had a male instructor and the second year a young female teacher. Both teachers were fine pianists. The second year it was made clear that all the piano students would be in a springtime recital. I had one piece to learn, I believe a Bach composition. It wasn't a complicated piece, but we were to play from memory.

Dodie at Blackstone College, 1946.

Blackstone Graduation, 1947.

The recital came and with it the anxiety of appearing before my peers, never having felt confident with my ability. My turn came, and I started to play, getting about twenty measures into the piece. At that point, my mind froze. I could not go on. The music simply would not come to me. I looked in the wing at my instructor, and with her finger waving slowly up and down, she was telling me to start over. So I began again and reached that twenty measure place, and again I could not continue. Again I looked at my teacher facing me from the wing, and again she beckoned me to start over. I started again and the same thing happened. The notes would not come to me. With that I stood up, went to the edge of the stage facing the auditorium of students and faculty and bowed my deepest bow. The applause was deafening. I was appreciated. My music was a failure, but I was not. My friends came backstage and congratulated me, all laughing and smiling.

One would think that my interest in taking piano lessons would have died. That was not the case, as about four years later I found a teacher in Carmel, New York, and continued to study with him. It was the first time that I had played duets, which we did regularly. I enjoyed my weekly lessons until just before I married. There were to be no more lessons in the future.

I had learned enough piano that for many years I enjoyed playing for my own pleasure. It had simply been a persistent desire, but I had finally learned my limitations and would have to find other creative outlets. The love of piano music nevertheless has been lifelong.

After the war my dad spent time in the workshop he had set up in the recreation room that never was used much for its original pupose. He had a work bench many tools and a lathe. He enjoyed many hours turning out beautiful dishes and bowls, always made of exotic woods. Always watching for a burl growing on a tree, he was able to find one from which he cut and polished a sectioned platter and other flat pieces. One project was making the wooden base that holds the round fluted tray he had sent home from French Morocco. I enjoy seeing it used as a coffee table in our home.

Begging burrs from a dentish friend in town, he started experimenting with boring into small blocks of acrylic, a new plastic material being produced. It seems he was often ahead of the time.

Before mushrooms because so plentiful in markets, my father interested Mr. Charles Darlington of Mount Kisco, New York, in the potential of growing mushrooms in one of the old mines in the area. It was a perfect place, dark and dank. I remember Ambassador Darlington coming to our home a few times to discuss the project as my father went to his home.

As a test, my father prepared an area at the foot of the outdoor stairway beneath the cellar door. It had a similar environment. He planted mushroom spores and waited. After a period of time he asked me to go to the basement and look at his experiment and report back about the mushroom growth. What I found, to my amazement, was one mushroom about five inches across and possibly some tiny ones. We were perplexed over this. It was as though all the spores had gotten together to form one large one.

They did go into business and successfully produced mushrooms, having them delivered by truck to markets in New York City. For some reason this enterprise that may have lasted three years was discontinued. I do not know whether the appetite for mushrooms was not there at that time or whether there was a problem with production.

Eldest Sister Remarries

Jane had not learned to drive. There had been no need, since she commuted on the New York Central to her jobs. A few years later she decided to take a Drivers Education course. Her teacher was Neil Blackwood, who taught Industrial Arts at Brewster High School. The school was still K-12 at Garden Street.

It wasn't long before Neil asked Jane on a date, and other dates followed. Doing what we sisters were good at, when we saw Neil walking up the driveway while still sitting at the dinner table, Joan, Ross and I started calling out, "Here comes Neil, Here Comes Neil." Jane would try to shush us and was hoping Neil could not hear us. I am sure he did, but he did not let on. Neil grew up in Oswego, New York, with one sister. Sadly, his mother died when Neil was very young. He graduated from the State University of New York at Oswego.

We learned that as an Army soldier he fought in the Battle of the Bulge in WWII and was stranded with some buddies in a stone building while being surrounded by Germans. The building happened to be a storehouse for the farmer's cognac. They ran out of food quickly and survived by drinking the liqueur. That is all I knew of his experiences. I never got to thank him for his service to our country.

When they decided to marry, Jane wanted to be married in our St. Andrew's Episcopal Church. It was the diocesan policy not to marry a divorced person in the church or be blessed by the church. At the time Reverend Basil Law was the rector, and Jane went to him and said that she did not intend to marry unless her marriage would be blessed by the church. Basil Law went to the presiding Bishop and spoke on her behalf. Jane waited patiently. In time she was granted dispensation and was able to be married by our family friend Reverend Basil Law. Her two sisters, dressed alike in aqua with matching shoes and hats, were beside her in the living room of our home.

The week before the wedding I went to our garage and reached for a tool on the wall. A small, dull, rusting sickle fell from the wall and cut my wrist. I went to the doctor who taped up my half-inch gash with no stitches. The day of the wedding, having made a special trip to the store, I opened the hood of Neil's automobile and placed a partially opened package of

Limburger cheese, figuring that the heat of the engine would carry the unpleasant smell throughout the car—my last act of sisterly love!

It wasn't long before Jane and Neil purchased the house known as the Drum House on Putnam Avenue that was owned by P. F. Beal Sr. Before moving in they made improvements and painted all the rooms. After my grandfather died, they were able to buy his summer cottage. They winterized it and made many improvements there. They had one son, Neil Jr. Neil Sr. developed serious rheumatoid arthritis and could not lift heavy objects such as stones, and as a result he became the cook, and Jane worked outdoors, even building stone walls.

Life was getting back to normal. However, my mother decided she no longer wanted to rent out the apartments. When Joan was released from the Navy, she became a licensed practical nurse and took a job at the Mahopac Emergency Hospital and lived at home. It was decades later that I was told by Robert Palmer of Brewster how much his family appreciated Joan. When his wife Jean was delivering her baby at the hospital, Joan was very compassionate and helpful during the delivery. As a result, when it came to naming the new baby girl, they decided to name her after my sister, Joan.

Joan married Paul Edward Peckham who had grown up in White Plains, New York. This wedding took place two years after Jane married, and my mother offered them an abbreviated apartment on the second floor. Paul worked in Brewster. Their apartment had a kitchen, bath, bedroom and small living room. A door was installed to separate their living quarters from my new bedroom and my grandmother's room.

In time Joan's and Paul's daughter, Susan was born. Paul went into the army and was assigned to Germany as a second lieutenant. While there, a son, Paul, Jr. was born. He enjoyed his career in the army.

My Life as a Young Adult

About 1951 I joined the Women's Club of Brewster and the Little Theatre Group. In 1953 I was made president of the Women's Club. My mother would calm my anxiety before the meeting of these older town ladies to whom I had to speak, and Mrs. Alexander (Gladys) Vanderburgh, a past president, was very helpful to me as I took over this position. During my tenure my suggestion of having a winter ball called the Snow Ball came to fruition, and it was a delightful event with the ladies dressed in formal attire. Hung from the ceiling of the old Brewster High School gymnasium was a huge white sparkling ball made of wire covered in cotton, designed by artist/member Florence Cooper, a very helpful and talented lady.

On occasion I would visit another member, Mrs. Benjamin Freeman, whose frequent guest was Dag Hammarskjold, Secretary General of the United Nations, who lived on Foggintown Road during his tenure. Through him she arranged a visit to the new United Nations building for members of the Women's Club.

From the time I made my first sweater in Miss Hubbard's knitting club, I continued to knit, often argyle socks. Seeing my Grandmother MacLean's lovely needlepoint pieces, I became interested in doing the same. Throughout the years I did many needlepoint pillows and chair seats, then bargello patterns, eventually designing some of my own. My grandmother taught me to sew, and before I married and afterwards, I made suits and dresses for myself and some children's clothes, even tackling a necktie for my husband and a bowtie for our son. Painting, photography, sculpting and writing were for the future.

In 1947 the area was hit with a long-lasting snowstorm, and it was cold enough to stay on the ground until the next snow came. There was so much snow that season that a rope tow started to operate in Somers, New York, six miles from Brewster. The hillside of the golf course facing Route One Hundred and the 19th Hole Restaurant became the ski slope. I had never skied, and this was my opportunity to start learning. I had participated in many sports and learned them quickly. One of the days that I skied down the hill, I was about to end my run when I noticed Betty Cleaver watching the action with her husband Jim Winters. I was only a few feet from them, when I fell face down at their feet. They must have been impressed with my skiing ability!

My Only True Love

One day leaving the church on a warm Sunday, people were standing around visiting, and I started talking with Mallory Stephens. I hadn't seen much of him, because he had gone to Deerfield Academy for his last two years of high school and had already graduated from Hamilton College. He was then in his second year of medical school in Syracuse, New York. We had a nice visit. I had also been away at school and college for most of three years. I had not known Mallory well, but our families had known one another for many years. Mallory's father having left farming as a young man had been Supervisor of the Town of Patterson. He later ran for the New York State Assembly, holding that seat for twenty-seven years.

When our family reached home that Sunday, my mother made a comment about the previous hour. She said, "That boy (meaning Mallory Stephens) is going to call you." Oh, mother! In a few days Mallory called me and invited me to a movie. Mother is always right! Then he took me to the Ringling Bros. circus in Manhattan, and what fun that was. (I had no idea at the time that he was a descendant of the Howes circus family of Brewster of whom I was aware and had passed the Howes Castle on Turk Hill numerous times). While walking on the street, a fleck of dust or whatever floats in the air in that canyon-like environment, went into my eye. Mallory decided he would remove it for me, and I leaned against a wall while this young doctor to be did a major procedure by taking the corner of his clean, white handkerchief, lifting my eyelid and removing the speck. A memorable experience. He reminds me that the day of the circus is when we fell in love.

After seeing him only during Easter, Thanksgiving, Christmas holidays and for a couple of weeks during the summer over a three-year period, he called me from Syracuse. He was excited to tell me that he had delivered five babies as a senior medical student. One call came in February during which he asked me to marry him and asked me to keep it from our families until he came home for Easter holiday. I was so excited. We became engaged, and an engagement party was held at my home in April of 1954. My mother and I had two months to prepare for the wedding, trousseau and reception. We worked together on everything. Mallory's parents were very welcoming, generous and helpful. When Mallory's mom was leaving our house after our engagement party, she said to my mother, "I thought he would never ask her."

Epilogue

Mallory Stephens and I were married on June 12, 1954, at St. Andrew's Episcopal Church. We decided to defy the convention of not seeing one another until the wedding was taking place by going together, just the two of us for Communion at eight that morning. Our friend Reverend Basil Law was studying in England, and the Rev. Chester Falby officiated. After the ceremony, everyone went outdoors and planted a young dogwood tree, a Bermudian tradition, we were told. Our reception was held at our home where my dad had made the outside of the house look beautiful. It was a clear and sunny day, and the eighty-five guests were at tables on the patio and the grass.

Young married couple, Mallory and Dodie.

Mallory and I had discussed what his four friends, as ushers would wear. Three of the four were to graduate from Syracuse Medical School with him, and he felt that he could not ask them to buy new suits for the wedding. His brother Willis and Mallory were to dress in new navy blue silk suits. We agreed to tell them to wear whatever suits they had. It turned out the three wore dark suits and one wore a light gray suit.

After the ceremony Mallory and I were driven by his brother Willis in his car to Somers where we were met by Mr. Stephens' secretary Ernie Buckstine. Ernie drove us to Manhattan. The next morning we were to fly to Bermuda for a week. We had to squeeze wedding and honeymoon into the two weeks between graduation and the start of his internship at Kings County Hospital, the largest hospital in the city.

Our apartment in Brooklyn would not be available until July 15, and we lived in the Stephens apartment in Manhattan generously offered by Mallory's parents. The night of our wedding we found the refrigerator stocked with several bottles of Champagne put there by Mallory's dad. Mallory opened a bottle (I did not like Champagne), and it was dead—and so was the second bottle and the third. There was a bar on the corner of the apartment building, and Mallory suggested we go there and have our Champagne toast. It didn't sound very romantic, but we went, had a toast and left.

The next morning, June 13th, we left for the airport on our way to Bermuda. July 1st was the starting date of his internship. We stayed at a private compound where the owners had their home and one other building with two apartments. On the first floor there was a refrigerator that we were welcomed to use. The first time I opened the door, two cockroaches flew around the inside of the refrigerator. Of course I let out a yelp—I had never seen a cockroach.

When we were in bed and the light was off, we heard a buzzing sound cross the room. Turning on the light we saw another cockroach zoom across the open space. Happy Honeymoon!

We had a great time driving the streets on the left-hand side of the road on motor bikes. We learned that the biggest industry in Bermuda was tourists being hospitalized after bike accidents. We enjoyed the white sandy beach and doing some touring of the island. It was to be our last relaxing stretch of time together for a long time.

We came back to the apartment where we were to stay until the apartment that we rented in Brooklyn was available. Mallory was commuting by subway wearing his white suit, sometimes falling asleep and passing his stop.

It was summer when we moved to the Brooklyn three-room ground floor apartment. We were fortunate to have a landlord and landlady who were very nice people. When Mrs. Farber knew that Mallory would be working all night, she invited me to their apartment upstairs to watch television with them. When I arrived, she would set a TV table in front of me and bring in cakes and tea. I can remember not being hungry but I ate, because she was being so hospitable and kind.

During this year Mallory had an acute attack of ulcerative colitis. He worked long hours, sometimes thirty-six on and twelve off. He was treated and continued to work.

Mallory loved medicine and was a dedicated and hard working intern and resident in internal medicine. His residency program started in July of 1955 at the Albert Einstein Medical complex in the Bronx earning fifty dollars a month. He was able to defer his military service while in medical training, but after one year of residency, he was called to serve in the Medical Corps. In 1956 we left by car for San Antonio, Texas, where he spent six weeks training in Army Medical combat conditions at Fort Sam Houston. We stayed the entire period at an inexpensive motel, where we met other couples who were there for the same reason. On weekends we could use the beautiful swimming pool on the post. From there we went to Frederick, Maryland, where Mallory was assigned to the Fort Detrick Medical Research Center.

The heat during the trip across country had been so uncomfortable that, when we saw an air conditioner for sale, we both envisioned a cool trip east. If we ever in our marriage made a bad purchase, that was it. It was made of metal, had a sort of barrel that spun around as the outdoor wind hit it. There was a container of water at the base over which the wind blew, and thus the air was to be cooled as it came into the car. Not many miles down the road on our way east the bugs from outdoors were hitting the "air conditioner" and were being blown over the water hitting us in the face. Oh, my gosh! What had we bought? We soon got rid of that modern marvel.

There was another bad mistake, when we decided we would need a second automobile in New York. We stopped where we saw a sign on an Austin Minor owned by a minister. We bought a true "lemon." Mallory used it to commute from the upper Bronx to the Bronx Municipal Hospital many miles south and later to Manhattan. It had so little power that it would slow nearly to a stop going up a hill. No wonder the minister wanted to rid himself of it. Mallory put up with it for five years.

Back in New York, Mallory's second year of residency began. A year later, after having completed a fellowship in rheumatology, he started to work at the Rockefeller Institute and was there for three years. After having to commute to lower Manhattan using the elevated and subway system, I was happy now to be working for an inventor nearby in Mount Vernon, New York. In 1963 we decided to move out of the city.

In February of that year our first baby, Mallory Jr. was born at Lying-In Hospital in Manhattan. What a beautiful baby and an indescribable experience to hold my baby son. We were thrilled. Unfortunately, he was born with a cleft lip, and we were told that it would be necessary over the years for him to undergo several operations. Fortunately the palette was not involved. The first operation took place when he was two and a half months old. The doctors and nurses at New York Hospital were skilled and wonderful. The parents held up pretty well, considering they had to see their baby with fifty-six stitches on his mouth and his arms held down close to his body by a restraining jacket to keep him from tearing the stitches. It actually was very upsetting to me, to both of us, to see our baby being unable to put his thumb in his mouth, and breast feeding from then on was out of the question. Being determined to alleviate some of this unnatural constriction, I went back to our apartment the first night with the idea of making a less restraining jacket for him. Without consulting my husband I took one of his light blue Brooks Brothers shirts, cut it apart and constructed a jacket with elastic bands from the sleeve to the body of the shirt opening in the back with cloth ties. I also made a second one. I thought this would at least allow our baby Mallory to move his arms, even slightly.

As it turned out, the nurse being very compassionate, told me that he could wear the jacket I had made when one of us was holding him, but he could not wear it when he was alone in the hospital crib. I understood that, but also realized that the jacket was not doing the job that I had intended. It was something that I had to do.

We held him almost round the clock, as we were so committed. It was actually an emotional drain to watch our little fellow going through what he did.

After eight years of marriage, having lived in Brooklyn one year and the Bronx for five years, we bought our first home in Mount Kisco, New York. Our daughter Diana Beal was born in May of 1964, and our family was complete. Doctor Mallory soon sub-specialized in rheumatology and took care of many patients with rheumatic diseases. He thoroughly enjoyed practicing medicine, and his patients were cared for with thoroughness and compassion.

Mallory gave me my first gourmet cookbook, *Gourmet's Basic French Cookbook*, by Louis Diat, when he was still in training in the Bronx. Was he trying to tell me something? Other gourmet books followed, as well as a subscription to *Gourmet Magazine*. Our son tells me that he was raised on gourmet food. In middle school as his contribution to a Christmas party, he made a *Bouche de Noel*, the chocolate Christmas log. I watched as he made it and learned from him.

Mallory's physical symptoms worsened while living in Mt. Kisco, and he took a year off, resting, reading and taking cortisone (similar to the medication my cousin Philip Beal III developed at Upjohn Pharmaceutical). He eventually decided to have an operation, and from then on he was well. While living in Maryland I was diagnosed with rheumatoid arthritis. Over the next several years the disease worsened, and I had my share of joint pain and medications to control it. After about thirty years, I started to exercise, and it was soon after that the disease became arrested. Regardless of illnesses, we had a good life and enjoyed raising our two children. Our son Mal, and Diana both graduated from Horace Greeley High School in Chappaqua, New York, and Hamilton College in upstate New York, Diana also receiving a Master's Degree in western classic literature from St. John's College in Santa Fe, New Mexico and a two-year certificate from the New Hampshire Art Institute. Our son now teaches survival and primitive skills at the Maine Primitive Skills School.

With the children away, I took the opportunity to continue my education. With the memory of my early education dragging at my heels, I took my first class, a fiction-writing course at State University of New York at Purchase. My daughter, Diana, who was at home that year took the course also. An assignment was to write a fictional short story. As writers do, I used some of my own experiences in the story. I wrote about being in kindergarten and being put in a dark closet that was the toilet. Writing on I finished this bit of fiction. Our writings were critiqued by the professor at SUNY Purchase, and as he handed it back to me, he said that the episode of being punished by the teacher by putting the child in the dark closet is too unbelievable to be good writing. I took the paper back but missed the opportunity to say, "BUT IT REALLY DID HAPPEN EVEN IF IT IS UNBELIEVABLE!"

I then registered at Pace University for an oil painting course, as I had been doing some painting on my own. The following year I signed up for a course on sculpting and casting. I registered for academic subjects and enjoyed for the first time studying and learning—Biology, Psychology, Middle Eastern Studies and Geology—not all in the same year. I continued sculpting workshops until we prepared to move from Mount Kisco, New York.

After thirty-five years, Mallory closed his rheumatology practice in 1997, and in 1998 we moved to Tuftonboro, New Hampshire on the waters of Lake Winnipesaukee where we are busy volunteering, boating and having family members and friends visit. Mallory volunteers at the Kingswood Youth Center in Wolfeboro and is on the lay committee of an 1800s community church that holds summer services. I volunteer at the WWII Wright Museum where there is a military building, a large home front collection, and an addition with an art gallery, research library and small chapel on the second floor—truly a national treasure. We also play table tennis frequently and have entered The Senior Games in Florida and New Hampshire.

Brewster will always be my hometown and close to my heart. When I considered writing the stories of the Brewster veterans, it was exciting and the prospect of actually doing something about it stayed with me until Mallory and I left New York State and moved to New Hampshire. I am certain that starting to volunteer at the Wright Museum became the catalyst for contacting the veterans of Brewster. After three and a half years, doing interviews in Brewster and writing up stories sent to me, my efforts came to fruition with the publication by Heritage Books, Inc. of *Those Who Served; Those Who Waited*. It was a very big project, but one I enjoyed from beginning to end. I have enjoyed speaking at various groups and organizations about growing up in Brewster during the Depression and WWII. After speaking at the VFW in Brewster I was presented with the Veterans of Foreign Wars Americanism Award, a cherished and appreciated moment. Another meaningful experience was talking to the veterans at the New Hampshire Veterans Home in Tilton.

Writing this book was a trip back in time many years. It is my hope that some of what I have said will trigger good memories for those who grew up in Brewster and other small towns, as it did for me. I also want people to know the importance of family and community—the friendships and experiences of youth; for whatever these experiences are, they become the roadmap of our future and an influence on our children.

www.ingramcontent.com/pod-product-compliance
Lightning Source LLC
Chambersburg PA
CBHW071422150426
43191CB00008B/1016